Augustine of Hippo

To the memory of Giovanni and Concetta Guglietti,
Father Ottavio Scaccia
and
Father Evasio Pollo

Intellectum vero valde ama.
Ep. 120, 3, 13

א ALEF
Series of works on universal logic and philosophy directed by
Michele Malatesta and Rocco Pezzimenti
A   **A**llgemeine Logik Und Philosophie
L   Universel **L**ogik Og Filosofi
E   Logica Universale **E** Filosofia
F   Logica Universal Y **F**ilosofia

Volume 1: V. Pacioni, OSA, *Augustine of Hippo. His Philosophy in a Historical and Contemporary Perspective*

Augustine of Hippo

His Philosophy in a Historical and Contemporary Perspective

Virgilio Pacioni, OSA

GRACEWING

First published in Italian in 2004 as
Agostino d'Ippona, Prospettiva storica e attualità di una filosofia
by
Mursia Editore, Milano

First published in English in 2010
by
Gracewing
2 Southern Avenue, Leominster
Herefordshire, HR6 0QF
United Kingdom
www.gracewing.co.uk

All rights reserved. No part of this publication may be reproduced, stored in a retrieval system, or transmitted in any form, or by any means, electronic, mechanical, photocopying, recording or otherwise, without the written permission of the publisher.

© 2004, 2010 Virgilio Pacioni
English translation © 2010 Gracewing Ltd

The right of Virgilio Pacioni to be identified as the author of this work has been asserted in accordance with the Copyright, Designs and Patents Act 1988.

The translation was begun by Prof. Brian Williams, continued and completed by Prof. Philip Rand.

Texts of Saint Augustine are taken from *Writings of Saint Augustine*, in *The Fathers of the Church*, ed. R. J. Deferrari (Washington, D. C.: Catholic University Press, 1947–)

978 0 85244 737 6

Typeset by Millstream

Contents

Contents v

Acknowledgements ix

Preface xi

Introduction xv

I THE ROUTE TO CONVERSION 1
1. From Childhood to the Reading of "Hortensius" 1
2. Adhesion to the Manichaean Gnosis. 4
3. Departure for Italy and Sojourn in Rome 10
4. From Doubt to the Certainty of Faith 12

II THE HERMENEUTICAL CIRCLE: METHOD 27
1. The reasonable Act of Faith 27
2. Two Ways toward Understanding: Auctoritas and Ratio ... 31
   (a) Intelligens omnis etiam credit. 33
   (b) Credit omnis et qui opinatur. 34
   (c) Non omnis qui credit intellegit. 35
   (d) Nullus qui opinatur, intellegit. 36
3. True Authority and genuine Philosophy 37
4. Distinction between Knowledge and Wisdom 40

III BEGINNINGS OF AUGUSTINIAN SPECULATION .. 49
1. The Criterion of Truth 49
2. Nature of the supreme Good 58
3. Divine Providence and Evil in History 64

IV ANTHROPOLOGICAL DOCTRINE ... 79
1. Reciprocal Influence of Soul and Body ... 79
2. Immortality of the Soul ... 86
3. Spirituality of the Soul ... 96
4. Human Nature as a dynamic Principle of Appetites ... 102

V THEORY OF KNOWLEDGE ... 115
1. Sensible Perception ... 115
2. Phenomenology of Signs ... 119
3. Imagination ... 122
4. Memory ... 125
5. Rational Knowledge ... 129
6. Role and Function of Dialectic ... 133
7. Intellectual Knowledge and the Nature of Illumination . 135

VI FREE WILL AND THE MORAL PROBLEM ... 149
1. Rational and Free Judgement of Will ... 149
2. Nature of the Passions ... 152
3. Prima naturae and Doctrine of Tria vitia ... 154
4. The uti/frui Distinction ... 159
5. Eternal and natural Law ... 169

VII NATURE AND EXISTENCE OF GOD ... 175
1. Metaphysical Notion of God ... 175
2. "Sicut creator ita moderator" ... 181
3. Proof of the Existence of God ... 191

VIII "ORDO SAECULORUM": TIME AND HISTORY .. 207
1. Nature of Time ... 207
2. Time as a historical Process ... 216
3. "Duo amores": "duae civitates" ... 221

IX POLITICAL PHILOSOPHY ... 231
1. Origin and Function of the civil Laws ... 231
2. Nature and Limits of the State ... 235

Contents

   3. Relationship between Church and State 242

Biography 253

Appendix 257

CRITICAL INTERPRETATIONS OF
AUGUSTINIAN PHILOSOPHY 257

   1. The mediaeval Heritage of Augustine 257
      (a) The first four centuries after the death of Augustine 258
      (b) From the mid-ninth century to the end of the twelfth .. 258
      (c) The thirteenth century 260
      (d) The fourteenth and fifteenth centuries 264
   2. Augustine in the Renaissance and the first Centuries
   of the Modern Era 265
   3. Liberal Interpretation and Viewpoint of the
   historiography of Catholic Origin 268
   4. Philosophical Turning Point 272
   5. Philological Turning Point 273
   6. Logical-formal and analytical-linguistic Turning Point . 277
   7. Conclusion 278

Conclusion 281

Bibliography 289

   1. Repertories 289
   2. Miscellanies 289
   3. Works of Augustine 290
   4. Editions 292
   5. Lexicons and Encyclopedias 293
   6. Translations into modern languages 294
      In English 294
      In Italian 295
      In German 295
      In French 296
      In Spanish 296
   7. Monographs and Critical Studies 296

    a) Monographs and general critical Studies 296
    b) Monographs and critical Studies of individual Subjects..301

Index of Names 311

Acknowledgements

This publication is dedicated to the memory of Giovanni and Concetta Guglietti, Father Ottavio Scaccia and Father Evasio Pollo, who have recently passed away. Their friendship, their humanity and Christian solidarity contributed to the pleasure and fruitfulness of my three-month stays for scientific and pastoral work in Toronto over the last twenty years. Thanks to them, my service to the Canadian Catholic Church in the Toronto Diocese, and to the Augustinian Order, particularly in the Marylake Monastery (King City, Ontario), has been all the more effective.

I am particularly indebted to my colleagues, Professors of the *Istitutum Patristicum Augustinianum* (Pontificia Universitas Lateranensis) in Rome, and to the Fathers of the Italian and Canadian Augustinian Province for their constant encouragement so that this work, already published in Italian by Mursia in Milan, could also be translated into English.

I am indebted to several friends in Toronto whose support made possible the publication of this work. The Guglietti Family and Mrs Filomena Chiovitti hastened to offer a generous financial contribution; Mrs Gianna Patriarca, author and poet, Mr Michael Spensieri, former Member of Parliament in Queen's Park Toronto, Mr Vito De Simini, Mrs Carmelita Bucci Santolino, Ms Kristy McCague and Mrs Connie Sanita assisted me with their linguistic competence.

Father John Borean, Parish Priest of the Church of St Clare of Assisi in Woodbridge, Ontario, always a highly important and estimated point of reference for the Italo-Canadian Catholic community, has been the indispensable contact with most of the aforementioned people.

The translation into English, was begun by Prof Brian Williams (d. 2004) of John Cabot University in Rome, continued and completed efficiently and professionally by Philip Rand, language instructor and translator.

Daniel Harmon, Professor Emeritus of Classics at the University of Washington (Seattle), and Sister Colomba Cleary, former high school teacher in the UK, generously offered their expertise for a total rereading of the text.

I am also grateful to my niece Mrs Regina Monika Weichert Coggi, to Mr Maurizio Perfetti, Mr Fabio Magalini and Mr Alessandro Bongarzoni who offered their technical assistance for the completion of the final draft of the manuscript.

Preface

Only rarely does a book bring together qualities and features that are, at first glance, opposed and heterogeneous. Virgilio Pacioni's volume on Augustine belongs to this category. This book constitutes an introduction to the complex themes of a philosophy, and, at the same time, presents chapters and paragraphs in which the most rigorous and up-to-date developments of the articles, monographs, and new research on particular aspects are taken into consideration.

Pacioni's approach involves not only a first-hand knowledge of the sources in the original language assiduously read, studied and taught, an arduous task when one considers that Augustine wrote over 120 works, but also a continuous updating of the related literature and its critical revision.

Two further difficulties arise in addition to those of undertaking a study which claims to provide an organic view of a thinker, in this case, the African philosopher: the interaction between the existential itinerary of the man Augustine and the intellectual itinerary of the philosopher Augustine, and that between these two itineraries and the more challenging theological and pastoral path taken by Augustine the bishop.

An observation should be made about the first difficulty. There are two types of philosophers: those for whom life is not relevant to the intellectual itinerary (remember some German thinkers of the seventeenth and eighteenth century whose hours of monotonous existence were overcome only through study and teaching); those whose intellectual itinerary cannot do without the existential one, since they are both aspects of a single *trend*. In this latter case, it is not the philosopher but the *homo totus* that seeks not the answers to idle intellectual queries, but the answers to the questions about the human being in all his dimensions. Augustine belongs to the second category.

Concerning the second difficulty mentioned above, Augustine's philosophy must first be observed in its context, then extrapolated, separating it from the pastoral preoccupations and the theological reflections, which are a feature of the African's later works, after the exquisitely and exclusively philosophical works of his youth.

With the expertise of one who has devoted years of study to the subject and thus clarified the *status questionis* for himself first and then for others, Pacioni has overcome both these difficulties: a) he has outlined the philosophical itinerary of Augustine intertwining, when necessary, with the existential one in order to enhance our comprehension; b) he has distinguished the philosophical reflections of Augustine the pastor from the pastoral context or the reflection of the revealed theology, with which they are closely connected, but different in their objective.

But the difficulties do not end here. The work faces one or the other of two hazards: Augustine's works could have been studied in chronological order. But in that case each subject would have trickled off into a thousand rivulets and it would have been extremely difficult, if not impossible, to identify them through a process of *reductio ad unum*. Or they could have been treated thematically, each one by itself, thereby confining Augustine's thought to closed compartments at the expense of the unity and organic nature of Augustinian philosophical speculation.

Once again, Pacioni has shown his expertise: without losing sight of the biographical and/or autobiographical references to Augustine, whenever these were necessary to an understanding of his philosophical itinerary, he has dealt with the material in nine chapters, focusing on a central philosophical theme but seen in relation to other themes, and examined in its diachronic development.

The following subjects are analyzed in this order: Augustine's philosophical vision before his conversion to

Catholicism; the hermeneutic circle between faith and reason; the philosophical problem of truth, of the supreme Good, Providence, anthropology, epistemology, ethics, natural theology; time and history; political philosophy. Each one of the nine marvellous studies constitutes a monograph *in nuce*.

Readers will see for themselves, in the foot notes, the constant references to Augustinian sources as well as to studies of specialists on individual subjects. They will discover that the author not only has first-hand knowledge of the texts of Augustine, but also discusses and assesses the hermeneutic stereotypes of Augustine's thought, which have been uncritically reiterated for generations and which, unfortunately, continue to be repeated by those who claim to know everything about the history of philosophy.

It is noteworthy that Pacioni uses the critical contributions of N. Cipriani, who, with the scrupulousness of a rigorous philologist, has traced the inspiration of Varro for Augustine's anthropology, going back to Antiochus of Ascalon. These studies constitute another milestone in the dismantling of the concept of a Neoplatonic Augustine.

The work appropriately concludes not only with a bibliography divided according to the subjects studied — repertories, miscellanies, lexicons and encyclopaedias, translations etc. — that enable the aspiring reader to amplify his knowledge, without getting lost in the *immensa silva* of Augustinian studies, but also and above all, with a history of criticism from the Middle Ages to the present: the final paragraphs analyze the three turning points (philosophical, philological and logical-linguistic and formal-logical) which revolutionized studies on Augustine from the nineteen forties on and which are the *terminus a quo* for any further reflection that claims to be rigorous on the thought of Augustine, the last thinker of the classic world and the first of the modern period.

MICHELE MALATESTA
University of Naples «Federico II»

Introduction

This work differs from many introductions to St Augustine's thought because it is not limited to performing a purely archaeological investigation. It is well known that any historical investigation worthy of that name is always rooted in a real need. My book is intended to draw inspiration from that principle, and for that reason I openly declare that it arises from a present interest and not out of mere erudite curiosity.

While I was writing my doctoral thesis in 1985 on the subject of theoretical philosophy in *Il problema del male in A. Camus, Echi di una problematica agostiniana?"* at the University of Rome *"La Sapienza"*,[1] I noticed the considerable presence of the Bishop of Hippo in the French thinker's works, which represent the most perceptive point of modern atheism. Later, I extended my investigation on contemporary thought and discovered, to my surprise, not only the disconcerting modernity of some Augustinian studies such as the one, for example, concerning the theory of signs,[2] but I also noticed Augustine's presence in directions of thought, oriented towards anything but Augustinian ideas, for example, existentialism[3] and phenomenology.[4] It is certainly true that M. Heidegger and E. Husserl make a non-Augustinian use of Augustine's thought, since they capture the African in the net of immanence; however they cannot do without it.

However, the presence of Augustine in contemporary philosophical thought can be perceived, above all, in that speculative movement that goes under the name of Christian Spiritualism. Both in the French and Italian versions, rethinking Augustine from a rigorous theoretical point of view in the light of demands made by modern philosophy, turned Augustine into a modern philosopher. In this movement the one who has rethought Augustine more than anyone else from a speculative post-phenomenological point of view is M. F. Sciacca (Giarre 1908–†Genoa 1975). This Italian philosopher, who had already dealt with Augustine (*Sant'Agostino*, Brescia 1949, the first volume of a monumental work never completed), in penetrating theoretical works such as *Filosofia e Metafisica* (1950), *L'interiorità oggettiva* (1952) and *Atto ed Essere* (1956), for Augustine scholars has become the main, theoretically fruitful interpreter of him. In, *Filosofia e metafisica* the existence of God is assumed, in the wake of Augustine, as constituting the roots of the problem of knowledge itself, without which this remains unfounded, metaphysically unintelligible. The *objective interiority* is Augustinian, assumed as determining the overcoming of immanentistic rationalisms and forms of subjectivism, idealism and existentialism. Augustine, seen again through Pascal and Blondel as well, removes M. F. Sciacca from metaphysical spiritualisms, phenomenologies, existentialisms, personalisms that have no foundation. Furthermore, it is Augustine himself who urges Sciacca to construct a *Metaphysics of Integrality*, which will be developed above all in the theoretical works *L'uomo, questo squilibrato* (1958) and *Morte e immortalità* (1959). The theses of the transcendence of the objective being over the finite existing one and infinite truth over the thinking existent one, thus form the basis of his anthropological metaphysics, which is developed in two other fundamental works: *La libertà e il tempo* (1965) and *Ontologia triadica and trinitaria* (1972). The problem of evil and the two civitates is also central in all the works of Sciacca, from *L'ora di Cristo* (1954) to *L'oscuramento dell'intelligenza* (1970).

Urged on by Sciacca's interpretation of Augustine as the philosopher of objective interiority, self-awareness and integrality, I wanted to research the sources, studying the *opera omnia* of Augustine, to see if this interpretation was philologically and historically based, or only due to the ingenious reconsideration of the Italian philosopher.

Introduction

Once again and with great surprise I had to ascertain that if the Sciacchian instances of Augustine's thought were due to exigencies that arose from the crisis and the aporias of modern thought, yet, unknown to Augustine, the themes of objective interiority and integrality, self-awareness, evil and time were acquired by the Philosopher of Hippo already in the *Dialogues*, genuinely philosophical and written just after his conversion.

Aware of the novelty of this approach benefitting from reconsideration of Augustine in contemporary speculation, I realized that in order to investigate Augustine's paternity of those achievements, I had to fight a battle on two fronts: philological and methodological.

As far as the first is concerned, I recognize Augustine's debt towards Platonism and Neo-Platonism, and maintain that calling Augustine a Platonist or Neo-Platonist tout court is limiting. This is what those, who do not have a knowledge of Augustinian historiography of the last few decades or a first-hand knowledge of the *opera omnia* of the African Father of the Church do. This is an *immensa silva* in which all the streams of late-ancient culture flow: it is certainly true that among the streams that converge, the main one is Platonist—Neo-Platonist, but it is not the only one. In Augustine Pythagorism is present,[5] as well as Aristotelianism[6] and Stoicism.[7] In this volume I have benefitted from a whole series of studies carried out in the last few decades, especially, by G. Madec, L. Hölscher, G. O' Daly and, above all, by N. Cipriani.[8] The latter scholar discovered that Augustine's anthropology was neither Platonist nor Neo-Platonist, but that it had come from Varro. Following indications offered by Book XIX of the *De civitate Dei*, in which Augustine investigates the anthropological and moral model, presented by Varro in his *De philosophia*, and attributed to Antiochus of Ascalon, N. Cipriani found several texts from Augustine's first works, by means of a very careful philological investigation, texts in which signs of Varro's influence on the Augustinian anthropological and moral model appear clear. The philological investigation of the Augustinian scholar from the *Institutum Patristicum Augustinianum* of Rome demonstrated that as far as anthropology is concerned, Augustine's main source is Varro and not Plato, Plotinus or Porphyry, even if the latter remains the main source for the rational demonstration of the immortality of the soul. The results of the philological research of the Roman scholar enabled me to indicate that through Varro himself and also through Cicero, Aristotelian and Stoic material reached the African, and it helped Augustine to reduce the dualistic expressions greatly if not to eliminate them entirely.

As far as the second point is concerned, the reading of Augustine with contemporary philosophy as a point of departure convinced me that the philological method is not enough in order to gain an understanding of the African thinker. It is well-known that Augustine makes ample use of Aristotelian—and above all—Stoic logic, as well as schemes of inference that cannot be traced back to those thought tendencies. The studies of Aristotelian logic by J. Lukasiewicz,[9] G. Patzig,[10] and many others, and those on Stoic logic by Lukasiewicz,[11] B. Mates[12] and M. Frede,[13] to mention a few, taught me that a total understanding of ancient logic is possible only through the use of modern symbolic logic.[14] Contemporary symbolic logic is none other than the development, made rigorous by symbolization, of Stoic, Aristotelian, Scholastic, and Leibnitzian logic, with the addition of numerous unknown branches of the Ancients and of people in the interim period. Ancient logic, whether Aristotelian, Stoic or Medieval, when rigorously symbolized, become actual subsets in contemporary logic. Hence, using modern symbolic logic does not mean violating the texts. It is just the realization that Aristotle already symbolizes the variables even though he does not symbolize the constants, and that the Stoics use variables even though they do not symbolize them, and this does not mean falling into anachronistic interpretations. The comparison between the ancients and the moderns—See for example the comparative terminology table of the Stoics with that of Frege and Carnap in *Stoic Logic* by Mates[15] — if it is useful for noting the analogies it is always useful for taking note of the differences.

As for the first point I used the studies of G. Madec, G. O' Daly and N. Cipriani, etc. here, I used those of T. G. Bucher, d. M. Malatesta.[16] There is more, however. Reading Augustine in the light of the theory of the linguistic acts and propositional attitudes, logical and linguistic research has made it possible to establish analogies but also differences between Augustinian philosophy and that of other modern and contemporary philosophers.

I have tried to reconstruct the framework of Augustine's speculation in all of its most original philosophical traits, following philosophical, philological and logical-linguistic suggestions performing a point by point analysis of the texts not only from a philological but also a historiographical, cultural and logic-formal point of view as well.

The three lines of development that inspired my book have benefitted from three steps forward in the orientation of Augustinian studies of the last few decades. The first I call philosophical, and M. F. Sciacca is its representative. Here, not only has the question of Augustine's philosophy been the subject of historiographic investigation, but it has also been a point of departure for theoretical research from a modern point of view. The second one I call philological, of which N. Cipriani is a representative. The original portrait of Augustine the philosopher has been recreated thanks to a reading of the Augustinian *opera omnia*. The third line of development I call logical and formal. M. Malatesta is its representative. Here, Augustine's use of Stoic logic, the rigor of his reasoning, and its relevance to Augustinian argumentation were discovered for the first time.

I believe that it is useful for the English-speaking reader to be made aware of the historical context in which such original, scientific contributions developed, since they have led to the working out of a new paradigm of interpretation.

From the nineteen-fifties on, Italy was the centre for numerous symposia, conventions, and seminars for the study of Augustine's works. They were sponsored by the Augustinian Order together with patristic scholars, those dealing with the history of philosophy as well as philosophers themselves.

In 1954, a convention on Augustinian philosophy was held on the sixteen hundredth anniversary of the birth of St Augustine. The subject was *St. Augustine and the major trends in contemporary philosophy*, and scholars from all over the world took part. The opening speech was given by M. F. Sciacca, who pointed out the relevance of Augustine's thought in modern philosophy, his presence in Idealism, Phenomenology and Existentialism in particular. Summing up the proceedings, Sciacca made two proposals, both of which were carried out: a) translation of the Bishop of Hippo's *opera omnia* into Italian with the Latin text on the facing pages; b) the creation of an Augustinian chair. After several years, this idea led to the creation of the *Institutum Patristicum Augustinianum* thanks to the efforts of Father Agostino Trapè.

In 1969, Sciacca, along with the Augustinian Fathers of Pavia, sponsored the *Lectio Augustini* (the Pavian Augustinian Week) for the purpose of presenting the language and thought of Augustine, especially to university students. The distinguished Professor from the University of Genoa delivered the first paper on Augustine and the Platonists. Scholars of international fame have taken part in these annual study weeks, which are still taking place. Among them are F. J. Crosson, A. Solignac, R. Holte, G. Madec, E. L. Fortin, J. K. Coyle, G. Balido, N. Cipriani and others. These events have given rise to interesting avenues for further investigation of an anthropological, logical and philological nature; often, these have been the result of the involvement of young participants in the study meetings. Some of them have since then become full professors holding university chairs. Several contributors brought out the purely instrumental role played by Plotinian and Porphyrian Neo-Platonism on Augustine, which a previous and widespread historiography had identified as basic in his intellectual as well as spiritual evolution. Out of this came, for example, a reformulation of Augustinian anthropology and the possibility of reconsidering the matter of sources not only from a philological but also a philosophical point of view.

In 1986, for the sixteen hundredth anniversary of the conversion of St Augustine, the *Institutum Patristicum Augustinianum* offered an International Meeting on the Saint for the purpose of investigating the philological, philosophical, theological and historical aspects of Augustinian thought. Scholars from the top universities in the world made important contributions. Among these were: G. Madec, A. Mandouze, V. J. Bourke, E. Kevane, R. O'Connell, T. G. Bucher, N. Cipriani, R. J. Teske and others.

At the end of the nineteen eighties, with the Institute of Philosophy of the Department of Literature and Philosophy of the University of Perugia as well as the Augustinian Fathers of the Province of Umbria, a new initiative was taken: the Center of Augustinian Studies of Perugia, which complemented the one in Pavia was set up. While a given work of Augustine was dealt with in Pavia every year, in Perugia the investigation involved the diachronic approach to a subject from the work of the Bishop of Hippo.

A few years later, a third avenue of studies came into being. The University of Urbino, together with the Augustinian Monastery of the St Catherine, offered an annual series of lectures concerning Augustine and contemporary philosophy. M. Malatesta, a Professor of Logic at the University of Naples *"Federico II"*, gave the first lectures. He brought out not only the modernity of Augustine by using logical inferences translatable into symbolic language, but also the need to read Augustine with the tools of semiotics, linguistics and the philosophy of contemporary language. That approach freed Augustine from the negative legacy of prejudices of some scholars, undeniably competent in their areas, but not capable of dealing with the interpretation of passages in which Augustine's genius anticipated the modern theories of linguistic acts and propositional attitudes.

In the nineteen nineties there was a growing conviction among scholars that Augustinian texts could be better understood by making use of the *Quellenforschung* method put forth by P. Hadot in *Porphyre et Victorinus*, Paris 1968.

According to the *Quellenforschung* method, to the extent that the scholar keeps close to the characteristic conceptual structure and to what in the literary and lexical formulation is indissolubly related to it, it is possible to arrive at a certain reconstruction of a source.

N. Cipriani took a leading role in this direction. As a Full Professor of the *Institutum Patristicum Augustinianum*, he performed a series of philological investigations, discovering new sources of Augustinian thought. In the nineteen nineties, the Augustinian scholar provided original contributions in which he pointed out that the method put forth by P. Hadot constituted a step forward and a safer path than the one used by several European and North American scholars in the nineteen sixties and seventies. These had maintained that it was enough to keep in mind the coincidences or similarities of the thought pattern to reach the source of an ancient author. The result of this attempt, which went beyond the prospects offered by P. Courcelle in the sixties, was the discovery of a new paradigm of interpretation based on the study of a comparison not only with conceptual structures, but also grammatical and lexical ones. Thus, new pagan and Christian sources for the Augustinian Dialogues were discovered and the Christian faith of Augustine, in some texts interpreted by previous historiography in Neo-Platonic terms or even neglected because of not being significant, was emphasized.

According to N. Cipriani, that hermeneutical paradigm, resulting from a conceptual, grammatical and lexical study leads to three significant conclusions, that can be summarized as follows:

> 1) in his first works, the author of the Dialogues accepts ideas and doctrines from Neo-Platonic philosophers

Introduction

and, at the same time, takes a marked distance from these in important points of doctrine;

2) the African continues to draw on both Neo-Platonic philosophers and classical Latin authors, such as Cicero and Varro, especially as far as the anthropological model, different from that of the Platonists, is concerned;

3) the author of the Dialogues draws inspiration not only from pagan writers, but also Christian ones. He does not limit himself to listening to the preaching of St Ambrose or speaking with the priest Simplicianus, as the French scholar P. Courcelle had maintained, but also reads works of St Ambrose and Marius Victorinus, which have a strong influence on his Christian faith and, especially, his Trinitarian doctrine.

In these years it was possible to discuss these new sources that official historiography had neglected and it has been shown that there are even literal and lexical parallels between passages from St Ambrose, Cicero, Varro and other authors with selections by Augustine.

It should be added that attention to logical and formal structures has increased. Heretofore, these had been neglected in specialized research. In Augustine, they can be brought out with modern syllogistics, in consideration of the widespread use of Stoic and Aristotelian logic used in works written during the African period.

As far as this third line of development is concerned, M. Malatesta deserves the merit of having been the first to carry out research on the Augustinian texts using the tools of modern formal logic. During the nineteen eighties and nineties, he devoted two monographic courses to the *Contra Academicos* at the University of Naples, "*Federico II*", which led to two publications: (*St. Augustine's Dialectic from the Modern Logic Standpoint. Logical Analysis of* "Contra Accademicos" III, 10, 22–13, 29, "Metalogicon", VIII, 1995 pp. 91–120; *La problematica linguistica del* "Contra Accademicos" *alla luce della filosofia del linguaggio contemporanea*, "Metalogicon", X, 1997, pp. 46–63). Reading Malatesta's works on formal logic, while I was writing my book, *L'unità teoretica del* "De Ordine" *di sant'Agostino*, Rome 1996, I discovered the presence of schemes for inference of Stoic logic in Augustine's philosophical works already utilized by Marius Victorinus in *Adversus Candidum*. Those contributions to formal logic were further enhanced in this study.

Notes

1. V. Pacioni, OSA, *La presenza di S. Augostino nell'opera letteraria and filosofica di Albert Camus* in *Congresso Internazionale su S. Agostino nel XVI centenario della conversione; Atti* III, SEAug, Rome 1987, pp. 369–379.
2. A complete monograph on the Augustinian theory of *signs* is still lacking, although there are highly valuable studies on semiotics and semantics especially in the *de magistro* and in *de doctrina Christiana*. See in particular F. G. Crosson, *The Structure of De magistro*, "Revue Des Etudes Augustiniennes", XXXV, 1989, pp. 120–127.
3. M. Heidegger taught a course on *Augustine and Neo-Platonism* in the summer session of 1921.
4. See E. Husserl, *Cartesianische Meditationen* und *Pariser Vorträge*, edited by S. Strasser, Haag, Nijhoff, 1963, pp. 178–183.
5. See *De musica*.
6. See *Contra academicos*.
7. See *Contra academicos* and *De ordine*.
8. For information on the above-mentioned scholars see the *appendix* to this volume.
9. J. Łukasiewicz, *Aristotle's Syllogistic from the Standpoint of Modern Formal Logic*, Oxford, Ad Clarendon Press, 2nd ed., 1957.
10. G. Patzig, *Aristotle's Theory of Syllogism. A Logical-philosophical Study of Book A of the* Prior Analytics, Dordrecht, Reidel, 1968.
11. J. Łukasiewicz, *Zur Geschichte der Aussagenlogik*, in "Erkenntnis", 15, 1935, pp. 111–31.
12. B. Mates, *Stoic logic*, Berkeley-Los Angeles, University of California Press, 1973.
13. M. Frede, *Die Stoische Logik*, Goettingen, Vandenhoeck & Ruprecht, 1974.

14. For an overall view, see I. M. Bochenski, *Ancient Formal Logic*, Amsterdam, North Holland, 1951.
15. B. Mates, *Stoic logic*, cit. p. 20.
16. As for the above-mentioned scholars see the *appendix* to this volume.

I

THE ROUTE TO CONVERSION

1. From Childhood to the Reading of "Hortensius"

Augustine was born on November 13th 354, at Thagaste, a Roman *municipium* situated on the Mediterranean side of proconsular Numidia. The ruins of the ancient city lie buried beneath the white buildings of the present-day town of Souk-Ahras in Algeria. His father, whose name was Patricius, a man of generous and impulsive character, was a small landholder, and a member of the municipal council.[1] His mother, Monica, a Christian richly endowed with human qualities, was educated in modesty and sobriety.[2] The family, which included a brother, Navigius, and a sister whose name we do not know, was of African origin, but had become Romanized: the language spoken at home was Latin. The children received a Christian education from Monica. When Augustine, while still a child, was on the verge of dying because of an intestinal blockage, he insistently asked to be baptized but the sacrament was deferred because he recovered.[3] From the first years of his life he showed himself to be "a child of good hope",[4] endowed with a sharp memory and lively intelligence.

When he completed his education at Thagaste in the modest school of a private tutor (*litterator*), he was sent to the Roman colony of Madaura, to continue his studies in grammar and rhetoric. Here, in the homeland of Apuleius, he studied passages from Latin poets and prose-writers, which were commented on and committed to memory. His school experience provided him with a good literary basis, as well as knowledge of elementary notions of mathematics, music and physics. While the study of literature appealed to him, he was bored by Greek language study, and he showed no sympathy at all for mathematics:

> Then, indeed, 'one and one are two, two and two are four' was a hateful sing-song, but very attractive was the vain image of a wooden horse filled with armed men, and the burning of Troy, and 'the shade of Creusa herself'.[5]

Because of economic difficulties, he was summoned back to Thagaste in 369 by his parents, and there he spent his sixteenth year in idleness, without any scholarly activity, troubled by the feelings of love "What else delighted me then but to love and be loved?"[6]

In the year 371, his father sent him to Carthage to pursue his studies. Thanks to the financial help of a family friend, Romanianus,[7] he was able to enrol there in the School of rhetoric of north Africa, the equivalent of a present-day university, an educational center for the western part of the Empire and then surpassed in importance only by Rome itself. Here, at seventeen years of age, he continued his studies. At this time he was dominated by three great passions: study, theatrical performances, and the search for sensual pleasure.

The following year he decided to live together with a local girl, to whom he seems to have sworn "fidelity as to a legitimate wife". From the union with this unnamed Carthaginian girl, he had a son named Adeodatus.[8]

Despite his passion for the performances produced in great numbers in the capital of Numidia, Augustine's commitment to study was steadily growing. "Already I was first in the school of rhetoric, and I found exceptional joy in it".[9]

An excellent training in the knowledge of rhetoric was a condition, in the fourth century, for a secure career, both in education and in the imperial civil service. The scholastic program for the years 372–373 included the reading of the Cicero's *Hortensius* (a work now lost to us) which contained a ringing exhortation to the study of philosophy and detachment from material goods. The study of this work was to lead Augustine to an unexpected discovery.

In *Confessiones* we find his enthusiastic account of this reading:

> (...) at that unstable period of my life, I was studying the books of oratory, in which I was eager to excel, because of a detestable and empty purpose, a joy in human vanity. In the regular course of study, I came upon the book of a certain Cicero, whose tongue nearly all admire, but not his heart. But that book of his contained an exhortation to philosophy. It was called *Hortensius*.
>
> In fact, that book changed my mental attitude (*mutavit affectum meum*). It altered my wishes and my desires. Suddenly, every vain hope became worthless to me and I yearned with unbelievable ardor of heart for the immortality of wisdom. For, it was not to sharpen my tongue (this was the apparent object being bought at my mother's expense, for I was in my nineteenth year and my father had died two years before) it was not, I say, to sharpen my tongue that I used that book. It was not its style of speech which influenced me, but, rather, what it spoke about.[10]

The reading immediately produced an illumination which re-awakened his intelligence and guided his most profound aspirations in a new direction. Augustine became convinced that philosophy is the highest ideal of thought and of life; since it is the search for and love of wisdom, it forms the pre-condition for attaining happiness. The two principal terms of the exhortation to philosophy were, in fact, wisdom and happiness. He embraced this philosophical ideal with a passion which from then onwards was to give a new dimension to all other human ideals in his eyes, ideals of success, pleasure and wealth. The sole disappointment that he felt was the absence in those pages of any mention of the name of Christ.

> The only thing to dim my ardor was the fact that the name of Christ was not there, for this name, my youthful heart had drunk in piously with my mother's milk and until that time had retained it in its depths; whatever lacked this name could not completely win me, howsoever well expressed, and polished, and true appearing.[11]

Dominated by a new intellectual interest and persuaded that human existence at its most profound level is defined by the desire for truth and happiness, he decided to open the *Scriptures*. He was disappointed, however, at the obscurity of their content, and at the rough style, not worthy of comparison with Cicero's majestic language.[12] He thought it would be better to entrust himself to those who teach rather than those who order one to believe (*docentibus potiusquam iubentibus esse credendum*).[13] These words explain the long time that Augustine spent far from the Church, whose teaching he initially considered incompatible with rational enquiry.

2. Adhesion to the Manichaean Gnosis.

Having set aside the Scriptures, Augustine did not return to Cicero, but turned rather to the Gnostic writings of the Manichaeans, in the hope of attaining wisdom through reason alone. He was to write later to his friend Honoratus:

> You know, Honoratus, that I feel among these people for no other reason than that they declared that they would put aside all overawing authority, and by pure and simple reason would bring to God those who were willing to listen to them, and so deliver them from all error. What else compelled me for nearly nine years to spurn the religion implanted in me as a boy by my parents, to follow these men and listen diligently to them, than that they said we were overawed by superstition and were bidden to believe rather than to reason, while they pressed no

The route to conversion

one to believe until the truth had been discussed and elucidated?[14]

The nucleus of the doctrine of Manichaeism consisted in a dualism perceived at four levels: metaphysical (there are two eternal principles, good and evil, in eternal struggle between themselves); cosmological (the heavens and the earth, men and things, derive from two metaphysical principles); anthropological (man is torn between two elements, light and darkness, the soul and the body); and moral (the two elements of soul and body are in conflict with one another, because the body, because of the passions, tends to hold back the divine light). The philosophical and religious message of Mani, the founder of the Manichaean sect, aimed at liberating man from evil by means of rational knowledge, and through a naturalism which took ascetic form: in this way man would be able to win, within himself, the domination of matter, and liberate the light that is imprisoned in his body. For this purpose Mani taught a system of naturalistic precepts: renunciation of marriage and procreation (*signalaculum sinus*), abstinence from eating flesh (*signalaculum oris*), respect for nature, in particular, water, fire, trees, and human beings (*signalaculum manuum*), and the obligatory consumption of vegetable foods. According to Mani and his followers, both the *Old Testament* as a work of the evil principle, and faith in the Incarnation ought to be rejected; however, a fervent religious sentiment should be cultivated, and sometimes this was expressed in extravagant fashion.[15]

Augustine was attracted to Manichaeism by two seductive promises: liberation of reason from all forms of conditioning, and the resolution of the problem of evil. His adhesion to the sect, however, was not without reservations: in fact he wrote:

> A childish superstition deterred me from thorough investigation, and, as soon as I was more courageous, I cast off the darkness and learned to trust more in men who taught than in those who

> ordained obedience, having myself encountered persons to whom the very light, seen by their eyes, apparently was an object of highest and even divine veneration, I did not agree with them, but thought they were concealing some important secret which they would later divulge.[16]

From the beginning of his encounter with the Manichaeans he realized that they were more eloquent and had a better stock of arguments to confute the teachings of others than they were firm and unshakable in demonstrating their own. It is likely that the need for rationality, as dictated by Cicero's *Hortensius,* was the factor which allowed Augustine to avoid being completely subjugated by the attractions of the Manichaean myth.

As a consequence of these reservations, he remained at the level of *auditor* for nine years, without ever rising to the ranks of the *elect*. Despite this, Augustine attended and listened to the classes of the Manichaeans, and made insistent efforts to persuade as many people as he could to follow him in the path he had chosen.[17]

When his studies in rhetoric were completed in 374, he thought of returning to Thagaste to teach grammar and dedicate himself to the spread of the sect. In the following year he returned to the valley of Megerda, and went back once again to Carthage. The death of a friend[18] and the desire for greater professional stability contributed to his decision to leave his native city. Writing to his friend Romanianus, to whom he was to dedicate his *Contra Academicos*, he recalled those days in this way:

> When I was bereaved of a father, you consoled me with your friendship, roused me with your encouragement, and aided me with your resources. By your favor and friendship, and by the sharing of your home with me, you made me almost as renowned and prominent a personage as yourself in our town. And when I was returning to Carthage for the sake of a more illustrious profession, and had revealed my plan and prospect to you alone,

and to no member of my own family, you, indeed, hesitated for a while—by reason of your innate love of homeland, because I had already begun to teach there. Nevertheless, by a marvelous tempering of good will, you became a helper instead of a dissuader when you were unable to subdue the yearning of a young man striving for what seemed to be better things: you furnished my journey with everything it needed. And you, who had tended the cradle—or, as it were, warmed the nest of my earliest studies in that city—you now again supported my first faint efforts when I dared to fly.[19]

In 375 he decided to open a school of rhetoric in Carthage. A number of devoted students followed him, in particular Licentius, the son of his friend Romanianus, as well as Alipius, Eulogius and Nebridius. It was a period in which he passed most of his time in study, teaching and care for his partner and child: meanwhile the network of his friendships was gradually spreading. While at the end of his studies Augustine had a mainly literary training, this was now enriched with fresh knowledge, thanks to his great commitment to the study of philosophy, science and history. He read and understood by himself the *Categoriae* of Aristotle,[20] he studied all the treatises he was able to find concerning the liberal arts,[21] as well as the treatise *De Philosophia* by Varro; the philosophical works of Cicero, and the greatest exponents of the Roman Stoic School, the *Noctes Atticae* of Aulus Gellius, and probably the *Introductio arithmeticae* by Nicomachus of Gerasa.[22] He was not content with going from one book to another, but reflected deeply on the various questions regarding his profession of teacher, for example, the nature of language, rhythm and meters (*de musicis et numeris*), and logic.[23] Meanwhile he was accumulating the necessary material for the composition of several subsequent works such as the *De dialectica*, the *De Magistro* and the *De Musica*. It should be noted that he added an interest in astronomical research to that in the fields of literature and philosophy, and it was in fact the results of these investigations that spurred him to perceive some of the internal contradictions of Manichaeism.

> Of course, I retained many things that were said by them, drawn from creation itself. The rational principle as suggested by numbers, the order in moments of time, and the visible evidence of the stars struck me. I made a comparison with the statements of Mani—for he wrote many things about these matters, being very prolix in his delirium—but I did not come upon the rational explanation of the solstices, or of the equinoxes, or of eclipses, or anything such as I had learned in the books of profane wisdom. What I was commanded to believe, in these writings, did not jibe with those rational explanations using numbers or with the discoveries I saw for myself. It was far different.[24]

Between 380 and 381 he wrote *De Pulchro et apto*, a treatise dedicated to Hierius, a Syrian orator resident in Rome. Augustine had not met this person, but he looked up to him as the model of a successful public speaker. In this work, which has not survived, he presented a number of views on aesthetics and metaphysics. Possibly drawing on Platonic sources, he proposed that the source of beauty is the 'being' in what exists. He distinguished between the beautiful (*pulchrum*) and agreeable (*aptum*): the one attracts us in and for itself, while the other does so in relation to what is in agreement with it. In metaphysics Augustine was chiefly indebted to Manichaean and Pythagorean sources: he opposed good and evil in parallel with unity and division and argued that the supreme unity, or *monad*, is the origin of order and all good things, whereas division or *diad* is at the root of disorder or bad things. Augustine thus came to identify the Manichaean principles of unity and duality with the Pythagorean antithesis of *monad* and *diad*. He then explained his anthropological vision, according to which man is divided within himself, because he possesses two basic tendencies, one good and one evil.[25] The work ended with a discourse relating to the problem of good and evil, according to the dualistic scheme which was particular to the Manichaean gnosis.

The faith of Augustine in the sect was weakening little by little, according to what he tells us in *Confessiones*,[26] mainly because of two factors: the intellectual sterility of the Manichaeans and the weakness of their theory in the field of the physical sciences. The doubts put before the Carthaginian Manichaeans remained unresolved on various occasions; however he was looking forward to meeting one of the most illustrious of the sect's exponents, Faustus of Milevis, who, according to what he had been led to believe, would be able to resolve all his queries. Finally in 383, Faustus arrived in Carthage from the Imperial Capital. In a private conversation, Augustine, explained all the doubts which troubled him, and realized that he had before him a man who was lovable and simple, but ignorant of the liberal disciplines other than grammar. Thus the encounter proved disappointing, and his disillusionment with the sect was complete.

> And so, when the interest which I had directed to the works of the Manichaeans was turned aside, and I was less hopeful of their other teachers, because, in the many problems which I had, that renowned master made this poor showing, I began to spend some time with him because of his own enthusiastic interest in that very literature which I was then, as a rhetorician, already teaching to the young men of Carthage. Thus, I read with him either the things he knew by repute and wanted to hear, or which I judged suitable to his natural bent. For the rest, any desire of mine to make progress in that sect was definitely killed when I came to know that man.[27]

While continuing to call himself a Manichaean and to conceive of God and the human soul as material realities and evil as a principle independent of God, his belief in Manichaeism was by now severely shaken.[28]

3. Departure for Italy and Sojourn in Rome

The immediate consequence of this disappointment was the desire to leave for Rome. The reasons for this decision are known to us: to distance himself from the Carthaginian scholastic environment which had become unbearable because of the presence of turbulent students, and to find better possibilities of pursuing an honorable career.[29] In his eyes, Rome provided the opportunity for a more serene life and one that would be more brilliant from the professional point of view. In *Confessiones*, Augustine has left us an account of his departure, and his separation from his mother Monica:

> She complained bitterly at the prospect of my leaving, and followed me to the seaside. But I deceived her, while she was urgently trying to get me either to change my decision or to take her with me. I pretended that I did not wish to leave a friend until he could set sail with a fair wind... Yet, when she refused to return without me, I persuaded her with some difficulty to spend the night in a place which was near our ship, at a shrine dedicated to blessed Cyprian.
>
> But, on that night, I set out secretly, while she remained behind in prayer and tears. The wind blew, filling our sail, and the shore line was lost to our sight. In the morning, she went wild with sorrow upon this shore. Yet, after blaming my deceptions and cruelty, she turned round again to pray to Thee on my behalf. She went away to her own home and I to Rome.[30]

He was accompanied by the good wishes of his friend Martianus, to whom he had said farewell with a verse from the Latin writer Terence, almost as if to prefigure the events of the future:

> This day now introduces another life, it requires another code of conduct.[31]

In the autumn of 383, Augustine disembarked at the harbor of the Capital. From Ostia Tiberina, sailing up the sacred river and crossing through the Roman *campagna*, already brown at the end of the summer season, he arrived in Rome. One can easily imagine the feelings of the African newcomer at the sight of Aventine hill, of the seven hills, the pagan temples, the imperial palaces, the arch of Constantine, the Colosseum, the Forum, and his amazement at the bustling of the crowds which animated the streets of the city. In his imagination he will have conjured up Cicero, intent on delivering his speeches in the Senate Palace, or Caesar as *Pontifex Maximus*, engaged in presiding over some religious rite. He could also admire the Roman landscape, which he had encountered in his studies and in Latin literature, the center of civilization which he had been taught to love. Here beat the heart of the great Empire which he was preparing to serve.[32]

In Rome he was a guest in the home of a Manichaean *auditor*. After some time he fell seriously ill.[33] After his recovery, he was able, with the help of the Manichaean sect, to open a school of rhetoric. Sadly his experience with the Roman students was no more fortunate than it had been with the Carthaginians: in Carthage the students were turbulent; in Rome, they left the school when it came to paying the agreed fees and went off to other teachers instead.[34] Meanwhile, the doubts concerning Manichaean teaching became stronger, even though he continued to enjoy friendships not only with the *auditors,* but also with those who were called the *elects*. He planned to direct his studies more towards the academic philosophers.

> Indeed, the thought even arose within me that those philosophers called the Academics were more prudent than other men, in thinking that one should doubt everything and in judging that nothing of truth can be grasped by man. For that was clearly the way that they seemed to me to think, as they are commonly regarded, though I had as yet no real understanding of their meaning.[35]

Even though the philosophers of the New (or Middle) Academy, held that it was necessary to doubt everything because the truth appears to be totally unknowable to man, Augustine did not go so far as to share the Skeptics' theory of universal doubt. However, he identified his state of uncertainty and intellectual confusion with the actual skepticism of the Academics.[36] In the fall of 384, his relations with the Manichaeans had definitely cooled, though he was still unable to overcome their materialism and dualism, and was attracted more by academic skepticism. Despite the intellectual restlessness of the moment, he managed to attract the attention of important members of the Roman aristocracy, such as the prefect Symmachus.[37] The latter, a politician and a literary figure, an adversary of the Christians, who had received from the imperial headquarters in Milan a request for a teacher of rhetoric, decided in his capacity as prefect and consul in Rome, to name Augustine as official professor of rhetoric at the Court of Milan.[38] Under the high protection of a pagan, the African scholar was now awarded the prize of a career that promised great success.

4. From Doubt to the Certainty of Faith

At the end of 384, having followed the Via Flamina and Via Emilia, Augustine arrived in Milan. At the beginning of the next year, he performed his first official task as Rhetorician at the Milan Court by delivering the panegyric for the consulate of Bautonis,[39] a friend of Symmachus. After some time he was joined in Milan by his mother, his brother Navigius and his African friends Alipius, Nebridius, Trigetius and Licentius, the son of Romanianus. In Milan, he discussed, especially with his friends Alipius and Nebridius, the foundations of morality.[40] Furthermore, having in practice already abandoned the metaphysical dualism of the Manichaeans, he turned towards a way of conceiving the presence of God within reality in the manner of Stoic

The route to conversion

pantheism, known to him above all through the philosophical works of Cicero. He writes:

> So that I was forced to think, not in terms of the shape of a human body, but of some corporeal being in local space, either spread out in the world or even infinitely diffused outside the world.[41]

In that period he conceived the created world in this way:

> One great mass, adorned with different kinds of bodies, whether the things were in fact bodies, or whether I imagined them as such instead of spirits. I made it great, not as great as it was, for I could not know this, but as great as seemed convenient, and bounded on all sides, of course. I imagined embracing it in every part and penetrating it, but remaining everywhere infinite. It was like a sea, everywhere and in all directions spreading through immense space, simply an infinite sea. And it had in it a great sponge, which was finite, however, and this sponge was filled, of course, in every part with the immense sea.[42]

In Milan, Monica found her son in a state of total prostration:

> She found me in grievous danger. I was despairing of ever finding truth.[43]

Although he had passed beyond Manichaeism, Augustine was still assailed by questions and doubts of a philosophical nature.

At that time the Bishop of Milan who had held the see for the last ten years, was Ambrose, son of a high official of the imperial administration, and a member of the *Gens Aurelia*, related to the Prefect Symmachus. Already a famous personality in his own right, he was influential, learned, and had had a good training in Latin and Greek literature, in rhetoric and in law. He knew both eastern and western Christian literature, as well as Neoplatonic philosophy.[44] Around Ambrose a group of intellectuals had formed, who united the study of Platonic philosophy with Christian religious practice. This group included the priest Simplicianus, who had been a close friend of Marius Victorinus, Manlius Theodorus, Xenobius and Hermogenianus. From early on in his stay in Milan, Augustine began to attend the Sunday liturgy, with the aim of listening to Ambrose:

> I carefully listened to his public discourses, not with the attitude that I should have had, but, as it were, to try out his eloquence; as to whether it was in keeping with his fame, whether he was more or less fluent than rumor had it. Upon his words I hung attentively, but of his subject matter I stood by heedless and contemptuous. I was delighted by the sweetness of his language, which, though more learned, was less entertaining and charming than that of Faustus. However, in subject matter there was no comparison between them, for Faustus was carried away by Manichaean fallacies, while this man taught the soundest way of salvation.[45]

The preaching of Ambrose helped: on the one hand it caused him to rid himself of two prejudices with which Manichaeism had infected his mind; the anthropomorphic representation of God[46] and the aversion to the Old Testament,[47] on the other hand it clarified in his mind the spiritual notion of God:

> For I have noticed frequently in the sermons of our priest, and sometimes in yours, that, when speaking of God, no one should think of Him as something corporal, nor even of the soul, which in the world is the only thing very near to God;[48]

the method of allegorical or spiritual interpretation of the *Scriptures*:

> When, having lifted the mystic veil, he laid bare the spiritual meaning of those things which seemed to teach error when taken literally, he said nothing that offended me, though I still did not know whether his statements were true;[49]

and finally the notion of free will:

> I turned my attention to observe what I heard: that the free choice of the will is the cause of our committing evil, and Thy right judgment, the cause of our suffering it. But I was not able to see this clearly.[50]

Listening to the sermons of the Bishop of Milan, Augustine was progressively introduced to new ideas: the conception of unearthly realities, the act of faith understood as something reasonable, the credibility of the books of the *Old* and *New Testaments*. He was thus gradually becoming aware that the teachings of the Catholic Church were not those that he had heard in his youth expounded by the Manichaeans, and that the criticisms leveled by them at the Church were without foundation.

However, some uncertainties remained with him:

> Often it seemed to me that truth could not be found, and my thoughts like a great flood tended to carry me over to the best of my ability how lively was the human mind, how wise, how penetrating, I could not believe that the truth must ever elude its grasp. Possibly the manner of seeking truth might be concealed and would have to be accepted from some divine authority.[51]

The obscurity and the unadorned style of the *Scriptures* no longer constituted a difficulty as far as he was concerned; the prejudices accumulated over the years of his youth gradually fell away one by one. From this point he began to undertake an important step, becoming convinced that the authority of *Scriptures* presupposes that of the Church.[52]

After abandoning the theology of the Manichaeans and the philosophy of the Sceptics, various obstacles of a speculative kind remained to be overcome. What is the nature of the only God of goodness? If we admit that no divine principle of evil exists, what then is the origin of evil itself from a metaphysical point of view? If God is the good principle, why does man find himself in a condition subject to limitation and to pain? Why does man sometimes consent to evil and oppose good? In May or June of 386, Augustine was immersed in these questions, when he came to discover several books of Platonic philosophy (*Libri Platonicorum*).[53] He himself recalls in *Confessiones*:

> Thou didst provide for me, by means of a man who was puffed up with the most monstrous pride, certain books of the Platonists which were translated from Greek into Latin.[54]

These books had a decisively important effect on him, because on the one hand they permitted him to resolve the remaining difficulties of a speculative kind, while on the other hand they led him to discover the ontological status of the whole of reality:

> Thus admonished to return unto myself, I entered into my innermost parts under Thy guidance. I was able, because Thou didst become my helper. I entered in and saw with the eye of my soul (whatever its condition) the Immutable Light, above this same eye of my soul, and above my mind, not this common light which is visible to all flesh, nor was it a brighter light of somewhat the same kind, as if it were one which shines much more clearly and fills the whole of space with its magnitude. It was not this, but something different, quite different from all these. Nor was it above my mind in the way that oil is above water, nor as the heavens are above the earth, but superior in the sense that it has made me, and I was inferior in the sense that I was made by it. He who knows the truth knows it, and he who knows it knows eternity. When I first knew Thee, Thou didst take me up to Thee, so that I might see that there was something to see, but that I was not yet ready for the vision. Shining Thy light upon me so strongly, Thou didst strike down my feeble gaze, and I trembled with love and with awe. I discovered that I was far from Thee in the area of unlikeness, as if I heard Thy voice from on high. There was no reason for me to doubt. I could more easily have doubted that I was alive than that there is non truth, 'which is clearly seen being understood

> through the things that are made'. I looked closely at the rest of things below Thee and saw that they are neither wholly in existence, nor wholly out of existence: they exist, indeed, for they are from Thee, but they do not exist, for they are not what Thou art. For that truly is which endures immutably. It was made manifest to me that it is because things are good that they can be corrupted. If they were the highest goods, they could not be corrupted. Unless they were goods, they could not be corrupted. For, if they were the highest goods, they would be incorruptible, but if they were not goods, there would be nothing in them to be corrupted. (...) All things which are corrupted are deprived of good.[55]

From the reading of the *Libri Platonicorum*, he derived not merely bookish information, but an illumination which permitted him to discover aspects of reality which were previously quite unknown to him: the certainty of the existence of the self in the interior nature of self-awareness, through which the human mind, in the act in which it finds itself, also goes beyond itself, to reach the ultimate foundation, the absolute Being; the discovery of God as a transcendent and spiritual Being, an incorporeal Truth; the metaphysical distinction between the changeable world of the senses, and the intelligible and unchangeable world; the principle of participation; the metaphysical notion of evil as the deprivation of good. Finally although he could obviously not find in those writings the Christian truth concerning the incarnation of the Word,[56] nevertheless he realized that they were of help in explaining, partially and in certain aspects, the immutability of the Word. Certain doctrinal points of the preaching of Ambrose, which had seemed obscure to him at first hearing, began to be illuminated. By continuing to question himself on the essence of an evil disposition in mankind, he became convinced that it is a perversion of the will, in that the latter detaches itself from the highest good in order to turn toward corruptible things.[57] It is likely, as the illustrious scholar G. Madec stresses,[58] that for Augustine this experience came as a sort of a flash of lightning, and that he saw things clearly only very slowly, little by little as he pursued his readings and deepened his reflection, during months of intense cultural activity. The difficulties of a speculative kind began to dissolve, the last obstacle on the path toward the personal God of the Christian faith, to Whom he could turn:

> I marveled that I now loved Thee, and not a phantasm in place of Thee. Yet, I did not stand still in the enjoyment of my God; rather, I was snatched up to Thee by Thy glory, but was soon snatched away from Thee by the natural weight of my will, and I fell back on these lower things with a groan. This was the weight of carnal custom. However, Thy memory was with me; I was in no way doubtful that there was someone to whom I should cling.[59]

Finally, the reading of the Letters of St Paul brought an end to another difficulty which, as he himself testifies, he had experienced in conceiving the union of the divine immutability of the Word with mutable humanity.[60] The conversations which he had during the summer months of 386 with the priest Simplicianus[61] were decisive in bringing about the final clarification. He thus came to identify the Wisdom of *Hortensius* and the Intellect of the *Enneads* with the incarnate Word of the Scriptures. From that moment Augustine was in possession of the guiding principle of his teaching, that is Jesus Christ, the Incarnate Word, who saves and illuminates. Furthermore, Simplicianus himself, drawing attention to the condensation of the Christian teaching about the Incarnate Word which is the *Prologue* to St John's Gospel, contributed to make Augustine realize, on the one hand, the originality of Platonism in comparison with other philosophical doctrines, especially for what regards the nature of the divine transcendence, and, on the other hand, the elements of distinction between Christianity and Platonism.[62]

According to recent research,[63] Augustine did not confine himself to reading the Scriptures, nor to listening to the sermons of Bishop Ambrose and conversing with the priest Simplicianus and with Marcus Theodorus, but he also devoted himself to reading Christian writers such as Ambrose, Marius Victorinus and Tertullian, to reflect on the arguments which were particularly dear to them: the doctrine of the Trinity, the meaning of the divine authority of Christ, the problem of the soul and that of evil. In fact in the early dialogues there are already verbal and doctrinal traces of these readings, which show the influence on the new convert not only of pagan literature, but also of a part of Christian literature.

In the summer of 386 a few obstacles of a practical nature still remained in the way of a complete adherence to the Christian revelation. It was in this period that Simplicianus told him the story of the conversion to the Christian faith of Marius Victorinus, a very learned rhetorician and expert in philosophy, honoured by the Roman political authorities with a statue in the Forum. In 362 the Emperor Julian had forbidden Christians to teach literature and rhetoric. As a result of this decree, in order to dedicate himself completely to Christ, Victorinus decided to give up teaching. This story caused Augustine great astonishment.[64] Some time after, he received a visit from a certain Ponticianus, an African official at the Palace, and a convert to Christianity. This visitor recounted him the story of the Egyptian monk Anthony, and the numerous monasteries which had been built by him in Egypt.[65] In August 386, Augustine was in the garden of his house. His attention was attracted by a strange and mysterious sing-song voice which repeated "Tolle, lege" ("Take up and read"); perturbed, he went back to pick up the book he had momentarily left aside, and read the first verse in it:

> "Not in revelry and drunkenness, not in debauchery and wantonness, not in strife and jealousy; but put on the Lord Jesus Christ, and as for the flesh, take no thought for its lusts". No further did I desire to read, nor was there need. Indeed, immediately with the conclusion of this sentence, all the darkness of

> doubt were dispersed, as if by a light of peace flooding into my heart. Then, having marked it either with my finger or with some other sign, I closed the book and, with a now peaceful face, informed Alypius. Then, he gave an account of what was going on within him, of which I was in ignorance. He asked to see what I had read. I showed him and he paid attention even beyond that part which I had read. I did not know the section which followed. Actually, the continuation read: "But receive he who is weak in faith". This, he applied to himself and he disclosed it to me. But he was strengthened by this admonition, in a decision and resolution which was good and most suitable to his moral qualities in which he had far surpassed me for a long time, and he joined in without any trouble or delay. After that, we went to my mother and told her; she rejoiced. We gave her the story of what had happened; she was exultant, triumphant, so that I sought no wife nor any ambition for this world, standing on that rule of faith where Thou hadst shown me in the revelation of so many years before.[66]

When the academic year ended, Augustine resigned from his teaching post and retired with his family and friends, to a villa which had been placed at his disposal by a friend and colleague, the grammarian Verecondus, at Cassiciacum in Brianza (Milan).[67] In this "philosophical retreat",[68] lasting approximately five months, Augustine and his companions prepared themselves for baptism, praying, dedicating themselves to light work in the countryside, and debating on certain matters of philosophy: the nature of truth, of happiness, of order of the world, and of soul.

> Then, when the time came at which it was required that I should submit my name, we left the country and returned to Milan. Alypius, also, decided to be reborn in Thee, along with me. We also included with us the boy, Adeodatus, born of me in the flesh as a result of my sin. Thou hadst fashioned him well. He was almost fifteen years old and surpassed many serious and learned men in his mental endowment.

> I am but confessing to Thee Thy gifts, O Lord my God, Creator of all, who hast much power to reform our deformities, for I was responsible for nothing but the sin in that boy. Thou, and no other person, hadst inspired us to have him nourished by us in Thy teaching: to Thee I confess Thy gifts. There is a book of ours written under the title, *on the Teacher*. In it, he converses with me. Thou knowest that all the views which are included in it as coming from the person of my interlocutor are his, when he was in his sixteenth year. I found many other more amazing qualities in him. His talent was for me a matter of awe, and who but Thee is the worker of such wonderful things? Thou didst take his life quickly from this earth and my memory of him is more free from concern, since I have nothing to fear for his boyhood or adolescence, or anything for him as a man. We associated him with us as our contemporary in Thy grace, to be trained in Thy studies. So, we were baptized and the anxiety for our past life fled from us.[69]

In the light of the journey that we have described so far, we can say without hesitation that the encounter of Augustine with Christianity was not a mere change of route from a philosophical point of view, but the irruption within him of the Truth itself. As Karl Jaspers rightly states,[70] it was a datable biographical fact, an event so unique as to form the beginning of a new existential journey, and the presupposition for all his subsequent intellectual output.

Notes

1. Possidius, *Life of Saint Augustine 1,1*.
2. *conf.* IX, 9, 19–22.
3. Ibid., I, 11, 17.
4. Ibid., I, 16, 26.
5. Ibid., I, 13, 22.
6. Ibid., II, 2, 2.

7. Ibid., III, I, 1; *Acad.* II, 2, 3; cf. G. Bonner, *St. Augustine of Hippo. Life and Controversies,* Norwich UK 1986, p. 53.
8. *conf. IV,* 2, 2.
9. Ibid., III, 3, 6.
10. Ibid., III 4, 7; cf. M. Ruch, *L'Hortensius de Cicéron. Histoire et reconstitution,* Paris 1958, pp. 135–166; M. Testard, *Saint Augustine et Cicéron,* Paris 1958; H. Chadwick, *Augustine,* Oxford 1986, pp. 9–10; B. Stock, *Augustine the Reader. Meditation, Self-Knowledge and the Ethics of Interpretation,* Cambridge (MA) — London (England), 1996, pp. 37–38.
11. *conf.* III, 4, 8.
12. Ibid., III, 5,9.
13. *beata v.* 1, 4; cf. A. Trapè, *S.Agostino, L'uomo, il pastore, il mistico,* Fossano (CN) 1976, pp. 61–62.
14. *util.cred.* 1,2; cf. P. Courcelle, *Recherches sur Les Confessions de Saint Augustin,* Paris 1968, pp. 64–65 and 272–274.
15. For further research on Manichaean doctrine, consult H. C. Puech, *Histoire des Religions,* VIII, Paris 1970.
16. *Beata v.* 1, 4.
17. *c.ep.Man.* 3, 3.
18. *conf.* IV, 4,7–8.
19. *Acad.* II, 2, 3.
20. *conf.* IV, 16, 28.
21. N. Cipriani, *Sulla fonte varroniana delle discipline liberali nel "De Ordine" di S. Agostino,* "Augustinianum", XL, 2000, pp. 203–224.
22. *conf.* V, 3, 3 ; cf. A. Solignac, *Doxographies et manuels dans la formation philosophique de Saint Augustin,* "Recherches Augustiniennes", 1, 1958, pp. 113–148.
23. *conf.* IV, 16, 30; cf. G. Madec, *Saint Augustin et la philosophie. Notes critiques,* Paris 1996, p. 32.
24. *conf.* V, 3, 6.
25. Ibid., IV, 15, 24; cf. K. Svoboda, *L'esthétique de Saint Augustin et ses sources,* Brno 1933, pp.10–16; M. F. Sciacca, *S.Agostino,* Brescia 1949, pp 24–25.
26. *conf.,* V, 3,3; cf. G. Bonner, *St. Augustine* op.cit., pp. 66–69.
27. Ibid., V, 7, 13.

The route to conversion

28. J. J. O'Meara, *The Young Augustine*, London 1965, p. 102.
29. *conf.* V, 8, 14.
30. Ibid., V, 8, 15.
31. *ep.* 258, 5.
32. J. J. O'Meara, *The Young* op. cit., p. 106.
33. *conf.* V, 9, 16.
34. Ibid., V, 12, 22.
35. Ibid., V.10, 19. With regard to the history of the ancient Academy, refer to G. Reale, *Storia della filosofia antica III. I sistemi dell'età ellenistica*, Milano 1983, pp. 465–556.
36. G. Madec, *Saint Augustin* op.cit., p. 33.
37. P. Brown, *Augustine of Hippo*, Berkeley and Los Angeles 1967, pp. 54–61.
38. *conf.* V, 13, 23.
39. *c.litt.Pet.* III, 25, 30; cf. P. Courcelle, *Recherches* op. cit., pp. 80–83.
40. *conf.* VI, 16, 26.
41. Ibid., VII, 1, 1; cf. Ch. Baguette, *Une période stoïcienne dans l'évolution de Saint Augustin*, "Revue des Études Augustiniennes", XVI, 1970, pp. 47–77.
42. *conf.*, VII, 5, 7.
43. Ibid., VI, 1, 1.
44. P. Courcelle, *Recherches* op.cit., pp. 93–138.
45. *conf.* V, 13, 23.
46. *beata v.* 1, 4.
47. *conf.* V, 14, 24; VI, 4, 6; cf. A. Trapè, *S. Agostino* op. cit., p. 105.
48. *beata v.* 1, 4.
49. *conf.* VI, 4, 6.
50. Ibid., VII, 3, 5.
51. *util. cred.* 8, 20.
52. *conf.* VII, 7, 11.
53. The reading of these books has constantly attracted the attention of scholars of Augustinian thought, who have sought by philological subtlety, and with an apparatus of remarkable erudition to find out whether Augustine had read only Plotinus (cf. P. Henry, *Plotin et l'Occident. Firmi-*

cius Maternus, Marius Victorinus, Saint Augustin et Macrobe Louvain 1934, pp. 69–77, or only Porphyrius (cf. W. Theiler, *Porphyrios und Augustin*, Halle 1933, pp. 1–70) or Plotinus and Porphyrius (cf. P. Courcelle, *Recherches*, op. cit., pp. 157–159), or yet again, first of all Plotinus and then later Porphyrius (cf. O. Du Roy, *L'intelligence de la foi en la Trinité selon s.Augustin. Genése de sa théologie trinitaire jusqu'en 391*, Paris 1966, pp. 68–71). Very probably Augustine had read the following treatises from the *Enneads*: 1, 6, *The Good*; 1, 8, *Nature and the origin of evil*; III, 2–3, *Providence*; III, 7, *Eternity and Time*; V,1, *The primary hypostases*; V, 2, *Genesis and order of things which are after the First*; VI, 6, *Numbers*. From Porphyrius he had read *The return of the soul*, *The philosophy of the oracles*, the *Sentences* and the *Commentary on Plato's Parmenides*.

54. *conf.* VII, 9, 13.
55. Ibid., VII, 10, 16 – 12, 18.
56. Ibid., VII, 9, 13–14.
57. Ibid., VII, 16, 22.
58. G. Madec, *Saint Augustin* op.cit., p. 39.
59. *conf.* VII, 17, 23.
60. Ibid., VII, 18, 24 – 19, 25.
61. *civ.* X, 29, 2.
62. G. Madec, *La Patrie et la Voie*, Paris 1989, pp. 43–46.
63. On this question, we would refer to two fundamental essays by N. Cipriani which appeared in the 1990s: *Le fonti cristiane della dottrina trinitaria nei primi dialoghi di S.Agostino*, «Augustinianum» XXXIV, 1994, pp. 253–312, and *L'ispirazione tertullianea nel «De libero arbitrio» di S. Agostino*, in *Il mistero del male e la libertà possibile: lettura dei dialoghi di S.Agostino*, Roma 1994, pp. 165–178.
64. *conf.* VIII, 2, 3.
65. Ibid., VIII, 6, 14.
66. Ibid., VIII, 12, 29–30.
67. Ibid., IX, 3, 5–4, 7. With regard to the localization of the ancient *Rus Casiciacum*, cf. L. Beretta, "Rus Cassiciacum": *bilancio e aggiornamento della "vexata quaestio"* and

S. Colombo, *Ancora sul* Rus Cassiciacum *di Agostino*, in *Agostino e la conversione cristiana*, Palermo 1987, pp. 67–92.
68. *Acad.* II, 2, 4.
69. *conf.* IX, 6, 14.
70. K. Jaspers, *Drei gründer des Philosophierens. Plato, Augustin, Kant*, München 1957, pp. 101–107.

II

THE HERMENEUTICAL CIRCLE: METHOD

1. The reasonable Act of Faith

Tertullian's influence on Augustine, for example, regarding the solution of the problem of evil, is well-known.[1] However, on one point there is a quite significant difference. From the period of his conversion to Christianity on, Augustine counterpoised to the *credo quia absurdum*, the expression into which scholars have condensed the viewpoint of the third century apologist, his own *rationabile obsequium* with regard to faith, expressed in lapidary fashion in the well-known formula *credo ut intellegam, intellego ut credam*. In the final part of the *Contra Academicos* one can already find a link of a biunivocal kind between faith and reason.[2] This dynamic relationship continues in the philosophical dialogues, and despite the change in the notion of knowledge of Augustine as a pastor, both as priest and bishop, it is always the paradigm on which he operates, until it reaches its definitive form in the *Enarrationes*:

> There are in effect things which, if we do not understand them, we do not believe, as there are other things which, if we do not believe them then we do not understand them. (*Alia sunt enim quae, nisi intellegamus non credimus; et alia sunt quae, nisi credamus, non intellegimus*).[3]

As a Christian intellectual, Augustine favours philosophical enquiry guided by faith in order to reach wisdom. As a pastor, he studied to the *Scriptures* scientifically according to the hermeneutical and exegetical principles expounded in *De Doctrina Christiana*, in order to establish the correct faith, and he also reflects through reason on faith itself, to understand God insofar as this is possible. As a layman, he traveled the route of the intelligibility of philosophical reflection inspired by faith; as a presbyter he favors that of reflection based on the Scriptures. Between the two viewpoints, in which the unifying element is the rationality of enquiry, there is a difference, but at the same time a harmony.

Reason is a necessary condition for philosophy as an enquiry *iuxta propria principia,* but it is not sufficient, because it requires the guidance of faith; just as it is a necessary condition for positive theology,[4] but not sufficient, because in this second case, the authority of the Scriptures precedes that of reason. We can penetrate more deeply into Augustine's position, as alien to a crude fideism as well as to a sterile rationalism, if we look at some observations which Augustine sent to Consentius a few years after his conversion. To this friend who took his inspiration from a kind of fideism *ante litteram,* he wrote:

> God forbid that He should hate in us that faculty by which He made us superior to all other living beings. Therefore, we must refuse so to believe as not to receive or seek a reason for our belief, since we could not believe at all if we did not have rational souls. So, then, in some points that bear on the doctrine of salvation, which we are not yet able to grasp by reason—but we shall be able to sometime—let faith precede reason, and let the heart be cleansed by faith so as to receive and bear the great light of reason; this is indeed reasonable. Therefore the Prophet said with reason: "If you will not believe, you will not understand; thereby he undoubtedly made a distinction between these two things and advised us to believe first so as to be able to understand whatever we believe. It is, then, a reasonable requirement that faith precede reason, for, if this requirement is not reasonable, then it is contrary

to reason, which God forbid. But, if it is reasonable that faith precede a certain great reason which cannot yet be grasped, there is no doubt that, however slight the reason which proves this, it does precede faith.[5]

Let us take a close look from a philosophical viewpoint at this text which illustrates very well how the act of faith, for Augustine, is not absurd but reasonable.[6]

For what goes beyond the limits of reason i.e. the truths concerning the doctrine of salvation, faith precedes, reason follows. We may put the consideration just stated between inverted commas, and write: "For what goes beyond the limits of reason, faith precedes, reason follows." We now ask ourselves: is the expression placed between the inverted commas reasonable or unreasonable? If we had said that for what goes beyond the capacity of reason, reason precedes faith, this statement would undoubtedly be unreasonable; but here we have stated the contrary. So then we have this sentence: "'For what goes beyond the limits of reason, faith precedes, reason follows': this is a reasonable sentence." Now let "For what goes beyond the limits of reason, faith precedes, reason follows" be a sentence of the object language, and let "It is a reasonable sentence" be a sentence of meta-language; we ask ourselves: who precedes in the sentence of the object language? We answer: faith. What precedes in the sentence of the metalinguistic language? Reason. As for what concerns the content (for example, the Trinity, the Incarnation), faith precedes reason, says Augustine, but when we assert that "in the things which go beyond reason, faith precedes", in this case it is reason which precedes faith; in other words, in Christian discourse concerning the content, faith precedes; in the epistemology of religion, reason precedes. As can be seen, here the reasoning is on two levels.[7]

During his stay in Milan, gradually reflecting on his own experience and on the contents of the preaching of Bishop Ambrose, Augustine learnt to reformulate the agreement between faith and reason. Contrary to what he had thought until then, he realized that adhering to the authoritative teaching of the Church was a fact compatible with rational demands. Freeing himself from his distrust of faith, he embraced Christianity and at the same time began his commitment to philosophical research. In this context, it is appropriate to recall the role that was played by both the cultural background of certain personalities in the Christian community of Milan,[8] and by the reflection on the birth and development of natural ties and social processes. He himself bears witness to this in *Confessiones*:

> Then, gradually, with a most gentle and merciful hand, Thou didst influence and settle my heart in the consideration of so many things. I believed without seeing them or being present when they occurred—for instance, so many things in the history of peoples, so many things about places and cities which I had not seen, so many things in my relations with friends, with physicians, with these men and those, which, unless believed, would render it impossible for us to do anything in this life, and finally with what faith I held an unshakeable conviction concerning the parents from whom I had taken my origin, something which I could not know unless I believed what I heard. By all this Thou didst persuade me that the men who are guilty and unworthy to be heard are not those who believe in Thy books, which Thou hast established as authoritative amongst nearly all peoples, but rather those who do not believe.[9]

Augustine stresses that faith in itself is reasonable, because social life and culture rest on it; the Christian faith is reasonable because the authority of Christ, being reasonably credible, is manifested as the true divine authority.

Faith itself was the point of departure for philosophical enquiry. The complex route that he followed to conversion in Milan was not a kind of reawakening, like that aroused in him by the reading of Cicero's *Hortentius*, or a blessed transformation of thought into spirituality aroused by the reading of Plotinus' *Enneads*. Nor was it in the first instance a cathartic experience.[10] It was a unique event which radically changed his way of thinking,[11] and allowed him to free himself from the rationalist prejudice in the light of which he had abandoned his mother's faith and as a young student, considered it to be a "childish superstition".[12]

The encounter with Christianity marked the passage from a phase of conflict to the discovery of a constructive or fertile relationship between faith and reason. In the paragraphs which follow, we shall attempt to show in more detail the various points concerning the circular relationship existing between the two ways of knowledge, faith and reason, stressing the new insights that Augustine introduced in the years when he was a presbyter.

2. Two Ways toward Understanding: Auctoritas and Ratio

In his *Contra Academicos*, he set forth the method of speculative enquiry. In order to attain the rational knowledge of the soul and of God, it is necessary to begin from the authority of Christ, using elements of philosophical doctrines which are not in conflict with the Christian faith.[13]

In *De ordine* he begins to demonstrate the validity of the method based on the reasonableness of the act of faith. A double impulse drives us to learn: that of *auctoritas* and that of *ratio*. In fact, he writes:

> It remains for me to declare how instruction is to be imparted to the studious youths who have resolved to live after the manner described above. Likewise, with regard to the acquiring of knowledge, we are of necessity led in a twofold manner: by authority and by reason. In point of time, authority is first; in the order of reality, reason is prior. What takes precedence in operation is one thing; what is more highly prized as an object of desire is something else.[14]

In the process of learning the use of the faculty of reason is not sufficient, but it is necessary to follow an authority as well. Even though this seems to be the most suitable means for inexperienced persons, whereas reason is the best suited to educated people, nevertheless, because of the fact that we are all born ignorant, only authority may open the door of knowledge to those who wish to learn what the "great and mysterious goods" are. He goes on:

> But, after one has entered, then without any hesitation he begins to follow the precepts of the perfect life. When he has become docile through these precepts, then at length he will come to know: (a) how much wisdom is embodied in those very precepts that he has been observing before understanding; (b) what reason itself, which he—now strong and capable after the cradle of authority—follows and comprehends.[15]

Giving assent to an authority is a property of human nature, which, immersed in temporal realities, perceives the truth of things after a long process of learning which begins with the act of faith in an authority. This is an indispensable factor of knowledge, not only in the sense that it is the basis of human and social ties, but also because it is the condition for setting off the activity of reasoning. Since it is not possible to know everything by direct experience, the scientific knowledge to which the wise person may aspire implies two orders of knowledge: that of things seen and that of things believed because of the witness of others.[16] Faith is distinguished both from *credulitas* and from *opinio*: the former is the mark of those who adhere without any verification to what they do not know; the latter is the mark of those who believe and affirm that they know what in fact they do not know. Faith means admitting something to be true, knowing that one does not know it and cannot know it, at least for the moment.[17] Augustine introduced a change in the concept of faith as taught by Plato (*pistis*) even in his earlier works. According to Plato faith signified belief, or a form of opinion (*doxa*) which corresponds to the degree of knowledge relative to sensible objects.[18] Faith understood as opinion is almost always deceptive and a cause of error; it may be true but can never have in itself the guarantee of

The hermeneutical circle: method

its own correctness, and it always remains unstable, as the sensible object to which it refers is unstable.[19]

In his work *De utilitate credendi*, Augustine illustrates more analytically the relation and the difference existing between three intentional acts: *credere, intellegere* and *opinari*. In fact he formulates four enunciates which may be analyzed with the tools of modern logic. He stresses that:

> (...) what we understand we owe to reason (*quod intellegimus igitur debemus rationi*); what we believe we owe to authority (*quod credimus, auctoritati*); what we opine, we owe to error (*quod opinamur, errori*);

in order to deduce:

> (...) but whoever understands, also believes (*sed intellegens omnis etiam credit*); whoever believes, and (believes) also whoever opines (*credit omnis et qui opinatur*); but not everyone who believes, understands (*non omnis qui credit, intellegit*), and no-one, who opines, understands (*nullus qui opinatur, intellegit*).[20]

This passage, of prime importance for understanding the gnosiological value of faith, gives rise to a whole body of expressions, which can be symbolized by the tools of modern logic, and to a corresponding series of diagrams. We shall seek to examine the meaning of the four expressions.

(a) Intelligens omnis etiam credit.

If we symbolize the predicate "understands" by 'Int' and the predicate "believes": by 'Cr', (a) becomes

$$\forall x\, Int\,(x) \longrightarrow Cr(x)$$

For every x, if x understands then x believes.

Let 'I' be the class of those who understand, and 'C' be the class of those who believe; the class of those who understand is included in the class of those who believe.

See the following diagram:

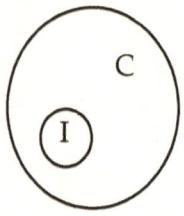

Fig.1

(b) Credit omnis et qui opinatur.

There are two sentences: *Credit omnis* et *(credit) qui opinatur.* Symbolizing the predicate "opines" by O_p, (b) becomes

$$\forall x \, Cr(x) \, \& \, \forall x \, O_p(x) \longrightarrow Cr(x)$$

for every x, x believes and for every x if x opines then x believes.

From the fact that Augustine has expressed two sentences here, we must create two diagrams, of which the second is a specification. Let 'O' be the class of those who opine, and 'C' the class of those who believe; the class of those who opine is included in the class of those who believe. Thus we have:

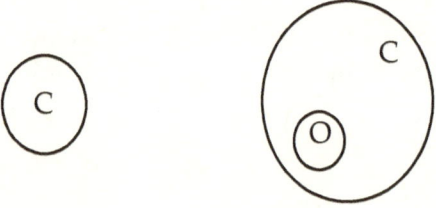

Fig. 2

The hermeneutical circle: method

Comparing Fig. 1 with Fig. 2, it emerges that the class of those who understand and the class of those who opine are actually sub-classes of those who believe. Thus the two diagrams could be combined in one, as follows:

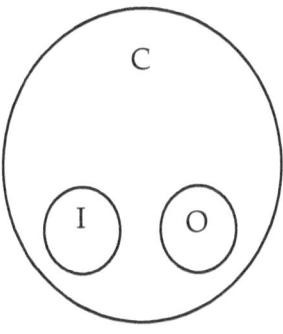

Fig. 3

(c) Non omnis qui credit intellegit.

Making use of the symbols already established above, we have:

(c.1) $\neg \forall x\; Cr(x) \rightarrow Int(x)$

It is not the case that for every x, if x believes then x understands. In fact in Fig. 3, we can see that the class of those who believe is far more extensive than the class of those who understand. Now keeping in mind that the negation of a universal affirmative is a particular negative, the symbolized expression becomes:

(c.2) $\exists x : Cr(x) \,\&\, \neg\, Int(x)$

There is at least one *x*, so that *x* believes and it is not the case that *x* understands.

The expressions (c.1) and (c.2) are of diverse form only on the linguistic plain, but have exactly the same meaning.

From Fig. 3 we can deduce as follows: since the class of those who understand and that of those who opine are actual subclasses of the class of those who believe, it can be deduced that for Augustine the largest class is the class of those who believe. In a few words, the context of faith—that is faith in general and not faith as a supernatural virtue—permeates the whole dimension of man, and consequently his intentional acts. If man understands, he believes; if man opines, he believes; whether he understands or opines, he believes.

(d) Nullus qui opinatur, intellegit.

Using the symbols we established above, we have:

$$\forall x \, O_p(x) \longrightarrow \neg \, Int(x)$$

For every x, if x opines, then it is not the given case that x understands.

In short, as can be deduced from Fig. 3 above, the class of those who understand and the class of those who opine are separated; i.e. there is no element which can belong simultaneously to the two classes. This may be expressed in formal mathematical terms as follows:

$$I \cap O = \emptyset$$

The intersection of class I and class O (i.e. the class of those who opine) is the empty class.

From the whole of this enquiry, conducted by means of the analysis of logic, it emerges that faith as a general category permeates all intentional acts of humankind.[21]

In the 48th question of *De diversis quaestionibus octoginta tribus* Augustine explains more clearly the difference between believing (*credere*) and understanding (*intelligere*), beginning from the type of content which is under discussion. There are certainties which are always believed without hope of their being understood; these are the ones concerning the facts of the past; there are others, on the contrary, which are understood as soon as they are believed, such as human reasoning on numbers, and other disciplines for example. Finally, there is a third type of certainty which must first be believed and then understood, such as the certainties concerning divine matters,[22] and for this reason Augustine distinguishes a dual faith in the Christian: faith in the eternal things (*fides rerum aeternarum*) and faith in temporal things (*fides rerum temporalium*) which have been undertaken for our salvation.[23]

3. True Authority and genuine Philosophy

Having demonstrated the need to follow an authority in philosophical enquiry, Augustine has no reservations about maintaining that the true authority to be followed in order to attain wisdom and happiness is not a human authority but a divine one, identified, from the *Contra Academicos* onwards, with the Incarnate Word:

> And I am resolved never to deviate in the least from the authority of Christ, for I find none more powerful.[24]

In following the authority of Christ, however, we must not despise the authority of mankind, even though much of the time this may be deceptive. With regard to philosophical enquiry into intelligible realities (the soul and God) he confirms his fidelity to Platonic teaching, without, however, excluding contributions which may come from other philosophers on various aspects of philosophy.

In *De ordine* Augustine begins the demonstration regarding the credibility of the divine authority of Christ, with arguments that were to be developed more fully in *De utilitate credendi* and in the tenth book of *De civitate Dei*. The reflections that Augustine makes here aim on the one hand to show the true, unique and supreme divine authority of the Incarnate Word, and on the other hand to confute the arguments of the Neoplatonist Porphyrius in favor both of theurgy as knowledge and of traditional polytheism as a religion possessed of philosophical substance.[25]

He writes:

> Authority, is, indeed, partly divine and partly human, but the true, solid and sovereign authority is that which is called divine. In this matter there is to be feared the wonderful deception of invisible beings that, by certain divinations and numerous powers of things pertaining to the sense, are accustomed to deceive with the utmost ease those souls that are engrossed with perishable possessions, or eagerly desirous of transitory power, or overawed by meaningless prodigies. 'We must, therefore, accept as divine that Authority which not only exceeds human power in its outward manifestations, but also, in the very act of leading a man onward, shows him to what extent It has debased Itself for his sake, and bids him not to be confined to the senses, to which indeed those things seem wondrous, but to soar upward to the intellect. At the same time It shows him what great things It is able to do, and why It does them, and how little importance It attaches to them. For, it is fitting that by deeds It shows Its power; by humility, Its clemency; by commandment, Its nature. And all this is being delivered to us so distinctly and steadily by the sacred rites into which we are now being initiated. Therein the life of good men is most easily purified, not indeed by the circumlocution of disputation, but by the authority of the mysteries.[26]

The reflections made in this paragraph can be correctly understood if they are analyzed in the light of the tenth book of *De civitate Dei*, where questions concerning the identification of the true divine authority are dealt with more fully from both philosophical and religious points of view.[27]

Porphyrius accepted the authority of the oracles as a divine reality, even though he had described theurgy as something to be feared.[28] Although he had perceived the need of man for a universal way to salvation, he held that this had not yet been indicated by any doctrine. Augustine, on the contrary, stated that Divine Providence had not abandoned humankind to its fate, but had intervened in the history of humanity, and made itself manifest in the Incarnate Word.

He also lists the criteria for distinguishing the superiority of Christ's authority to that of the demons. The latter, while not being superior to humans as far as reason is concerned, since they share that in common, are nevertheless capable of producing extraordinary sensible signs for humankind. On the other hand, the authority which not only transcends all human power in miraculous sensible signs, but also reveals to man the point to which it has lowered itself on his behalf by taking on the human condition itself, is divine and supremely worthy of belief. This authority commands humanity, moreover, not to allow itself to be drawn along by its senses, through which these extraordinary signs are perceived, but to go beyond, towards the intelligible world. At the same time, he shows how many great things (*quanta*) it can undertake here below, the reason why (*cur*) it undertakes them, and how little (*quam parvi*) it considers them to be. Finally, it must teach mankind about its power by concrete facts, its clemency by humility, and its nature by an authoritative word. These are characteristics which belong only to the authority of the Incarnate Word.

According to Augustine, such truths are transmitted in a certain way by the Scriptures, and satisfactorily interpreted by an absolutely true philosophical discipline,[29] which is shown, in method and content, to be the genuine philosophy (*germana philosophia*)[30] by the fact that it has inherited what Plato and Aristotle truly taught about the intelligible world, superior to and distinct from the sensible world. This philosophy, guided by the authority of the Incarnate Word:

> (...) philosophy sends forth reason, and it frees scarcely a few[31],

aims to reach the certain knowledge of truth,[32] similar to that of mathematical principles;[33] in particular it sets itself the task of the intellectual knowledge of the soul and of God. On the other hand, although making its enquiry under the guiding hand of faith, it frees only a few, because liberal education (*ordo eruditionis*) in the context of which it flourishes, is a privilege of the few, and also requires moral purification (*ordo vitae*). Augustine goes on:

> By itself it compels these not only not to spurn those mysteries, but to understand them insofar as they can be understood. The philosophy that is true—the genuine philosophy, so to speak—has no other function than to teach what is the First Principle of all things—Itself without beginning,—and how great an intellect dwells therein, and what has proceeded therefrom for our welfare, but without deterioration of any kind. Now, the venerated mysteries, which liberate persons of sincere and firm faith—not indiscriminately, as some say; and not harmfully, as many assert—these mysteries teach that this First Principle is one God omnipotent, and that He is tripotent, Father and Son and Holy Spirit.[34]

To sum up, genuine philosophy investigates the nature of the intelligible world with the intention of arriving, as far as possible in the present situation, at the actual knowledge of the mystery of God, according to the teaching of the Christian faith.[35]

4. Distinction between Knowledge and Wisdom

We must recognize that from the outset Augustine adopts a precise method of 'research', and at the same time a type of philosophy which, as it takes the "raw datum" of faith as its starting point, aims to reach a certain and indubitable knowledge of intelligible realities.[36] In this first stage of his quest, Augustine does not use faith as a source of arguments which must take the place of those proper to reason. The analysis of the various speculative problems is conducted by a method which has rightly been described as a "hermeneutic circle", or a "circular paradigm" to show the

The hermeneutical circle: method

dynamic of mutual integration and illumination between the two cognitive forces which man has available to him, namely authority and reason.[37]

It should be stressed that Augustine emphasizes the two different possibilities of living the Christian faith: that of the philosopher, who sets out to investigate intelligible reality, starting from faith, and that of Monica, in other words of the simple people who are satisfied with faith alone.[38] In this first stage of enquiry, the notion of knowledge (*scientia*) and wisdom (*sapientia*) coincide.[39] But in the years of his presbyterate, he underwent a major change in his thinking, passing from enquiry of a philosophical nature to enquiry of a biblical/theological nature. We are in the second stage of his thought. Ordination to priesthood brought him face to face with a new task, that of preaching, teaching and defending the faith against the errors and arguments of heretics. On the other hand it should be remembered that St. Paul distinguishes the gift of knowledge from that of wisdom, and thus it is necessary first to embark on a profound study of the truth of faith. While continuing to keep the same method of enquiry, Augustine changes the instrument, which is now identified with the deeper and more critical study of the Scriptures. Beginning from the criticism of the notion of wisdom as taught by certain pagan philosophers, he introduces a new concept of knowledge (*scientia*), which he opposes to that of wisdom (*sapientia*). This change, which as we have stressed does not substantially modify the scheme of his method, should not surprise us, above all if we remember the "progressive" character of Augustinian thought, defined by Augustine himself in the following testimony:

> Therefore I admit that I try to be of the number of those who write by advancing in knowledge, and advance by writing.[40]

In the human mind he distinguishes a double function of reasoning: the first presides over the activities of a material and temporal kind, the other over the activity of contemplating intelligible and immutable truths.[41] Beginning from this distinction, he reinterprets the definition of wisdom proper to some pagan philosophers, as "a science of human and divine things". Taking his inspiration from the apostle Paul, he states that it is necessary:

> To divide this definition in such a way that the knowledge of divine things is properly called *sapientia*, but the name *scientia* properly belongs to the knowledge of human things.[42]

This distinction is further illustrated in the twelfth book of *De Trinitate*, in which Augustine on the one hand investigates the depths of human psychology to discover within it the actual image of the Trinity itself, and on the other hand refutes the doctrine of reminiscence as taught by Plato and Pythagoras.

> Wherefore, whatever we do prudently, courageously, temperately, and justly, and whatever knowledge we gather from history, either as furnishing us with examples to guard against or to imitate, and with the necessary proofs respecting any subject or discipline, wherewith our action is conversant in avoiding evil and in desiring good.

Hence, when the utterance is about these thing I hold it to be 'the utterance of knowledge', to be distinguished from 'the utterance of wisdom', to which belong those things which neither have been nor shall be, but which are; and on account of that eternity in which they are, it is said of them that they have been, are, and shall be without any changeableness of times.[43]

In the thirteenth book of *De Trinitate*, beginning with a brief analysis of the *prologue* to St John's Gospel, he moves on from a general concept of historical knowledge to a more specifically biblical one, and clarifies the distinction between knowledge and wisdom in a definitive way. The first investigates the historical truths that are at the basis of faith; the second the eternal truths which are the object of contemplation by the human intellect. Before the final summing up, Augustine explains his thinking on the matter:

> But all these things which the Word made flesh did and suffered for us in time and place belong, according to the distinction which we have undertaken to point out, to knowledge, and not to wisdom. But because the Word is without time and without place, He is co-eternal with the Father and is wholly present everywhere. And if anyone is able, insofar as he is able, to bring forward a truthful utterance about this, then that utterance will belong to wisdom.[44]

The content of this *scientia* consists of the knowledge of certain historical/temporal realities, and in particular of the events of the History of Salvation, and of the moral precepts. The deeper knowledge of this history ("possessed, moreover, by a few"), put "to the profit of the good and to defence from the wicked", "generates, feeds, defends and fortifies the faith that leads mankind to happiness".[45] Understood rightly, this is the real knowledge which Augustine calls "scientia sacra", based on more profound reflection on the Scriptures, by means of which we may arrive at a rigorous knowledge of the Christian faith. Augustine is now convinced that only this kind of enquiry can prepare for and lead to wisdom. He also formulates a series of hermeneutic principles, which form the actual content of the first three books of *De doctrina christiana*, as a basis for this "scientia sacra", which must also make use of 'profane' or secular knowledge. Just as the Jews when fleeing from Egypt seized vessels of gold and silver, clothes and other objects which they destined for a better use, so the scholar of "scientia sacra" must not hesitate to seize all the knowledge which may be useful to true religion.[46]

Both knowledge and wisdom draw upon the content of the Scriptures; however the knowledge of the events of salvation precedes and provides an introduction to wisdom, that is, to the intellectual knowledge of divine reality. Man in fact speaks with greater wisdom in relation to the progress that he makes in knowledge of the Scriptures.[47]

We should remember that by the distinction between the two forms of knowledge which he developed from the time of his presbyterate onward, Augustine did not mean to separate knowledge and wisdom, but on the contrary to stress their intimate link. He dedicated a great part of his intellectual energy to the defence and development of this "scientia sacra", with which he was to interpret many books of Scriptures, with the aim of studying the doctrinal content of the Christian faith in greater depth. The scholars of the Middle Ages were to give the name of "theology" to this knowledge, to distinguish it from philosophy.

The uninterrupted commitment to illustrating the complexity of the method used is a clear witness to the importance attributed both to purely human or Christian faith, and to reason, as basic factors of knowledge. Although autonomous in its argumentational proceedings, reason finds itself strengthened in philosophical enquiry when it is guided by faith; it can extend its cognitive range as far as intelligible realities, on condition that it does not place obstacles in the way of interior illumination.[48] By making authority the departure-point for the activities of reason, Augustine draws up a method for enquiry into rational truths, and as far as possible, also into those of faith. He also resolves the radical opposition introduced by Platonic philosophy between the sensible and the intelligible world. In this way, the existence of a hierarchy in the ontological scale is also demonstrated, and he illustrates the importance of the mediation of the Incarnate Word, necessary to man, in order to attain salvation, both from a gnoseological point of view (by passing from the knowledge of sensible realities to intelligible ones), and from an ontological standpoint (by passing from a mortal condition to an eternal one).[49] In *De Trinitate*, Augustine recalls the proportion enunciated by Plato in *Timaeus*:

> As eternity is to that which has a beginning, so truth is to faith.

The hermeneutical circle: method

Certainly a true proportion, but one to be supplemented by the additional fact that Christ is the true mediator, the principle of coherence which sows the faith in temporal realities in humankind, and reveals the truth about eternal realities:

> But eternal life is promised to us by means of the truth, and once again our faith is just as far away from the clear knowledge of the truth as mortality is from eternity. Hence, we now practice faith in the things that were done in time for our sake, and by it we are cleansed, in order that when we have come to sight, as truth follows faith, so may eternity follow mortality.[50]

Notes

1. N. Cipriani, *L'ispirazione tertullianea* op.cit., pp. 165–178.
2. G. Reale—G. Antiseri, *Quale ragione?*, Milano 2001, pp. 201–204.
3. *en.Ps.* 118, s.18, 3.
4. For reasons of clarity we use here the terminology which was been formulated as time went on, to indicate what Augustine is saying with the term *scientia sacra*, as we shall see.
5. *ep.* 120, 1, 3.
6. R. Holte, *Béatitude et sagesse. Saint Augustin et le problème de la fin de l'homme dans la philosophie ancienne*, Paris 1962, p. 324.
7. With regard to object language and metalanguage, cf. R. Carnap: *Introduction to Semantics and Formalization of Logic*, Cambridge (MA)—London 1975; pp 3–5: cf. also M. Malatesta, *The Primary Logic*, Leominster (England) 1997, pp.16–17.
8. P-Courcelle, *Recherches* op.cit., p. 252.
9. *conf.* VI,5,7; cf. E.Portalié, *A Guide to the Thought of Saint Augustine* Chicago 1960, pp. 115–116.
10. O. Du Roy, *L'intelligence* op. cit., p. 456.

11. K. Jaspers, *Drei Gründer des Philosophierens* op.cit., pp. 101–108.
12. *Beata v.* 1,4.
13. *Acad.* III, 20, 43.
14. *ord.* II, 9, 26. We should remember that ancient rhetoric, like the neo-Pythagoreans, had spoken long before of the principle of authority as the beginning of knowledge. Augustine returns to this tradition of thought. On this, see the original essay of K. H. Lütcke, Auctoritas *bei Augustin*, Stuttgart 1968, pp. 13–58.
15. *ord.* II, 9,26.
16. *ep.* 147, 3,8; cf. G. Madec, *La patrie* op.cit., pp. 165–169; M. F. Sciacca, *S.Agostino* op. cit., p. 269; A. Carlini, *Le ragioni della fede*, Brescia 1959, pp. 8–35.
17. *util. cred.* XI, 22; cf. O. Grassi, Preface to *L'utilità del credere*, in Agostino. *Il filosofo e la fede*, Milano 1989, p. 237.
18. K. H. Lütcke, Auctoritas op. cit., p.70.
19. Plato, *Respublica* V, 476e–477b; cf. G. Reale, *Storia della filosofia antica* II, Milano 1979, pp. 96–98.
20. *util.cred.*, XI, 25; *mag.* XI, 37.
21. For further information, see my own essay Auctoritas e ratio: *via alla vera libertà*, in *Il mistero del male e la libertà possibile: linee di antropologia agostiniana*, Roma 1995, pp. 103–109; cf. also M. Malatesta, *La logica delle funzioni. Strumenti per un'indagine transculturale, I. Logica dei predicati, delle classi e delle relazioni*, Roma 2000, pp. 171–189.
22. *div. qu.* 48.
23. *f. et symbol.* 4, 6–8.
24. *Acad.* III, 20, 43.
25. M. Cutino, *I dialoghi di Agostino dinanzi al "De regressu animae"*, *di Porfirio*, "Recherches Augustiniennes", XXVII, 1994, pp. 41–74.
26. *ord.* II, 9, 27; cf. J. J. O'Meara, *St. Augustine's View of Authority and Reason in A.D.386*, "Irish Theological Quarterly", XVIII, 1951, pp. 338–346.
27. J. J. O'Meara, *Porphyry's Philosophy from Oracles in Eusebius' "Praeparatio Evangelica" and Augustine's Dialogues*

The hermeneutical circle: method

of *Cassiciacum*, "Recherches Augustiniennes", VI, 1969, pp. 103–139.

28. *civ.* X, 27; cf. N. Cipriani, *Il rifiuto del pessimismo porfiriano nei primi scritti di S.Agostino*, "Augustinianum", XXXVII, 1997, p. 133.
29. *Acad.* III, 19, 42.
30. *ord.* II, 5, 16.
31. Ibid.
32. *vera rel.* 24, 45.
33. *sol.* I, 5, 11 – 6, 12.
34. *ord.* II, 5, 16.
35. R. Holte, *Béatitude* op. cit., pp. 87–109; G. Madec, *Petits études augustiniennes*, Paris 1994, p. 168; G. Madec, *Saint Augustin* op. cit., p. 20; N. Cipriani, *Il rifiuto* op. cit., pp. 135–136 ; V. Pacioni, *L'unità teoretica del "De Ordine" di Sant'Agostino*, Roma 1996, pp. 212–217.
36. H.-I. Marrou, *Saint Augustin et la fin de la culture antique*, Paris 1958, pp. 368–376.
37. G. Reale – D. Antiseri, *Quale* op. cit., p. 202.
38. *ord.* II, 5, 15; II, 17, 45–46.
39. *Acad.* III, 3, 5; *sol.* I, 4, 9 – 5, 11; *lib. arb.* II, 9, 26–27.
40. *ep.* 143, 2. On this subject we agree with what E. Gilson wrote in *The Christian Philosophy of Saint Augustine*, New York 1960, p. 364: "There was a psychological evolution in St. Augustine; there were many variations of detail and a great number of these we have pointed out, but we have never discovered the slightest philosophical change in any of his essential theses. St. Augustine fixed his main ideas from the time of his conversion – even, we believe, regarding grace – and he always drew on the capital he had acquired".
41. *trin.* XII, 33.
42. Ibid. XIV, 1, 3.
43. Ibid., XII, 14, 22–23.
44. Ibid., XIII 19, 24.
45. Ibid., XIV 1, 3.

46. *doctr. chr.* II, 40, 60; cf. E. Gilson, *The Christian Philosophy* op. cit., p. 125.
47. *doctr. chr.* IV, 5, 7.
48. The theme of illumination will be given more extensive treatment in Chapter VI of this book.
49. R. Holte, *Béatitude* op. cit., p. 325.
50. *trin.* IV, 18,24; cf. G. Madec, «Christus, scientia et sapientia nostra», *Le principe de cohérence de la doctrine augustinienne*, «Recherches Augustiniennes», X, 1975, pp.78–79.

III

BEGINNINGS OF AUGUSTINIAN SPECULATION

1. The Criterion of Truth

In the autumn of 386, after abandoning teaching, Augustine decided to retire to Cassiciacum, in the villa owned by his friend Verecondus, together with his mother Monica, his brother Navigius, his son Adeodatus, his cousins Lasdidianus and Rusticus, his friend Alypius and two pupils, Licentius and Trigetius. Over a period of five months he wrote various philosophical works, commonly known collectively as *The Dialogues* of Cassiciacum: *Contra Academicos*, in which the theories of Carneades, chief exponent of the *Nova Academia*, are confuted; *De beata vita* in which he probes further into the nature of the highest good; *De ordine*, in which problems related to Divine Providence and the nature of evil are dealt with. Closely linked to these debates are the *Soliloquia*, an original dialogue between Augustine and reason, and several *Letters* written to distant friends.

In *Contra Academicos* Augustine aims at confuting the arguments of the Academics, and demonstrating the existence of an objective criterion of truth (*iudicium veritatis*). It is typical of Augustine's method that the discussion begins with questions directed to his interlocutors:

> Have you any doubt that it behooves us to know truth? (...) If we can be happy without understanding truth?[1]

Licentius, appealing to the doctrine of the *New Academy*, maintains that the search for truth is sufficient in itself to bring happiness. Trigetius, taking the opposite line, states that it is not the mere search but the possession of the truth that is the condition of happiness. The former, appealing to Cicero's authority, holds that man has one single criterion to follow, that of probability, since the truth is an unattainable target; the latter, noting that his friend's idea coincides with that of Cicero, claims the right to proceed in free enquiry, not bound by any author, and he adds that the incessant search, without arriving at an objective truth, leads to error. Licentius replies by stressing that error is the approval of what is false in place of what is true (*error mihi videtur esse falsi pro vero approbatio*), and the pure search is itself a sign of wisdom. Trigetius, aware that Licentius, an able dialectician, is not vulnerable on this point, decides to shift the object of the discussion to the notion of wisdom, suggesting the following definition: "wisdom is the right road that leads to the truth".[2] Licentius responds that wisdom is a pure road, pure method, pure enquiry. Then Augustine intervenes, proposing a different definition of wisdom: "wisdom is the knowledge of things human and divine".[3] Licentius also attacks the teacher's definition: if this were the case, in fact, we would have to confer the title of wiseman on the fortune-teller, Albericus of Carthage, a well-known libertine and pimp, but capable of magical responses. From this he concludes that wisdom is both knowledge and diligent enquiry of things divine and human; the former belongs to God while the latter is the task of man. God derives happiness from the former, man from the latter.[4]

Before ending this session, Augustine sums up the discussion that has taken place, and promises that when the debate is resumed, he will take part personally, defending the idea of Trigetius, and subjecting the philosophies of the New Academy, the defence of which Licentius has taken on, to critical scrutiny.

The debate is resumed after a week. Augustine, on a suggestion from Licentius, gives a summary exposition of the Academic philosophers as he had known them from the reading of Cicero's *Academica*.[5] According to the Academics, it is necessary to suspend assent to any representation, because neither thought nor sensory perception are capable of founding criterion for truth. With regard to practical conduct, it is sufficient to follow the doctrine of the probable or of verisimilitude. Alypius in turn explains the cultural and historical origins of the Academic philosophy, showing the difference between the *Middle Academy* of Arcesilaus and Carneades, and the *Fifth Academy* of Antiochus of Ascalona. In the reconstruction of the history of the Academy, Alypius attributes to the authority of Plato and Socrates themselves the idea according to which one may defend oneself from error on condition that one does not give assent to anything without a more profound examination. He continues by stressing that the Stoic Zeno had introduced the radical notion according to which nothing can be held to be certain if it is not true in such a way as to be distinguishable from the false, and that the wise person must never make assertions on the basis of opinion. Arcesilaos had become aware of this teaching, and derived from it that man does not have the capacity for such a knowledge, because the sole source of knowledge is the sensible world. Thus the wise man does not give assent to anything. Subsequently there appeared a disciple of Philo, Antiochus of Ascalona, who recovered the genuine thinking of Plato, maintaining against the innovations of the sceptical Academics, that the wise man can know the truth.

After this exposition by Alypius, Augustine resumes the critical theme of Antiochus, performing a rigorous critique of the doctrine of probability or verisimilitude.[6] The third book of the *Contra Academicos* opens with a strong appeal for the search for truth, which is the most noble and most necessary of tasks. After a series of questions posed by Augustine on the nature of knowledge and opinion, Alypius abandons scepticism and sets out to defend the actual theses of probabilism, but since he cannot succeed in finding further rational arguments to support his position, he evokes the myth of Proteus.[7] In classical mythology Proteus was a clairvoyant who granted the favor of his replies only under constraint. Having been captured, he used the stratagem of changing himself into a lion, a panther or a dragon, thus succeeding in liberating himself while the hunter, terrified, abandoned his prey. The secret was in standing firm despite all the transformations, until he resumed his natural semblance: only then did he resign himself to giving the required information, constrained by a higher power. The mythical Proteus is the image of truth, of which man is unable to take possession unless a higher power comes to meet him.

Surprised by this last reflection by Alypius, Augustine addresses some benign words to his friend, before beginning the confutation of the ideas of the New Academy:

> 'But Alypius, you have told us who it is that is able to show us truth, and I must sedulously endeavor not to disagree with you. Alike with brevity and piety, you have said that only some kind of deity is able to show a man what truth is. Wherefore, in this discussion of ours, I have heard nothing more pleasing, nothing more weighty, nothing more worthy of approval and—if, as I trust, that deity be present—nothing more true. For, with what depth of understanding, with what fixation of attention on the very best kind of philosophy, has the famous Proteus been mentioned by you! That Proteus, so that you, boys, may see that poets are not to be entirely disregarded in philosophy, is portrayed after the image of the truth. In poems, I say, Proteus portrays and personates the truth, which no one can lay hold on if he is deceived by false image, and loosens or loses his hold on the nodes of understanding. My most intimate friend is in accord with me, not only on the question of probability in human affairs, by also on religion itself; this is the most manifest sign of a true friend, inasmuch as friendship has been rightly

Beginnings of Augustinian speculation

and piously defined as 'a friendly and affectionate agreement on human things and on divine.'[8]

At this point Augustine goes on to investigate the premises of the philosophers of the *Middle Academy*. The section of *Contra Academicos* (III, 10, 22 – 13, 29) which we are about to analyse constitutes an ideal dialogue with certain philosophers. He decides to set aside the role of the maieutic philosopher for that of the teacher, turning himself from a subject of the debate into an instructor. The debate thus becomes a monologue by which the teacher aims to confute two premises of the Skeptic Academics: a) "Nothing can be perceived" (*Nihil posse percipi*) and b) "Assent must not be given to anything" (*Nulli rei debere assentiri*).[9] The first sentence is subjected to analysis in relation to the problem of certainty. Augustine maintains that, in order to prove validity of the statement according to which nothing may be perceived, Carneades appeals to the disputes and dissensions of the philosophers. Augustine replies that the diatribes between philosophers to which the Academic refers are of no interest to him; in fact he is certain of possessing certain notions in a clear fashion, though not yet being a philosopher. And he continues:

> I am certain that either there is only one world or there are more worlds than one. I am likewise certain that if there are more worlds than one, their number is either finite or infinite (*Certum enim habeo, aut unum esse mundum, aut non unum; etsi non unum aut finiti numeri, aut infiniti*).[10]

In order to understand the meaning of the first sentence, we have to begin from certain elements of Stoic logic used by Augustine. The Stoics used the logic of propositions which, although discovered after the death of Aristotle, is at the basis of the logic of terms elaborated by the latter.[11] Moreover the Stoics were accustomed to making a distinction: they spoke of simple propositions and non-simple propositions. We modern logicians speak of atomic sentences and molecular sentences. Among the non-simple propositions, the Stoics took into account conditional propositions (our 'implications'), copulative propositions (our 'logical product') and disjunctive propositions. An example of a conditional proposition: "if it is daytime, there is light". An example of a copulative proposition "it is daytime and there is light". An example of a disjunctive proposition: "either it is day or it is night".[12] It is also known that the Stoics discovered the tables of truth, without making use of a similar symbolization to that of modern symbolic logic, however. Thus, for example, a copulative is true if and only if all the simple propositions which make it up are true; a disjunctive is true if and only if one and one only of the simple propositions which make it up is true and the other is false, and so on. Finally, they discovered the relation between discourse or argument and sound connection (*sunemménon ygiés*) which is one of the possible forms that a tautology may take.[13]

The argument (logos) is a system consisting of premises and a conclusion. The premises are the propositions accepted for the demonstration of a conclusion; the conclusion is the proposition demonstrated by beginning from the premises. For example, in the following argument: "If it is day, there is light, but it is day, therefore there is light", the conclusion is "there is light"; the other propositions form the premises.[14] The tautology is a molecular sentence which is always true, true in all possible worlds, that is in all situations independently of the meaning and the truth value of the atomic sentences which make it up.[15]

Now we come to Augustine. In formulating the non-simple proposition, "the world is one or (*aut*) it is not one", he does not know which of the two simple propositions which compose it is the true one, but he does have the certainty that one of them must be true. Thus he knows that there is truth, and that this is guaranteed by the non-simple proposition, the latter being a tautology.[16] As we can see, Augustine is a step ahead of the Stoics. While for the latter, tautologies (correct connections) serve to prove the correctness of the arguments in their diatribes against the

Peripatetics and Neoplatonists, to Augustine, they serve to resolve the problem of certainty.

At this point Augustine, taking an ironic tone, imagines that Carneades has unexpectedly awakened (*evigilavit*) from a long sleep, and is asking insistently that one and only one of the simple propositions which make up the non-simple proposition shall be chosen. Augustine replies:

> I refuse to do that, for it is the same as saying: "quit what you know (*relinque quod scis*) and say what you know not (*dic quod nescis*)".[17]

Moreover, to Carneades' objection that in this way the non-simple proposition will remain in suspension, he answers:

> Better hanging in suspense than falling to the ground. While it is hanging, it is at least in plain view, and it can be pronounced either true or false. Because I know that it is true or false, I say that I know it as a proposition.[18]

With the assertion that "I say that I know this expression", Augustine wishes to make reference to the awareness with which he knows the non-simple proposition to be true.[19]

He then closes the discussion of the problem of certainty by reminding Carneades that the disjunctive proposition mentioned above is certain because it has nothing in common with falsity.

Having demonstrated that something can be perceived, at least on the logical view point, he then moves on to deal with the second assertion of the Academics relating to assent, because the problem of certainty is intertwined with that of assent. The solution of the first problem, regarding certainty, is based on a premise: the existence of the world. In fact, the disjunctives suggested above, the certainty of which cannot be contested by the Academic, concern the essence of the world and not its existence. The existence of the world is only presupposed.[20] As far as the problem relating to assent is concerned, the Academic advances three objections.

The first:

> But (...) if the senses are deceptive, how do you know that this world exists?[21]

Augustine replies:

> Your reasons will never be able to refute the testimony of the senses to such extent as to convince us that nothing is perceived by us. In fact, you have never ventured to try that, but you have strenuously exerted yourself to convince us that a thing can be something other than what it seems to be. So, by the term *world*, I mean this totality which surrounds us and sustains us. Whatever its nature may be, I apply the term *world* to that which is present to my eyes, and which I see to be holding the earth and the heavens... or the *quasi* heavens.[22]

The reply is further illustrated thus:

> If you say that nothing appears to me, then I shall never be in error: then is in error the man who rashly accepts as true whatever appears to him. Indeed, you yourselves say that to sentient beings a false thing can appear to be true, but you do not say that nothing can so appear to them.[23]

The Academic puts forward another objection:

> Is it the very same world that you are seeing, even if you are asleep?[24]

Augustine replies:

> I have already said that I am using the term *world* to designate whatever appears as such to me. But if you think that the term ought to be restricted to that which appears to those who are awake and of sound mind, then contend, if you can, that sleeping men and deranged men are not in this world while they are asleep or are deranged. My only assertion is that this entire mass and frame of bodies in which we exist is either a unit or not a unit, and that it is what it is, whether we be asleep or awake, deranged

Beginnings of Augustinian speculation

or sound of mind. Point out how this notion can be false.[25]

Then a third objection is put forward:

> But you can say that what I perceive when I am awake could appear to me also when I am asleep. Therefore, it can be very similar to something false (*ideoque hoc potest esse falso simillimum*).[26]

Augustine replies:

> However, if there are one world and six worlds, it is clear that there are seven worlds, no matter how I may be affected. And, with all due modesty, I maintain that I know this.[27]

He concludes that the deceit concerns sensible knowledge, never rational knowledge.

In paragraph 26 of the work in question, we have another imaginary dialogue between Augustine, an Epicurean and an Academic.

While in the first dialogue Augustine has given a brief description of pathological and hallucinatory illusions, he now deals with the problem of physiological illusions, taking certain examples from the Epicureans, such as the oar which appears to be broken in the water, the oscillation of war towers in movement, the wings of birds that change colour according to the position which the birds themselves assume. The Epicurean is the first to contribute, and he advances a rational explanation of these phenomena.

The Academic objects:

> I am deceived if I give assent (*ego tamen fallor, si assentior*).[28]

But Augustine makes the sceptic Academic observe:

> Restrict your assent to the mere fact of your being convinced that it appears thus to you. Then there is no deception (*noli plus assentiri, quam ut ita tibi apparere persuadeas, et nulla deceptio est*).[29]

And he concludes the diatribe with five assertions:

> I know (*scio*) that this appears white to me. I know (*scio*) that I am delighted by what I am hearing. I know (*scio*) that this smells pleasant to me. I know (*scio*) that this tastes sweet to me. I know (*scio*) that this feels cold to me.[30]

If the problem of certainty can be resolved by using the non-simple propositions of which the Stoics were speaking, the problem of assent can be resolved by reflecting on simple ones. When I say: this object seems to me to be white (which is a simple proposition) I *know* that this appears to me to be white (*hoc mihi candidum videri scio*); when I say this sound delights my ear, then I *know* that this sound delights my ear. In short, while the Stoic restricts himself to considering simple propositions as ingredients of non-simple ones, Augustine discovers in the analysis of the simple proposition the principle of self-awareness. The skeptic calls into question the object of sensory perception, but he cannot call into question the fact that I know that at that moment I am perceiving something. The problem of truth is thus shifted: no longer the truth as *adequatio* between *res* and *intellectus*, but as *adequatio* between the critical capacity and what I have experienced. While the Stoics begin from simple propositions to construct non-simple ones, Augustine takes the opposite path; he begins from the truth of the non-simple propositions to discover the truth of the simple ones. The Stoics move from the part to the whole; Augustine from the whole to the part. From the logical structure of thought he discovers that one of the two propositions is necessarily true. Once he has assured himself that one of the propositions of a contradiction must be true, he establishes the criterion of truth, by not permitting any assertion beyond what can be perceived, and referring the act of perception back to self-awareness.

2. Nature of the supreme Good

From the reading of Cicero's *Academica* Augustine had perceived that, once the problem related to the criterion for truth had been resolved, philosophical reflection must enquire into that concerning the ultimate goal (*télos*) of human nature, that is the highest good. In the dialogue *De beata via*, written after *Contra Academicos*, the psychological axiom which Cicero had advanced in his *Hortensius*, namely "everyone wishes to be happy"[31] is taken up again, with the intention of achieving the determination of the true nature of the object desired. The question of the ultimate goal of human life should be studied, beginning with the analysis relating to the nature of good things. In *Confessiones*[32] going back to the period of Cassiciacum, he was to say that this problem had been the subject of discussion with Alypius and Nebridius in the days before his conversion.

In *De beata vita*, the discussion is introduced by a brief exchange of questions and answers between Augustine and his interlocutors, to stress that human beings are composed of soul and body and that the unity of these two factors is provided by the awareness of self which the human being possesses. Both the body and the soul seek after their own nourishment: the body desires material food to ensure its health, the soul tends to nourish itself on reflection and virtue.[33] After these remarks of an anthropological kind, clearly derived from the Peripatetics,[34] the enquiry into the nature of the desire for happiness which is part of the human constitution gets under way. It is important to underline that the discussion unravels beginning from the analysis concerning the nature of the good things which man desires, not from the anthropological model in some ways suggested by the opening of the dialogue. Those present aknowledge that a person who does not have what he desires cannot be happy, and that the person who achieves what he desires is not necessarily happy. The only person who is happy is he who attains a permanent good (*semper manens*) which cannot be subverted by the change of fortune or the adversity of events.[35] Monica puts forward the idea according to which a person who possesses material goods in abundance may also be happy, but on condition that he places a limit on his desires. Although appreciating this definition of happiness (clearly of Stoic origin) Augustine goes much further, identifying "what is eternal and always stable" with God himself. Thus a happy person is one who possesses God. The development of this thought is in explicit polemic with the Academics: those who believe that the truth cannot be found, will not be able to possess either God or happiness.[36] In the thirty-fourth paragraph Augustine further illustrates his remarks, passing from the Stoic meaning of the term measure (*modus*) to the Platonic meaning. In fact Aristotle and the Stoics understood the significance of measure as a just mean (*mesótes*), by which the soul maintains itself in balance between two opposites, and in this just mean they had conceived virtue as the highest level of human behavior. For his part, Plato had already previously applied the term measure (*métron*) in a metaphysical sense to 'primordial unity' or 'the most exact measure'.[37] Augustine stresses that this 'supreme measure' constitutes the ultimate goal of humankind and its happiness.[38] Having corrected the eudemonistic trend of Peripatetic philosophy, Augustine concludes by introducing the expression *Deo frui*,[39] which constitutes his characteristic teleological formula, and providing a definition of happiness in the strictly Christian sense:

> This, then, is the full satisfaction of souls, this the happy life: to recognize piously and completely the One through whom you are led into the truth, the nature of the truth you enjoy, and the bond that connects you with the supreme measure.[40]

In the work *De moribus Ecclesiae catholicae et de moribus manichaeorum*, Augustine looks into the nature of the ultimate good, beginning from the notion of human nature, understood as a dynamic principle of tendencies (*appetitus*). He makes use of the anthropological model of Varro, the eudemonistic character of which he accepts, while rejecting the immanentist view point.[41] In this writing too, he starts from the assertion that the tendency to happiness (*appetitus beatitatis*)⁴² is a common characteristic of all humankind; he observes nonetheless that neither the person who does not possess what he loves, whatever that may be, nor the person who possesses what he loves, if it be harmful, nor the person who does not love what he possesses, even if it is a very good thing, can be considered happy. In fact, one who aims at what he cannot achieve is tormented; one who has obtained what should not be aimed for, is mistaken, one who does not aim for what he should achieve, is sick. This last possibility alone remains, therefore: one who both loves and possesses what constitutes his own supreme good, without fear of losing it, is happy.⁴³ To know the nature of this supreme good, it is necessary, however, to submit the ontological structure of the human being to investigation. Although he does not provide an exhaustive description of the essence of human nature in this context, Augustine stresses certain aspects of it:

> Rather, it seems to me that since nearly everyone agrees (or at least, and it is sufficient, those with whom I am now dealing agree) that we are composed of body and soul, what should be determined at this point is *what man himself is*. Of the two which I have mentioned, is he body alone or soul alone? For although they are two things, soul and body, and neither could be called man were the other not present (for the body would not be man if there were no soul, nor would the soul be man were there no body animated by it), it might happen, nevertheless, that one of these would be looked upon and be spoken of as man.
>   What do we call man, then? Is he soul and body like a centaur or two horses harnessed together? Or shall we call him the body alone in the service of a governing soul, as is the case when we give the name *lamp*, not to the vessel and flame together, but to the vessel alone on account of the flame within it? Or shall we say that man is nothing but the soul, inasmuch as it rules the body, just as we say that the horseman is not the horse and man together, but the

> man alone from the fact that he guides the horse? This is a difficult problem to solve, or, at any rate, even if its solution were simple, it would require a lengthy explanation involving an expense of time and labor which would not profit us here. For whether it be both body and soul or soul alone that goes by the name of man, that is not the supreme good of man which constitutes the supreme good of the body. But whatever is the highest good either of body and soul together or of the soul alone, that is the supreme good of man.[44]

Augustine agrees with Varro in maintaining that 'identification of the essence of human being should be sought not in the body, as the Epicureans taught, or in the soul, as the Platonists maintain, but in the integration of the soul and the body, without, for the time being, going more deeply into the characteristics of their relationship. Having established the anthropological premise, with which the Manichaeans too can agree, he passes on to investigate the nature of the highest good, beginning with a remark which is clearly derived from Varro: the body is a good entity, in possession of certain primary good things (*prima naturae*) such as pleasure, absence of pain, strength, beauty, agility; nevertheless, none of these goods constitutes the highest good of the body, but on the contrary, the highest good of the body is the soul:

> (...) by its very presence the soul provides the body with all the things we have enumerated and with that which excels them all besides, namely, life.[45]

The soul is the highest good of the body because it is better than the body, and communicates vigour and life to it (*corpore melius est et quo ei vigor et vita praebetur*). If however, the existence of a being superior to the soul is discovered, which perfects it and renders it better in its kind, then not even the soul can be considered the supreme good of humankind.[46] It is important to point out that here Augustine uses a particular notion of the supreme good, understanding it as a reality which not only satisfies the desire of mankind, but improves and perfects even the soul itself.[47] Varro, and before him, Antiochus of Ascalona and the Peripatetics had already recognised the existence of a natural tendency in man toward the perfection of his physical and intellectual capacities.[48] They had also taught that virtue, a habit or quality of the soul, acquired with the help of the teaching or guidance of a wise man,[49] constitutes the condition for improvement of the human soul. Augustine resumes this anthropological teaching, while proposing a correction of primary importance to it. He acknowledges that for the learning of virtue a moral doctrine and a wise guide are required, but he maintains that true moral teaching cannot be assured in any certain and stable way either by the subject himself or by a man who has attained virtue and wisdom, because one may be deprived of its presence against one's own consent and despite one's own resistance. Thus he concludes by affirming that only God can guarantee true moral teaching, and thus the perfection of the human soul.[50]

On one hand Augustine has taken to himself the principle according to which the supreme good must be sought, departing from human nature, in particular from the natural tendency to happiness (*appetitus beatitatis*), on the other hand he has identified the supreme good of humankind with God Himself. If the first theme, of an anthropological nature, is the result of the comparison with the eudemonistic viewpoint characteristic of the anthropology and morality of Varro, the second, of a metaphysical nature, is the result of the comparison with certain themes of Neoplatonic metaphysics, such as that relating to the natural vocation of man to God. In later writings Augustine was to go more deeply into these two aspects, until he saw in the original tendencies of human nature the sign of a superior finality which links man to God.

Many beings, Augustine wrote in *De vera religione*, have been created by the eternal Truth or Wisdom of the Father without being destined to it (*sunt per ipsam facta, ut non sint ad ipsam*): those equipped with reason, on the other hand, have been created by means of Truth or Wisdom so as to be destined to it (*sic sunt per ipsam, ut ad ipsam etiam sint*).[51] In *Confessiones*, this natural inclination of humankind toward God was to be illustrated by the image of specific weight:

> The body inclines by its weight toward its own place. A weight is not necessarily an inclination toward the lowest level, but to its proper place. Fire inclines upward; a stone, downward. They are moved by their weights; they seek their places. Oil poured out below water rises above the water; water poured on oil sinks beneath the oil. They are moved by their weights; they seek their own places. When not well ordered, they are restless; when they are in order, they are at rest. My weight is my love; by it I am carried wherever I am carried.[52]

While a substantial number of the pagan philosophers had considered man to be a being closed and resigned within the limits of his nature, constrained to search for the highest good in the practice of virtue, Augustine, in contrast, considered man as a being capable of happiness (*capax beatitatis*) because he is equipped with his own natural tendency towards it. In his work *De Trinitate* speaking of man as the image of his Creator, capable of "remembering, knowing and loving Him who made him",[53] he was to describe him as a being capable of the highest nature (*summae naturae capax*).[54]

3. Divine Providence and Evil in History

In editing the writings from Cassiciacum, Augustine notes:

> At this same time, in fact, between those (books) which were written, *On the Academics*, I wrote also two books, *On order*, in which I treated the important question of whether the order of divine Providence embraces all things, the good and the evil.[55]

We know that in Milan, Augustine read Plotinus' treatise concerning Providence and the nature of evil. In this writing, the Neoplatonic philosopher maintains that a universal fatalism governs the whole world and that an immutable and necessary order overcomes the initiative of individual human beings, subject to a fatal law which rewards and punishes them because they are responsible for the good and evil they perform. In illustrating the nature of Providence, Plotinus distinguishes a particular providence (*prónoia eph'ekásto*) and a universal providence (*tou pantós prónoia*). The former is the providence of man, which reasons before acting; this consists in asking whether it is necessary to perform an act or not necessary to do so, and what will be the outcome for us if we do or do not perform it. In short, particular providence is the providence of the wise man within the human sphere. The latter is universal providence. This can be conceived either by analogy with the human kind or in a different manner. Plotinus leaves aside particular providence, of the human kind, and rejects universal providence conceived by analogy to human providence on the basis of the dogma of Greek philosophy, according to which the world is eternal. It is clear that Plotinus on one hand assumes the notion of providence adopted by the Stoics, while on the other hand he attacks the Biblical notion of creation.[56]

Very closely connected with the problem of providence is the one related to the nature of evil. Plotinus observes:

> The conflict and destruction that reign among living beings are inevitable, since things here are derived, brought into existence because the Divine Reason which contains all of them in the upper Heavens— how could they come here unless they were there? —must outflow over the whole extent of Matter.[57]

During retreat at Cassiciacum, Augustine succeeded in pinpointing the connection between the problem of Providence and that of evil. The two problems constitute the main content of the dialogue *De ordine* up to Chapter 7 of the second book. Plotinus too, in his third *Ennead*, had seen this connection; however, if this is undeniable in the way he poses the two questions, the approaches diverge, and as we shall see, the conclusions are radically different.

After an acute criticism of the cosmological doctrine of the Epicureans and Stoics, Augustine also distances himself from that of Plotinus. He writes:

> Nor can we presume in the name of "a universal nature" (*per universam naturam*), according to some frivolous claims of a vain opinion, to remove from the secret control of the (divine) Majesty (*secretissimum Maiestatis arbitrium*) that which we admire well-ordered in every single thing without the intervention of any human craft whatever (*ullis nugis vanae opinionis*).[58]

It is interesting to note that at this point Augustine introduces, though only in very concise form, the problem of history:

> Yet, here is a point suggestive of even more questioning: that the organic parts of a flea are marvelously fitted and framed, while human life is surrounded and made restless by the inconsistency of countless disorders (*humana vita innumerabilium perturbationum inconstantia vexetur et fluctuet*).[59]

Plotinus, on the contrary, describes the dramas and the questionings that trouble the events of human history with great detachment, looking at them as if they were simply scenes from the theatre:

> Men directing their weapons against each other under doom of death, yet neatly lined up to fight as in the pyrrhic sword-dances of their sport, this is enough to tell us that all human intentions are but play, that death is nothing terrible, that to die in a war or in a fight is but to taste a little beforehand what old age has in store, to go away earlier and come back the sooner. So for misfortunes that may accompany life, the loss of property, for instance; the loser will see that there was a time when it was not his, that its possession is but a mock boon to the robbers, who will in their turn lose it to others, and

even that to retain property is a greater loss than to forfeit it.[60]

In the most important part of *De ordine* Augustine intends to show that divine Providence, while being transcendent, extends to the furthest and most minute things, while moral evils present in human life must not be attributed to the divine will nor can they be considered as the consequence of any kind of necessity. Furthermore, a distinction is introduced which will prove to be important in the development of the dialogue, and is related to the notion of order: there exists an order of things (*ordo rerum*) proper to each being and a universal order (*ordo universitatis*) by which the world is governed and directed. The understanding of the two *ordines* requires at least one of two conditions: morality (*ordo vitae*) or learning (*ordo eruditionis*).

The discussion begins with the presentation of the protagonists. Licentius, by now a long way from the philosophy of the Academy, is a rich young man of poetic tendencies: the character who takes the most active part in the debate, he now puts himself forward as a defender of the fatalist determination of the Stoics.[61] The other leading character, described less clearly than Licentius, is Trigetius: although he is young, he loves history as a mature man does; while not having the capacity for abstraction and comparison of the other, he places more importance in facts. He does not possess the passionate drive of Licentius, but is sober and realistic. The third character is Alypius, absent at the outset; he is to take part in the discussion at a later moment, as soon as he returns from Milan to Cassiciacum. Finally there is Navigius, Augustine's brother, while their mother Monica is not named but is to play an important part, to the point that at the end she in fact will represent the true philosophy.

The actual discussion begins with the third chapter. It is dawn; Augustine is lying on his bed in a room in the villa at Verecondus, deep in thought. He himself recounts:

> I was awake, therefore, as I said, when the sound of water flowing past at the rear of the baths came to my ears, and it was noticeably louder than usual. To me it seemed very strange that the sound of the same running water was at one time quite clear, and again less audible. I began to ask myself what was the cause.[62]

In the next room, Licentius wakes because of the mice that are scurrying around in search of food, and he persistently slaps the floor; Augustine calls his pupil's attention:

> For I see that your muse has given you a light by which to work at night—have you noticed how irregular is the sound of that water drain?[63]

Licentius answers him:

> It is nothing new to me at this time; for, awakened from sleep at times, and desirous of quiet, I have hearkened to learn whether it were pouring rain when that water was doing just what it is doing now.[64]

Trigetius, too, resting in another room, has woken up in the meantime. So Licentius improvises for the others an explanation of the phenomenon, observing that a constant flow of water is a manifest order, while an irregular flow is a manifest disorder; however, since there is a cause for the phenomenon of rhythm which is interrupted, in reality this situation is part of an order which escapes our immediate perception. The conclusion is that apparently there is disorder, but that nothing is, in itself, outside order.[65] The dialogue, which started quite by chance, is transformed into a passionate philosophical dispute. Disregarding the reservations of Augustine and Trigetius, Licentius deepens his thesis, inspired by the more rigid Stoic determinism already adopted by Plotinus[66]: nothing can occur outside order (*nihil praeter ordinem fieri posse*),[67] because the ultimate structure of things obeys the same universal law of order by which providence governs things. Thus, there is no effect which does not have a cause (*nihil fieri sine causa*), since order, by its nature, coincides with the succession of causes (*ordo causarum*).

Beginning with the fifteenth paragraph, when the cosmological problem has been set aside, the enquiry shifts to the relation existing between order and evil, between God and evils. Trigetius points out to Licentius that if nothing occurs outside order, then evils must of necessity come within (the framework of) order; if order derives from God, and is willed by Him, then the evils which afflict human life must be attributed to the divine will. To avoid reaching this conclusion, Licentius introduces a new notion:

> And because this orderly arrangement maintains the harmony of the universe by this very contrast (between good and evil), it comes about that evil things (lesser goods) must exist. In this way the beauty of all things is in a manner configured, as it were, from antitheses, that is, from opposites: this is pleasing to us even in discourse.[68]

Plotinus had already taught that, although moral evils constitute a disorder contrary to the nature of the soul, they are not outside the universal order.[69] Licentius goes on to affirm that the notion of divine justice is the rational test of the thesis he has expounded. Beneath the literary form of rhetorical questions, he puts the focus on a triple problem:

a) if there is no distinction, there is no retribution either, whereas we know that justice consists in retribution, or in giving each his own;

(b) if all things are good, then there is no distinction in them;

(c) if the justice of God consists in giving to each of the good and evil doers on the basis of their merit, then nothing exists outside order.

The logical structure underlying the first two questions is as follows: if all things are good, then there is no distinction; if there is no distinction, then there is no retribution: but there is retribution, then all things cannot be good.[70]

After some digressions, the discussion on this point is taken up again in the twenty-second paragraph of the second book of *De ordine*. It is a key moment in the dislogue.[71] Monica is also present at this point. After having recalled, in conformity with the previous statement of Licentius, that divine justice is an attribute by which God distinguishes the good from the evil and distributes to each and every one what one deserves, Augustine puts a dilemma to those present. With the clear intention of destroying Licentius' argument and directing the discussion toward a definitive conclusion, he asks: if God subjects the good and the evil of humankind to judgment because he is just, or good and evil always exist, or God was not just when evil did not yet exist.[72] According to a philosophy of a deterministic type like the one defended by Licentius, the reply to the dilemma put forward is a foregone conclusion. Trigetius intervenes, proposing a new distinction which marks the breaking point between the pagan vision of Licentius and the Christian one.[73] It is pointed out that God is always just, even before evil begins to exist, because he always possesses justice as an essential attribute of his nature; God, however, exercises justice through a just judgment only when evil is committed in time. The thesis is further illustrated with the example of Cicero: when the Catiline conspiracy had been exposed, the former came to exercise prudence, temperance and fortitude and justice, virtues which he had possessed before Catiline had prepared such ruin against the Roman state. Thus Trigetius concludes:

> Virtue is to be considered in itself, and not through some deed like this, in reference to man. How much more so with reference to God? (...) — if indeed in the inadequacy of our thoughts and speech it is permitted to compare the one class with the other in any way. (...) For — so that we may understand that God was always just — with the rise of evil, which He would distinguish from good, He did not delay giving to each one its due. Justice did not have to be learned by Him, but rather the justice He always had, was then to be put into practice.[74]

Beginnings of Augustinian speculation

When the distinction between justice as a divine attribute and the use that is made of it by God has been illustrated by Trigetius, Augustine provides a new contribution to the discussion, using the notion of order in a polysemantic fashion. He passes, in fact, from the use of the notions of *ordo rerum* and *ordo universitatis* to that of *ordo Dei*. Speaking to Licentius, he stresses:

> Where is that which you so strenuously asserted: that nothing is done apart from order? For, the fact that evil had a beginning is surely not brought about by the order of God (*ordo Dei*), but, when it had become a fact, it was included in God's order.[75]

Moral evil is a disorder which arises in contradiction to the divine order, and to the order pertaining to human nature. As it has a temporal origin, it cannot be considered necessary and coeternal with the order of God. However, it does not remain unpunished, because it is made to re-enter the order established by God himself through His just judgment. At this point Monica, gathering the thread of the argument, concludes the discussion with the definitive point of view inspired by the Christian faith:

> I think that nothing could have been done apart from the order of God (*ordo Dei*), because evil itself, which has had an origin, in no way originated by the order of God; but that divine justice permitted it not to be beyond the limits of order, and has brought it back and confined it to an order befitting it.[76]

To understand Monica's words properly, we must make three remarks, since traditional historiography, which lacks an in-depth reading of the *De ordine* dialogue has often given a Neoplatonic interpretation to its content, in particular the problem of evil.[77] While for Plotinus, moral evil is contrary to the nature of the human soul, but in conformity with the universal nature (*universa natura*), for Augustine moral evil is contrary both to the order of every being, and to the Divine and universal order. Secondly, it should be stressed that evils which have emerged in time outside the order of God, do not re-enter the order automatically, as result of universal nature, but are forced to do so by a mysterious but just judgment of God. Augustine makes it clear that the new order in which evils are made to re-enter is in fact a penal order.[78] In conclusion, he is opposed to the Plotinian theory of the necessity of evil: for the perfection of the universe neither moral evils (sins) nor penal evils are necessary; the world would be perfect, if evil had not in fact been introduced.[79]

From the most recent researches, it would seem that Augustine had derived from Tertullian[80] the notion of *ordinatio iudiciaria* as he was to define it later[81] as well as the relative distinction of evil, both as fault voluntarily committed by a human being, and as a punishment which a human being suffers because of a just divine condemnation. This distinction of evil, which here inspires Monica's conclusion, was to be specifically introduced at the beginning of the first book of *De libero arbitrio*.[82] In *Confessiones*, Augustine was to recall that he had heard mention of that distinction in the Milanese period before his baptism.[83]

We may conclude this *excursus* on the problem of Providence and moral evil with a final remark relating to *De ordine*: in the second paragraph of the first book Augustine already goes beyond the static and immutable Plotinian vision of time, reflection of the eternal divine intellect, to arrive at a genuinely historical vision which distinguishes a before and after in human existence. There was a time in which all was good, and the perfect order willed by God reigned; now, there is another order, established by God the just judge, in which the evil performed by humankind does not remain disordered and unpunished.

In his writing *De moribus Ecclesiae catholicae et de moribus manichaeorum*, with which he explicitly undertook his controversy against the Manichaeans, and once the question relating to the nature of moral evil has been resolved, Augustine begins to demonstrate the irrationality of the notion of substantial evil which belongs to Manichaean metaphysical dualism. While on the one hand certain doctrines taken from the Christian tradition were to prove useful in criticising some aspects of NeoPlatonism (e.g. on the problem of moral evil), on the other hand the use of certain Neoplatonic notions was to be determining in the controversy with the Manichaeans: that of God as the supreme Good, that of the substantial good of temporal things, and finally that of evil understood as the diminution and privation of good. Even at the time of his stay in Cassiciacum, Augustine perceived that such philosophical notions, corrected by the Christian faith, could constitute an effective speculative instrument for confuting the irrationality of the metaphysical and anthropological dualism of the Manichaeans.

Notes

1. *Acad.* I, 2, 5.
2. Ibid. I, 5, 14.
3. Ibid. I, 6, 16.
4. Ibid I, 8, 22.
5. J. J. O'Meara, *The Young* op. cit., p. 11.
6. *Acad.* II, 7, 19 – 13, 30.
7. Ibid. III, 5, 12.
8. Ibid. III, 6, 13.
9. Ibid. III 10, 22.
10. Ibid. III, 10, 23.
11. W. C. Kneale—M. Kneale, *The Development of Logic*, Oxford/Clarendon 1962; it. tr. *Storia della logica*, Torino 1972, p. 207
12. I. M. Bochenski, *Elementa logicae grecae*, Roma 1937, p. 84.
13. M. Malatesta, *The Primary Logic* op. cit., p. 55.
14. I. M. Bochenski, *Formale Logik*, Freiburg-München 1956; it. tr. *La logica formale*, Torino 1972, p. 166.
15. M. Malatesta, *Dialettica e logica formale*, Napoli 1982, p. 21.
16. for further examination of this theme cf. V. Pacioni, *La struttura logica del principio di autocoscienza*, in *Interiorità e intenzionalità in Sant'Agostino*, Roma 1990, pp. 64–67.

17. *Acad.* III, 10,23.
18. Ibid.
19. M. Malatesta, *St. Augustine's Dialectic from the Modern Logic Standpoint. Logical Analysis of* "Contra Academicos" III, 10,22 – 13, 29, "Metalogicon", VIII, 1995, p.103. See also, by the same author: *La problematica linguistica del* "Contra Academicos" *alla luce della filosofia del linguaggio contemporanea*, "Metalogicon", X, 1997, pp. 46–63, which is a reflection conveyed by modern hermeneutical tools into the propositional attitudes and linguistic actions examined by St. Augustine in the works written immediately after his conversion. The merit of having analyzed for the first time the texts of Augustine using the instrument of symbolic logic goes to T. G. Bucher. In this regard see T. G. Bucher, *Zur formalen Logik bei Augustinus*, "Freiburger Zeitschrift für Philosophie und Theologie", XXIX, 1982, pp. 3–45; T. G. Bucher, *Augustinus und der Skeptizismus zur Widerlegung* in "Contra Academicos", in *Atti del Congresso internazionale su S. Agostino nel XVI centenario della conversione*, vol. II, Roma 1987, pp. 381–392.
20. M. Malatesta, *St Augustine's* op.cit., p. 104.
21. *Acad.* III, 11,24.
22. Ibid.
23. Ibid.
24. Ibid. III, 11, 25.
25. Ibid. III, 11, 25.
26. Ibid.
27. Ibid.
28. Ibid. III, 11, 26.
29. Ibid.
30. Ibid.
31. *beata v.*, 2, 10.
32. *conf.* VI, 16, 26.
33. *beata v.*, 2, 8–9.
34. R. Holte, *Béatitude* op.cit., p.195.
35. *beata v.* 2, 10–11.
36. Ibid. 2, 14.

Beginnings of Augustinian speculation 75

37. Plato, *Leges* 716 c 4 –5.
38. *beata v.* 4, 35.
39. Ibid. 4, 34.
40. Ibid. 4, 35; cf. R. Holte, *Béatitude* op. cit., p.197.
41. N. Cipriani, *L'influsso di Varrone sul pensiero antropologico e morale nei primi scritti di S.Agostino*, in *L'etica cristiana nei secoli III e IV: eredità e confronti*, Roma 1966, p. 374. In the chapter which follows I shall give various illustrations of the character of this model, which Augustine is already using from the time of the writings composed after his conversion.
42. *mor.* I, 11, 18
43. Ibid. I, 3, 4.
44. Ibid. I, 4, 6.
45. Ibid. I, 5, 7.
46. Ibid.
47. N. Cipriani, *L'influsso di Varrone* op. cit., p. 376.
48. Cicero, *De finibus* V, 9, 25–26.
49. *civ.* XIX, 3, 1; see also Aristotle, *Ethica Nicomachaea* X, 9, 1179b 21 and 33–34; Cicero, *De finibus* V, 21, 59–60.
50. *mor.* I, 6, 9–10.
51. *vera rel.* 44, 82.
52. *conf.* XIII, 9, 10.
53. *trin.* XIV, 12, 15.
54. Ibid. XIV, 4, 6; 8, 11.
55. *retr.* I, 3, 1.
56. Plotinus, *The Enneads III*, 2, 1. With regard to the interpretation of this text of Plotinus, see my volume *L'unità teoretica* op. cit., pp. 86–98.
57. Plotinus, *The Enneads III*, 2, 4. The texts used here are taken from Plotinus, *The Enneads*, Penguin Books, London 1991.
58. *ord.* I, 1, 2. In our translation we deliberately distance ourselves from the published translation of R. P. Russell, *Divine Providence and the Problem of Evil. A Translation of St. Augustine's "De ordine"*, New York 1942, p. 9. With regard to the interpretation of this passage of the "De ordine", I

would refer readers to my volume *L'unità teoretica* op.cit., pp. 90–92.
59. Ibid. I, 1, 2.
60. Plotinus, *The Enneads* III, 2, 15.
61. A. Dyroff, *Über Form und Begriffsgehalt der augustinischen Schrift* "De ordine", in *Aurelius Augustinus*, edited by M.Grabmann and J.Mausbach, Köln 1930, p.27; see also J. Doignon, *Le "De Ordine", son déroulement, ses thèmes*, in *L'opera letteraria di Agostino tra Cassiciacum e Milano*, Palermo 1987, p. 120.
62. *ord*. I, 3, 6.
63. Ibid.
64. Ibid.
65. Ibid. 1, 3, 8.
66. Plotinus, *The Enneads* III, 3, 1.
67. *ord*. I, 3, 9.
68. Ibid. I, 7, 18.
69. Plotinus, *The Enneads* III, 2, 7.
70. *ord*. I, 7, 19.
71. A. Dyroff, *Über Form* op. cit., p. 38.
72. *ord*. II, 7, 22.
73. N. Cipriani, *Il problema del male in Sant'Agostino*, in *Agostino non è (il) male*, edited by G. Fidelibus, Chieti 1998, p. 31.
74. *ord*. II, 7, 22. Augustine, with the intention of confuting the "theory of historical cycles" went more deeply into the question relating to eternity of God "who creates new things without any change in his will" in *De civitate Dei* XII, 21.
75. *ord*. II, 7, 23.
76. Ibid.
77. On this we would mention the two following authors: G. R. Evans, *Augustine on Evil*, Cambridge 1982, pp. 93–98; K. Flasch, *Augustin Einführung in sein Denken*, Stuttgart 1980, pp. 92–98.
78. N. Cipriani, *Il problema del male* op. cit., p. 33.
79. *lib. arb.* III, IX, 26.

80. V. Pacioni, *L'unità teoretica* op. cit., pp. 231–236.
81. *c. Iul. Imp.* 1, 66.
82. N. Cipriani, *L'ispirazione tertullianea* op. cit., pp. 166–168.
83. *conf.* VII, 3, 5.

IV

ANTHROPOLOGICAL DOCTRINE

1. Reciprocal Influence of Soul and Body

The metaphysical relationship between soul and body, sometimes described as *ineffabilis permixtio*[1] and at other times as *connexio vinculi naturalis*[2] is introduced into the earliest works by two key terms: the first we find in *De immortalitate animae:*

> (...) all the inclination (*appetitus*) the mind has toward the body is either to possess it, or to build it up somehow, or in some form to advise it.[3]

This tendency is something natural to the soul itself, for which the body is not something extraneous. The second term is to be found in the *De musica:*

> (...) I think the body is animated by the soul only to the purpose of the doer (*nisi intentione facientis*). Nor do I think it is affected in any way by the body, but it acts *through* it and *in* it as something divinely subjected to its dominion.[4]

The term *intentio* signifies tension, a positive impulse, which arises out of the will to give life and governance to the body. As both A. Dihle[5] and G. O'Daly[6] have pointed out, the doctrine which inspired the Augustinian notion of *intentio* is probably of Stoic origin, *tónos*, tension of the soul, in which both the cohesion of the soul and its intellectual faculties are taken into consideration, even though, in contrast to the Augustinian vision, the *tónos* does not seem to have any relationship with the energy of volition which moves toward action. The doctrine concerning the unity between soul and body emerges more clearly if the definition of *anima* which is found in *De quantitate animae* 13, 22, and the definition of man which we find respectively in *De ordine* II, 11, 31 and in the *De moribus Ecclesiae catholicae et de moribus manichaeorum* 1, 27, 52 are analyzed. This is the text from *De quantitate animae*:

> (...) it must be understood that, although God made the soul, it has a definite substance which is neither of earth, nor of fire, nor of air, nor of water, unless, perchance, one should think that God gave to earth a nature that is exclusively its own and did not give to the soul a nature that is proper to it. If you wish a definition of what the soul is, I have a ready answer. It seems to me to be a certain kind of substance, sharing in reason, fitted to rule the body (*substantia quaedam rationis particeps, regendo corpori accomodata*).

It must be recalled that in Augustine, the term substance is synonymous with essence. The soul rules and governs the body. The two basic components making up the human being are not dualistically opposed to one another; that is, they are not extraneous. They are conceived as dimensions which integrate with each other, even though the incorporeal element prevails over the corporeal. Augustine does not accept the Aristotelian idea of the soul as *enteléchia*, as a *form* of the body; in accordance with the Neoplatonists, he does not believe in the doctrine of *hylomorphism*. In his eyes, this doctrine jeopardizes the immortality and incorporeal nature of the soul; nevertheless he agrees with the Aristotelian point of view in conceiving the soul as a principle of existence, of being, of movement of the body.[7]

While the soul for Plotinus is a substance extraneous to the body, which does not owe its existence to the fact that it is seated in a body,[8] for Augustine the soul has been called into existence and is destined to animate and govern the body. This goal is not a matter of chance but an essential condition of its being, while this or that act of its activity

Anthropological doctrine

in relation to the body may be due to change; on the contrary it is consubstantial in that the soul has been made in order to give life to its body.[9] The soul has been created by God in His image,[10] not to pay the price of wrongdoing prior to its present existence, as Plotinus taught, or to know the evil of which matter is constituted, as Porphyrius believed, but with the positive function of governing and animating the body.[11] The definition of a human soul which we have expounded here is certainly distant from Neoplatonic anthropology both in its formulation and in its content. The philological and speculative conclusions of N. Cipriani[12] have shown that the definition given in the *De quantitate animae* were very likely inspired by Varro. This is supported by an hypothesis suggested by Varro and mentioned three times by Augustine. The first is in *De ordine* II, 6, 18; a second is in *De moribus Ecclesiae catholicae et de moribus manichaeorum* I, 4, 6, and the third is in *De civitate Dei* XIX, 3, 1, where Varro is explicitly mentioned. Since these passages scattered among various works of Augustine are of primary importance and have not been subject of much attention by scholars, we shall analyse them here in full.

In *De ordine* II, 6,18, Augustine discusses the unity of the body and the soul with his pupil Licentius, who reminds the master that the soul is in the body, but in such a way as not to be commanded by it. This is the reply:

> "And I am not saying that", I replied. "But neither is the rider on the horse in such manner that the horse holds empire over him; although he drives the horse where he wants to go, yet, when the horse is moved, it must be (*necesse est*) that the rider is moved".

By using the image of the rider and the horse, Augustine shows that the unity of the soul and body is not accidental but necessary. The soul as principle is superior to the body, by analogy to the rider who is superior to the horse; nevertheless the soul is not free to move without the body, because the two principles, although they are metaphysically different, constitute one necessary unit.[13]

The image of the rider and the horse returns in *De moribus Ecclesiae catholicae et de moribus manichaeorum* I, 4, 6, to stress that the soul (the rider) may indeed be identified with man in that it is ordained to govern the body (the horse):

> What do we call man, then? Is he soul and body like a centaur or two horses harnessed together? Or shall we call him the body alone in the service of a governing soul, as is the case when we give the name *lamp*, not to the vessel and flame together, but to the vessel alone on account of the flame within it? Or shall we say that man is nothing but the soul, inasmuch as it rules the body, just as we say that the horseman is not the horse and man together, but the man alone from the fact that he guides the horse (*quod regendo equo sit accomodatus*)?

In *De civitate Dei* XIX, 3, 1, Augustine states explicitly that the image of the rider and the horse, used to explain the unity of the human composition, can be traced back to Varro, who used it to sustain that the soul is in a necessary relation to the body:

> First of all, he (Varro) thinks that a definition of man must be settled upon, since in philosophy it is the supreme good of man that is in question, not that of a tree or of an animal or of God. In man's nature he finds two elements, body and soul; and he has no doubt whatever that of these two the soul is the better and by far the nobler element. But he discusses the question whether man is the soul alone or the body alone or a combination of body and soul. In the first case, the body would be like the horse to the horseman, where the horseman is not both horse and man but only the man, though he is called a horseman because of a relation to the horse which he rides.

This way of conceiving is clearly inspired by Varro, according to whom the soul may be identified with man in that it is in close relationship with the body (*regendo corpori accomodata*).[14]

A similar idea had previously been put forward in *De quantitate animae*:

> In view of our discussion, who can reasonably offer any complaint that the soul was given to move and manage the body, since an order of things so great and so divine could not be better linked together?[15]

We now come to the two definitions of man, which have been the subject of often conflicting interpretations by scholars. The first, as we have mentioned, is to be found in *De ordine* II, 11, 31:

> Of particular interest to us ought to be the fact that man has been defined thus by the ancient philosophers (*veteres sapientes*): man is an animal, rational and mortal (*animal rationale mortale*).

The definition contains the term *animal*, which designates the genus. Two specific differences are added, *rational* and *mortal*, which enable us to distinguish man from the beasts (*a bestiis*) and from God (*a divinis*). They remind man in what direction he must go, and from what he take his distance. It is an Aristotelian/Stoic definition, going back to the *veteres sapientes*, philosophers who are more ancient than Neoplatonist thinkers.[16] There are various possible sources for Augustine's definition. Apuleius, in *De interpretatione* 271, 12–13, gives the same definition of man as we find in the *De ordine*. The Apuleian context is typically Aristotelian, as can be seen from the analysis of the predicables. Even before Apuleius, a similar but not identical expression can be found, as Doignon observed,[17] in Cicero,[18] where the Roman writer examines the Stoic doctrine of *comprehensio*. The same definition is also to be found in Quintilian[19] and re-appears in Sextus Empiricus,[20] where, in discussing the criterion of certainty, the Skeptic philosopher counterposes *others* to Epicurus. The *veteres sapientes*, then, should be identified in the line which, deep doctrinal differences notwithstanding, links Peripatetic logicians with those of the *Stoa* and those of other philosophical traditions. It is no accident that the definition reappears in the work of the Neoplatonist Porphyrius, in a text which forms the introduction to Aristotle's *Categoriae*. Recently, N. Cipriani[21] has pointed out that the source of inspiration for Augustine in formulating the above definition is to be found among the works of Varro, who in turn may have taken it from a Greek source.

In *De moribus Ecclesiae Catholicae et de moribus manichaeorum* I, 27, 52, another definition appears, which has reminded some scholars[22] of Neoplatonism:

> Man as he appears to us is a rational soul, making use of a mortal and earthly body (*anima rationalis est mortali atque terreno utens corporis*).

This definition does not seem like an alternative to the other, derived from Aristotelian/Stoic teaching,[23] since Aristotle says in the *De anima*:

> (....) all natural bodies are instruments of the soul (....).[24]

A similar concept is to be found in the *Nicomachean Ethics*:

> where there is nothing common between the ruler and the ruled, there is not even friendship between them, because there is no justice, for example, between a worker and instruments, between soul and body, between master and slave.[25]

In Augustine's anthropological point of view the two definitions are not alternative: they perform different but complementary functions. The first, in *De ordine*, is more specific in speculative terms, and shows the integration of the incorporeal factor with the corporeal; the second, in *De moribus*, stresses the primacy of the soul over the body understood in moral terms. In *De moribus*, Augustine was probing deeper into the notion of love for one's neighbour; a love which, if it is a benefit aimed at the body, is termed medicine, while if it is a benefit directed toward the soul, is then called discipline, instruction, teaching.[26]

On the one hand the Stoic and Aristotelian elements in Varro's anthropological model helped Augustine to reduce

Anthropological doctrine

dualistic expressions of his anthropology, which are to be found here and there in his early works, perhaps traces of his Gnostic-Manichaean past or consequences of his reading of Platonic books in Milan. On the other hand they also led him to offer a positive assessment not only of the good things of the soul, but also those of the body and of social life. The latter aspect is a further confirmation of the fact that for Augustine, the body is conceived as an integral part of the human being, as stated from the very start of his literary production, following Varro's lead: "(....) we are all agreed that there is no such thing as man without the body and without the soul".[27] In the first book of the *De libero arbitrio,* and the second of the *De moribus*[28] the positive nature of the good things of the body and social life is also stressed.

A brief mention should be made of the two types of good things concerning the civil life and the instinct towards sensible pleasure. We already find in the *De ordine*[29] the accent placed on civil commitment and on the necessity of an adequate training for the management of public affairs. Man must promote peace[30] within public life, develop work in order to favour learning, to cultivate the fields, to administer the *ordo civitatis,* and to spread exercise of the various professions.[31] Physical pleasure, considered by Augustine as a good thing even though of a low kind[32], possesses a positive function because it serves to satisfy certain natural needs (*prima naturae*). On this point Augustine differs[33] from Cicero,[34] for whom sensible pleasure does not enter among the good things of nature, and he finds himself, instead, taking the position of Antiochus of Ascalon, who considered *voluptas* a bodily good. We should note, finally, that differing from Varro, who located the aim of life in corporeal goods and in virtue, Augustine ascribes a relative value to such goods, subordinating them on the transcendent level according to a *uti-frui* doctrine on which, as we shall see, he founds his conception of morality (*ordo vitae*). This can become an *ordo amoris,* in the same degree in which the corporeal goods are subjected to the spiritual, the inferior to the superior, and the temporal to the eternal.[35]

2. Immortality of the Soul

Before dealing with the immortal and incorporeal dimension of the soul, which constitutes the primary factor in human nature, we must introduce a premise of a speculative nature. From the beginning, Augustine introduced into philosophical research a change of perspective in relation to classical philosophy. While for the ancients, the focus of philosophy is on the cosmological problem (if we except Socrates, and to a limited extent the Sophists), for Augustine the focus is on the anthropological problem, and hence its theological corollary. What Greek philosophy was searching for was a principle which would render the world comprehensible. From Thales to Plotinus, Greek thought had concentrated on the relation between the One and the Manifold. From this two other questions arose which would not change the meaning and character of the basic issue, but would define it with regard to the relation between the two terms which from the beginning were only implied: one was the problem of man, as far as the Socratic school was concerned, while the other, for the Neoplatonists, was the problem of God. The world cannot, in fact, be explained without God. But man and God, in Greek thought, intervene only to explain the world, to render it comprehensible to man as he contemplates it, so that he can also find the reasons for his own existence. For Augustine, on the other hand, the point of departure for philosophy is of an anthropological and theological nature: God is first and foremost the source and principle of the existence of man, and hence also the reason for the existence of the world.[36] In *De ordine* Augustine summarizes the scheme of philosophical enquiry:

> To philosophy pertains a twofold question: the first deals with the soul; the second, with God. The first makes us know ourselves; the second, our origin.

Anthropological doctrine

> The former is the more delightful to us; the latter, more precious. The former makes us fit for a happy life; the latter renders us happy.[37]

In the light of this change of viewpoint, Augustine uses the metaphysical premise of Platonic origin, already stated in *Contra Academicos*,[38] concerning the distinction between the sensible world and the intelligible world, in order to reflect on the immortal and incorporeal nature of the human soul, beginning with self-awareness.

In the second book of the *Soliloquia*, composed in Cassiciacum, the subject of the immortality of the soul is raised, later to be taken up in the small treatise *De immortalitate animae*. The theme of human self-awareness, already studied in *Contra Academicos*[39] and in *De beata Vita*[40] is the premise for the dialogue between Augustine and reason on the immortality of the soul:

> *Augustine.* Our labor has been interrupted long enough, and love is impatient, nor will there be surcease of tears until love is granted the object of its love. Let us begin then our second book.
> *Reason.* Let us start.
> A. May we believe that God will be with us!
> R. May we surely believe that, if it is in our power!
> A. He Himself is our power.
> R. Pray, then, as briefly and perfectly as you are able.
> A. O God, ever the same; may I know myself, may I know Thee. That is my prayer.
> R. Do you, who wish to know yourself, know that you exist?
> A. I know it.
> R. How do you know it?
> A. I do not know.
> R. Are you conscious of yourself as simple or composite?
> A. I do not know.
> R. Do you know that you are moved?
> A. I do not know.
> R. Do you know that you think?
> A. That I know.

R. Therefore, it is true that you think.
A. It is true.
R. Do you know that you are immortal?
A. I do not know.
R. Of all those things which you said you did not know, which do you prefer to know first?
A. Whether I am immortal.
R. Do you love life, then?
A. I confess I do.
R. Well, will it be enough when you have learnt that you are immortal?
A. It will surely be a great thing, but too little for me.
R. Just the same, how much will you enjoy this which is so little?
A. Very much.
R. Will you, then, not weep for anything?
A. Not a thing.
R. What if that life is discovered to be such that in it you will be permitted to know no more than you already know, will you control your tears?
A. On the contrary, I shall weep so much that it will be no life at all.
R. Therefore, you love life, not for the sake of living, but for the sake of knowing.
A. I grant your conclusion.
R. What if that same knowledge of things were to make you unhappy?
A. I believe that that can in no wise happen. But, if it is so, no one can be happy, for even now it is by reason of my ignorance of things and for no other reason that I am unhappy. But, if the knowledge of things makes one unhappy, then unhappiness is everlasting.
R. I see, now, all that you desire. Because you think that no one is unhappy by reason of knowledge, it is by this token probable that understanding makes one happy. But, no one is happy unless living; no one lives unless he exists. Therefore, you wish to exist, to live and to understand, but, to exist that you may live, to live that you may understand.

Anthropological doctrine

> Hence, you know you exist; you know you live; you know you understand. But, what you want to know is whether these things will always endure or whether none of them is to endure; whether some of them will remain for ever and some perish; and whether, if all are to continue, they can be increased or decreased.[41]

Augustine reveals to reason that he wishes to enquire into the nature of the immortality of the soul; of all the truths of which he is ignorant, this is the one above all others that he wishes to know. He does not know whether he is simple, single, or multiple; he does not know what the senses transmit; whether he is subject to becoming or not; however, he *does* know that he exists (*esse*) and he *does* know that he thinks (*cogitare*).

By a formula which contains three evident proofs which cannot be reduced to any form of deduction[42] Augustine points out that he knows three truths: that he exists, that he is living, and that he knows. Further, however, he also desires three things: existence, life and knowledge, in this order: he wishes to exist in order to live and to live in order to know; in knowledge, in fact, lies the aim of existence. He knows that he exists, he lives and he knows, but he does not know if existence, life and knowledge are transient or eternal, or partly transient and partly eternal,[43] In what follows we shall re-examine the principle of self-awareness in order to understand developments and extensions of thought which are the subject of reflection in *De vera religione* (39, 72), in *De civitate Dei* (XI, 26–27) and in *De Trinitate* (IX, 3; IX, 4, 9, 4, 5–6; X, 4, 6). I wish only here to underscore an aspect which may be useful for understanding the path of demonstration concerning the immortality of the soul which is followed both in the second book of the *Soliloquia* and in *De immortalitate animae*.

In these two works he seems to distance himself from the notion of interiority of which Plotinus speaks,[44] and to draw closer to the notion of *oikeiosis*, which originates with the Academics and Peripatetics, according to which we must love, preserve and know ourselves.⁴⁵ Here, the demonstration concerning the immortality of the soul is initiated.

Augustine proceeds in the following manner. He performs some preliminary demonstrations, which he then abandons, but which have a propaedeutic function with the final demonstration in mind. The first argument concerns the idea of the indestructibility of error. He begins from the statement that the truth exists. The whole argument, given in *Contra Academicos* against the Sceptics, had come to this certain conclusion: error (*falsitas*) also exists. Now error arises where the human soul assents to the deceit which the senses experience. Thus, if error exists, and it cannot be otherwise, it presupposes that sense exists as an imperishable *vis*. But the subject of sensual feeling is the soul and not the body, hence if the senses are imperishable, since, if the opposite were true, error would no longer exist in the world, the soul, as the subject of sensation, must also be immortal, and because the soul can feel, it must be alive, and so we deduce that the soul lives for ever.⁴⁶

Reason summarizes the argument as follows:

> You said that error cannot exist without the senses and you also said that error is not able not to exist; therefore, the senses always exist. Furthermore, there is no sense without a soul; therefore, the soul is everlasting. Nor is it able to sense unless it is living; therefore, the soul lives forever.⁴⁷

Augustine immediately realizes that it is not possible to base the immortality of the soul on the indestructibility of error. The first argument is therefore abandoned.

They then pass to the second argument. Augustine and reason go back to investigating the nature of the true and the false. According to common opinion, the true is what is as it appears to a knowing subject (*quod ita se habet ut cognitori videtur*) while the false is what appears different from what is (*quod aliter quam est, videtur*).⁴⁸ The true and the false exist through the intervention of a knowing subject. The existence of the awareness of the thinking subject, to whom whatever is appears, comes to be the condition for the true. But the existence of a body is also conditioned by the existence of a knowing subject. A. Guzzo comments:

> So that, if a body is true only if there is an awareness to which it seems such, and since it *is* a body only if it is a true body, it *is* a body only if there is an awareness for which it is a *true* body in that it appears what it is. In this way the existence of bodies is made to depend on the existence of the mind, for which they *are* bodies when they are true bodies.[49]

Reason intervenes with this specific point:

> Therefore, if nothing is true unless it is what it seems to be, and if something corporeal can be seen only by the senses, and if only the soul is able to use sense perception, and if a body does not exist if it is not a true body — if all these things are so, then a body cannot exist unless a soul had existed before it.[50]

Nothing, then, exists of itself. A body exists if it is a *true* body, i.e. if there is a *ratio* which thinks it. Reason and Augustine have arrived at a paradoxical position similar to that of contemporary idealism, by which we must deduce, as the disciple of reason immediately realises, that nothing exists by and for itself.[51] We must therefore believe that no stones exist in the heart of the earth, i.e. where there is no sentient subject who perceives them; these stones would not exist if we did not see them, or they will no longer exist when we have gone away and no-one else is present to see them.[52]

The disciple of reason realizes that the absurdities which have arisen come from the definition of the true which was previously put forward. And so the second argument is also abandoned.

Reason intervenes to point to this question:

> Therefore, consider which you choose to say: that corporeal things can be seen only by the senses, or that only the soul has sense perception, or that this is a stone or something else but it is not true, or that the true itself must be defined differently.[53]

Augustine pleads with reason:

> Let us examine this last, I beg you.[54]

After an exchange of questions and answers, a new definition of the true is suggested:

> The 'true' is that which exists.[55]

But this definition too is set aside; in fact there would not be anything that was false if everything that is were necessarily true. One must turn back again to investigate the notion of the false. We have reached paragraph 10.

The false is what has some similarity to the truth, without being the true. We call false a tree, which we see painted in a picture, or the face we see reflected in a mirror, or the motion of towers in the eyes, of those who sail, the apparent break in the oars beneath the water, and so on—for the sole reason that these phenomena are similar to the true. The similarity seems to be the reason of the error. It may be objected: if what we define as false at the same time is not dissimilar to what we define as true, it would be true; hence what is entirely similar to what is true is true. Two examples are produced: Two eggs, which are exactly identical, are true eggs; on the contrary, a woman seen during a dream is not true because she is different from the real woman whom we can touch, hear, and question when we are awake. We must deduce, stresses reason, that:

> Is not, then, similarity the mother of truth and dissimilarity the mother of falsity?[56]

After a few words of encouragement from reason, Augustine continues the discussion. Both the hypothesis concerning similarity as a cause of deception, and the hypothesis concerning dissimilarity as a cause of deception, lead us to the conclusion that everything is false.

> I do indeed see this, but, when I consider that what we call false contains something like and something unlike the true, I am unable to decide for which of these it should merit the name of false. If I should say that it is because it is dissimilar, there is nothing which cannot be called false, since there is nothing which is not dissimilar to something which we acknowledge to be true. If, on the other hand, I were to say that it should be called false because it is similar, not only will those eggs object which are true because they are most similar, but also will I be at the mercy of someone who would force me to admit that all things are false, since I cannot deny that in some respect all things resemble one another.[57]

Must we conclude, then, that the reason that certain things are described as false is both similarity and dissimilarity at once? But in this case too, we shall be forced to conclude that everything is false, because all things, among themselves, are similar in one sense and dissimilar in another.[58]

We must return to the first position: is the false what appears different from what is? But then we are back with the difficulty that a short while ago we had thought to avoid, since we have to state that a thing is true if there is a subject with knowledge, and a thing is false if there is a subject who deceives himself. Or do we have to fall back on the idea that it is true not that which appears to be what it is, but that which actually is, to conclude that everything is true and nothing is false, because everything that is, is true?

At this point Augustine, disappointed, turns to reason:

> And so my troubles return, and I do not see that I have made any progress, in spite of my forbearance of your slow pace.[59]

Reason suggests a different notion of the false, according to which there are false things in reality external to the awareness that errs:

> There remains nothing that can with justice be called false, unless it would be that which either feigns to be what it is not, or tends to exist and does not succeed.[60]

In the former case, we are faced with an act which is either deceptive (*fallax*) or untruthful (*mendax*). The deceptive is that which tends to deceive. The untruthful act arises from anyone who does not speak the truth, and differs from the deceptive act in that the latter always sets out to deceive, whereas someone who utters untrue things may not always intend to deceive. In the latter case, we are faced with the images which seek to be but are not, which seem almost to wish to be the persons of people whose images they are, but nevertheless remain images (for example a portrait, an image in a pond, the apparition in a dream). Let us focus our attention on the case concerning the phenomenon of the fiction, either with or without the intention to deceive.

The fox, for instance, deceives by natural instinct; man, on the other hand, at times deceives because of the cunning of the mind. But the actor on the stage, who represents Priam, feigns with an untruthful act, but without the intention of deceiving. Here we meet with a paradoxical fact: reason reminds Augustine that the actor Roscius on the one hand is a *false* Priam, and on the other hand is a *true* tragic actor; an example of things that are true in that they are false,[61] and what makes them true is simply the fact that they are false for a precisely defined purpose. The dialogue has now arrived at a surprising truth:

> That I do not know, and I will be very much surprised if it is not because I find in these examples nothing worthy of imitation. To the end that we may be true to our nature, we should not become false by copying and likening ourselves to the nature of another as do the actors and the reflections in a mirror and the brass cows of Myron. We should, instead, seek that truth which is not self-contradictory and two-faced so that it is true on one side, false on another.

Anthropological doctrine 95

Immediately reason replies:

You are in search of things great and divine (...).

The disciple agrees:

I agree willingly.[62]

A. Guzzo writes, commenting on this passage of the *Soliloquia*:

This leads finally to the concept, which must also be a different order from that of the sensible, in which it is possible to find truths which are simply truths, and not true for some and false for others. Thus Augustine too finds a way out of the difficulty, in which the problem of truth and error has embroiled him, by taking refuge in a different world from that of the sensible, where truth is pure truth, remote and separate from the possibility of error. Something similar had occurred to Plato in his *Theaetetus* to which this second book of the *Soliloquia* is closely similar. In *Theaetetus* as well, it is hypothesized that there is no truth, if not in relation to a subject that knows it. Also in *Theaetetus*, he pulses back from such a position and ascribes to himself the evil root of having wanted to seek truth in sensible knowledge, which, embroiled in appearances, is always true to some and false to others. Hence salvation is indicated in *Theaetetus* in the rigorous understanding that the truth should not be sought in the sensible world, which is always at one and the same time true or false, but in the reasonings which the soul makes of its own accord, far from the senses, and thus in the world of pure concepts.[63]

Pursuing his own path, Augustine arrives at the same conclusion which Plato had reached: on the one hand there exists an intelligible level, on which truth itself subsists; on the other hand there exists a sensible level, which we perceive with our sight and with our touch; the first is true and the second is similar to the truth. But while Plato made truth reside in ideas, Augustine, on the contrary, locates it in the dialectic already described, in *De ordine*, as *disciplina disciplinorum*—a knowledge which embraces both truth in itself and the rules which form the basis of the capacity of reasoning, including the laws of definitions, distinctions and partitions,[64] as it also regulates the relations among the sentences, and unveils inferences and logical laws.[65]

The path taken leads reason to conclude that the soul is immortal, because it is the necessary bearer of eternal truth:

> If whatever is in a subject endures forever, the subject itself must of necessity endure. Every branch of learning is in the soul as in a subject. If, therefore, learning endures forever, the soul must endure forever. But, learning is truth, and, as reason showed in the beginning of this book, truth abides forever. Therefore, the soul endures forever; if it died, we would not call it the soul. Consequently, only he can reasonably deny the immortality of the soul who proves that some point in the above reasoning was granted illogically.[66]

The demonstration of the immortality of the soul which is to be put forward in *De immortalitate animae* will follow the pattern of the one we have already found in the *Soliloquia*. The theme of the immortality of the soul is a constant of Augustinian speculation, even when he is dealing *ex professo* with other questions. What can be shown from the analyses of the texts is that there is a continuous passage from reflection on self-awareness, as an index of spirituality and hence a metaphysical premise for immortality, to the intelligible contents present in the soul.

3. Spirituality of the Soul

In *De quantitate animae*, a work which also takes the form of a dialogue, the enquiry is into the incorporeal nature of the human soul. At the beginning, the creatural character of the human soul, which is distinct from the divine reality and from the bodily substance, is emphasized:

Anthropological doctrine

> I believe that God, its Creator, is, so to speak, the soul's proper habitation and its home.[67]

Augustine rejects the idea that the human soul may be consubstantial with the divine reality, as Plotinus taught, or part of *universal nature*, which was the teaching of Varro and all the *Veteres Academici*. However, he did follow Varro and Plotinus in considering the soul as an incorporeal reality, capable of functions linked to the *sensus*, to the *ratio*, and to the *intellectus*.[68] In this argument too, the commitment is great, since the enquiry is moved not by curiosity of an empty erudition, but by an essential and speculative necessity.[69] In fact, before his conversion to Christianity, for a period of nine years, he came back again and again to reflection on this subject. Now that he had become a Christian, he realised the importance of philosophically basing the notion of the non-corporeal nature of the human soul on a position counter to the ancient materialist currents.[70] In *De ordine*, it was stated that to know the soul meant knowing one's self, and hence one's own ultimate origin. Plotinus, too, in the *Enneads*, had insisted on the importance of this issue for philosophy. Augustine is of the same opinion, and considers the study of the soul the pivot on which all of intellectual life turns, and the key to attaining knowledge of every other speculative issue.[71]

In *De quantitate animae*, the proof relating to the non-corporeal nature of the soul is expounded, and answers to certain objections are also provided. After repeating that the soul is immortal and created in the image of God,[72] he goes on to specify the departure point for the debate between Augustine and his interlocutor, Evodius.

Every corporeal reality possesses three dimensions: length (*longitudo*), breadth (*latitudo*) and height (*altitudo*). If it were possible to prove that there exist realities devoid of these spatial characteristics, we might perhaps be able to admit the existence of non-corporeal substances, and thus begin the enquiry into the incorporeal nature of the human soul.[73]

Evodius, like Augustine in earlier days, finds it difficult to admit the existence of incorporeal realities.[74] He allows that certain non-three-dimensional entities exist, such as justice, virtue;[75] however, the human soul cannot be numbered among these, considered as a material substance similar to wind.[76] The wind is a real but invisible entity, subtle materiality: the human soul could be something similar, an invisible force, co-extensive to the body to which it belongs.[77] To convince Evodius to accept that the soul is not a three-dimensional entity, the discussion is shifted to one of the faculties of the soul, memory, to arrive at the conclusion that this is not a faculty of a body. By memory we succeed in retaining images of distant places, which are not within the reach of our direct perception. This example introduces the idea that the soul and the body are structurally different substances.[78] The analysis of certain notions of geometry makes it possible to carry the discussion forward. There are three dimensional bodies because they possess length, breadth and height. If for example a cube is deprived of one of the dimensions we obtain a flat figure with two dimensions only. If we remove the second dimension from the flat figure, we obtain a line. This figure possesses only the dimension of length. Now if we reduce the line to a point, we obtain an entity which does not possess either length or breadth or height. The point, in fact, is a totally indivisible geometrical entity (*id erit igitur quod dividi nequeat*), intelligible only to the reason. Evodius concludes his reflection with a procedure which can be reduced to Stoic logic; if the point is divisible, then the point has length or the point has extension; if the point has length, then the point is a line; if the point has extension, then the point demands another centre; the point is not a line; the point does not demand another centre; hence the point is not divisible.[79] On the basis of the principle by which the similar perceives the similar it can be concluded that the human mind does not have a corporeal nature, because it perceives non-corporeal entities, and at the same time is superior to the actual geometrical entities which it intuits.

Anthropological doctrine

Augustine stresses that there is nothing to be wondered at in the fact that the soul is not corporeal, does not extend in length, does not spread itself in the surface, does not become solid with volume; and yet it is so powerful within the body as to govern all its members and to be its driving force. But there is yet more. The soul not only knows intelligible entities, but also possesses the power to know itself, by force of the presence within it of truth itself.[80]

The conclusion is judged to be an important step forward in the proof concerning the incorporeal nature of the soul. Evodius is convinced by the argument, however, he points out two difficulties:

> Yet I wonder about this: while it is so clear to me that the soul has no corporeal quantity that I show not the slightest resistance to those arguments, and while I am entirely unaware of any point which I cannot grant, why is it that, as the body grows with age, the soul grows, too, or at least, would seem to grow? Who would deny that small children are not to be compared in cleverness to some animals? Who would doubt that as they grow older their soul also seems to grow? Then, if the soul is extended through the space of the body, why does it not have quantity? If, however, it is not extended, how does it feel all over anything that strikes it?[81]

These are serious objections, because in the past they have caused great problems for Augustine. To the first, he replies by stressing that the growth of the soul should not be conceived in the same way as physical growth is; the growth of the soul is not tied to the various mutations to which the body is subject, but takes place through the exercise of its faculties.[82]

Once the spatial extension of the soul has been excluded, the question concerning its development is studied with reference to the acquisition of language.[83] The assertion which states that children learn to speak at the same time and with the same rhythm as they grow bodily is refuted. Augustine confirms the contrary theory, with a series of examples which show how the phenomenon of language is a power which is acquired regardless of any type of physical growth. The argument is aimed against the idea of any possible concatenation between the various phases of physical and psychological development.[84] The acquisition of language may be impeded by environmental and psychological factors; however, it should be remembered that the art of imitation, the capacity of observation, the following of a master, are the factors which determine the development of the linguistic capacity.

> To let you hear the truth, the soul is rightly said to be enlarged, as it were, by learning and to grow smaller by unlearning, but in a metaphorical sense, as we have discussed. You must avoid this misconception that the growth of the soul means that it fills out, as it were, a larger space, whereas in fact a more skillful soul has a greater power to act than a less skillful one.[85]

Evodius continues to put forth objections to the position taken by his teacher, stating that the strength which is in the body grows in proportion to what which lies in the soul. The teacher denies that there can be a close relation between corporeal growth and the proportional increase of strength, pointing out that the growth of strength is to a large extent dependent on exercise, on training rather than on automatic increase by the body. In fact the strengths in the human being have will, impulse, and desire as their genetic factors, which as emotional drives can increase the urge towards movement or slow it down. Strengths are a psycho-somatic phenomenon, which can be controlled through training and physical health: however, they are strongly conditioned by the efficacy of the psychical impulse, from which we must deduce that the soul possesses a "strength" of its own which gives it courage and daring.[86]

Anthropological doctrine

These problems do not prevent the formulation of a definition of soul borrowed from Varro,[87] who taught that the soul as such could be considered and said to be 'man' in that it is in relation with the body:

> It seems to me to be a certain kind of substance, sharing in reason, fitted to rule the body.[88]

In paragraph 26, a second objection by Evodius was put forward, and this is now brought up again in paragraph 40:

> (...) why the soul feels wherever the body is touched, if the soul's magnitude has not the same spatial extent as that of the body.[89]

The analysis of the mechanism of sensory perception responds to the objection which claims that the soul, through sensation, would be totally limited to the body to which it belongs:

> But, the experience of the eye in a living body, namely, the experience of sight, is an experience of something that is there where the eye is not. From this argument it is clear to anyone that the soul is not contained in place, since the eye, which is a body, experiences something that is outside the eye and only things that are outside, an experience it never has without the soul.[90]

It follows that the soul is not diffused throughout the whole body, as is blood; the relationship (*contemperatio*) between soul and body must not be conceived as a sort of physical mixture.[91]

Finally, an analogy is suggested to Evodius to drive home the point that the soul remains indivisible despite the division of the body. In the work we are studying, Augustine arrives at the non-corporeal nature of the soul by reflecting also on Stoic semiotics as well.[92] For the Stoics, the word as sound is corporeal, while the meaning, or the significant entity—the *lektón*—which may be true or false, is incorporeal.[93] Augustine begins from this Stoic teaching, and establishes an analogy between the *lektón* and the word as sound, on the one hand, and the soul and the body on the other. Just as a word is extended in time, and thus is composed of elements, so, in the same manner, is the body. However, as the meaning of a word lives in this extension, but is not extended, the same can be proved for the soul with regard to the body. The Stoics used semiotics with the aim of building a logic of the sentences: Augustine uses semiotics for a metaphysical purpose, in other words, to demonstrate the non-corporeal nature of the soul.

4. Human Nature as a dynamic Principle of Appetites (appetitus)

In order to understand the originality introduced into anthropology, we must point to two ontological premises which are at the basis of the expansion of Augustinian thinking. The human being has in his structure, as a constituent element, the tendency to be, in order and in unity, as a primary dynamic which allows him to exist:

> And so, whoever confesses there is no nature of any kind, but desires (*appetat*) unity, and tries as much as it can to be like itself, and holds its salvation as a proper order in place or time or weight of body.[94]

The second premise, consequence of the first, can be stated in this way: in a human being the natural strength is not expressed as an undifferentiated *impetus* that can be directed toward objects of all species; on the contrary, it is only displayed following a hierarchy of tendencies, each of these having an object, a well-defined aim.

These natural dynamisms are governed, according to Augustine, by the *ordo rerum*, which he has already described in *De ordine*, a work written immediately after his conversion.[95] In these ideas, we can aknowledge the Stoic influence which conceived human nature as a principle of growth, by which the *pneuma*, which pervades all things, becomes a principle of life, *sensus, psyché*, and in human beings, *lógos*.[96] The notion of human nature considered

Anthropological doctrine

here is different from those of Plato and Aristotle. For the former, *physis* is an essence which possesses the principle of movement in itself; it coincides with the immaterial soul which is united with the body as an alien factor. This dualistic trait present in Platonic anthropology is weakened in Aristotle, for whom *physis* is a strength which operates through an immanent finality. Human nature coincides with the soul, *eidos*, of a particular body; but the soul as *enteléchia*, as form, belongs to the body in a strictly necessary manner.

In *De moribus Manichaeorum* we find the following general definition of nature:

> A nature is nothing else than that which a thing is understood to be in its species. And just as we call what a being is by the new word *essence* or, more often, *substance*, so the ancients who did not have these terms used the word *nature*.[97]

However, when Augustine passes on to enquire in concrete terms into human nature, this is conceived as a dynamic principle of primary tendencies or *appetitus* or *amores*. This dynamism is a force orientated in two basic directions: on the one hand it drives us to satisfy certain appetites within the temporal horizon; on the other hand it moves towards the level which transcends the temporal sphere. There is, in fact, in us a primary tendency to find satisfaction over and beyond the reality of the temporal world.[98] As for the appetites, as N. Cipriani has underlined,[99] Augustine, in working out his anthropology has taken for himself the doctrine of the primary tendencies (*prima naturae*) expounded by Varro in his *De philosophia*, but going back further, to Antiochus of Ascalon. The latter, in turn, had derived it from the Stoics, but he applied some Aristotelian corrections. This anthropological model, freed from the trap of immanentism, was to be used by Augustine as a premise for enquiry into various problems. At the same time, the eudemonistic pattern would be transfigured into an opening to transcendence. It is interesting to examine these primary tendencies in detail.

The primary native impulse which moves the human being is the appetite for his own preservation, awareness of himself, his own physical integrity, his *quies*, as repose ordered by the appetites (*appetitus*).

In *De musica*, the master puts it to his disciples as follows:

> But what manner of man do you think this is, referring all those numbers from the body and over against the body's passions and held from them by memory, not to carnal pleasure, but only to the body's health? A man referring all those numbers operating on souls bound to him or those numbers put out to bind them, and therefore sticking within the memory, not to his own proud excelling, but to the usefulness of those souls themselves? A man also using those numbers in either kind as directing, in the role of moderators and examiners of things passing in the senses, not for an idle or harmful curiosity but for a necessary approval or disapproval? Doesn't such a man work all these numbers and yet not get caught in them? For he only chooses the body's health not to be hindered, and refers all those actions to the good of that neighbor he has been bidden to love as himself in the natural tie of common right.[100]

Behind pleasure (*voluptas*) which accompanies the dynamic of the corporeal senses, there is hidden the natural *appetitus* for *quies*:

> Bodily pleasure seeks nothing but rest (*quies*).[101]

The natural tendency to self-preservation, physical integrity aimed at *quies*, is nothing other than a determination of the *oikeiosis* or *amor sui*, a desire by which every living being tends to safeguard itself and its own freedom from harm.[102] The nature of every person possesses the impulse to defend its own freedom from harm, to love itself. Later, in the impassioned confrontation with the anthropologi-

Anthropological doctrine

cal doctrine taught by the ancient Academics, in particular by Antiochus of Ascalona, Augustine repeats the same thought:

> These philosophers say—and rightly say—that the first and most fundamental command on nature is that a man should cherish his own human life and, by his very nature, shun death; that a man should be his own best friend, wanting and working with all his might and main to keep himself alive and to preserve the union of his body and soul.[103]

A second natural *appetitus* is the tendency to find out the truth. Expressions which bear witness to this inclination of human nature are scattered throughout almost all Augustine's philosophical works:

> Why should we have such a dread of falsities and desire truth as if it were a great good?[104]

The first dialogue *Contra Academicos*, written in Cassiciacum, testifies to an irrepressible urge rooted in human reason to find out the truth. This impulse, which is sometimes called *cupiditas veri*[105] or *amor inveniendi veri*,[106] drives us on to enquiry, and to a laborious search. Under present conditions, however, the human being often finds himself in difficulties in understanding and recognising the truth:

> Well, then, are we to take lightly a punishment entailing such consequences as these, where passion lords it over the mind, dragging it about, poor and needy, in different directions, stripped of its wealth of virtue, now mistaking the false for the true, even defending something vigorously at one time only to reject at another what it had previously demonstrated, while all the while it rushes headlong into another false judgement; now withholding all assent, while fearful for the most part of the clearest demonstrations; now in despair of the whole business of finding the truth while it clings tenaciously to the darkness of its folly; now at pains to see the light and understand, and again falling back out of weariness to the darkness?[107]

Nothing, though, can destroy the *notitia veritatis*[108] or *notio sapientiae* carved in the reason of every human being, despite the contradictions inherent in human nature. Later, Augustine was to write:

> All men desire the joy arising from truth. I have been acquainted with many men who wish to deceive, but not one who wished to be deceived.[109]

The third natural *appetitus* is described as follows:

> We want to be unconquered (*invicti*) and rightly so, for the nature of our mind is unconquerable though only as we are subject to God in whose image we are made.[110]
>
> No man is unconquerable in himself, but by the unchangeable law which makes free those who serve it and them only.[111]

The desire not to be conquered, to be free, coincides with the natural tendency to act with facility. Augustine speaks of an *appetitus actionis*, which directs man and woman towards social activity, and of an *appetitus ad agendum cum facilitate* or of *amor actionis*.[112] From the concept of invincibility, Augustine passes on to that of freedom and facility of action. There is a tendency in us to act and to act with facility, by which we are driven from purely physical activity to cognitive and social activity, with the aim of attaining victory, peace,[113] *utilitas proximi*,[114] social good. This impulse towards action leads man and woman to build the family as a *societas amoris*, society as *ordo civitatis*, and to collaborate in the running of public affairs. This conception of human nature open to all levels of social life is defended not only against the Neoplatonists, but is also introduced in the controversy with the Stoics:

> So much for the philosopher's 'happy life'. What we Christians like better is their teaching that the life of virtue should be a social life.[115]

The impulse toward social life has made man progress, who has invented things for technical and handicraft use,

Anthropological doctrine

has learned to cultivate the fields, to build cities with varied buildings and monuments, has created a variegated range of signs in *litteris, in verbis, in gestu*, to convey the memory of the past and with the aim of promoting the growth of family experience in civil society.[116] The inclination to act motivates sensory, cognitive and social action.

> I turn now to real wild beasts. They, too, keep their own particular genus in a kind of peace. Their males and females meet and mate, foster and feed their young (…). It is even more so with man. By the very laws of his nature, he seems, so to speak, forced into fellowship and, as far as in him lies, into peace with every man.[117]

This doctrine of human nature, devised by Antiochus of Ascalon by the use of Aristotelian and Stoic ideas, reached Augustine through Varro's *De philosophia*. He welcomed this conception of human nature, with its eudemonistic hallmark, but at the same time he gave it a transcendent opening which was lacking in the Stoic philosophy with which Varro was linked. Even in the earliest *dialogues*, Augustine took over this vision of human nature for himself, according to which man and woman possess various *appetitus*, the full satisfaction of which can only be attained in a world which is not that of temporal things. The corrections to Varro's point of view were possible for Augustine, thanks to the metaphysical dimension attained through the reading of Platonic books. So the *appetitus cognoscendi* becomes a desire to know the ultimate foundation of reality, the *appetitus* for *salus* and for *quies* becomes desire for happiness (*appetitus beatitatis*),[118] for supreme Good, for real *Quies*, and the impulse to be invincible and free becomes free submission to Truth. The anthropological model of Varro is thus corrected and enriched, starting with the Platonic metaphysical principle according to which reality is divided into two levels, one sensible and the other intelligible or transcendent.[119]

Notes

1. *Gn.litt.* III, 16, 25.
2. *ep.* 238, 2, 12.
3. *imm.an.* 13, 20; cf. N.Cipriani, *L'influsso di Varrone* op. cit., p.284.
4. *mus.* VI, 5, 9; *Gn. litt.* VIII, 21, 42.
5. A. Dihle, *The theory of will in Classical Antiquity*, in *Sather Classical Lectures*, Berkeley—Los Angeles—London 1982, p. 62.
6. G. O'Daly, *Augustine's Philosophy of Mind*, Berkeley and Los Angeles 1987, pp. 44–45; see also C. Di Martino, *La intentio nella psicologia di Agostino: dal "De libero arbitrio" al "De Trinitate"*, "Revue des Études Augustiniennes", XLVI, 2002, pp. 173–198.
7. *imm.an.* 15, 24; cf. N. Cipriani, *L'influsso di Varrone* op.cit., p. 390.
8. Plotinus, *The Enneads* IV, 7, 8 (5), 40–47.
9. M. F. Sciacca, *Introduzione a S. Agostino. La Trinità* Roma 1973, p. LXVIII.
10. *an. Quant.* 1,2 – 2,3.
11. Ibid. 36, 81.
12. N. Cipriani, *L'influsso di Varone* op.cit., pp 383–396.
13. V. Pacioni, *L'unita teoretica* op. cit., p. 220.
14. N. Cipriani, *L'influsso di Varrone* op. cit., p. 387; see also G. O'Daly, *Augustine's philosophy* op. cit., p. 57.
15. *an. quant.* 36, 81.
16. V. Pacioni, *L'unità teoretica* op. cit., p. 258; see also N. Cipriani, *Sulla fonte varroniana* op. cit., pp. 205–206, and G. M. De Durand, *L'homme raisonable mortel: pour l'histoire d'une définition*, "Phoenix" XXVII, 1973, pp. 328–344.
17. J. Doignon, *Le "De Ordine"* op. cit., p. 134.
18. Cicero, *Academica* II, 7, 21.
19. Quintilian, *Institutio oratoria* VII, 3, 15.
20. Sextus Empiricus, *Hypotyposeon Pyrrhoneion* II, 25–26; Porphyrius, *Isagoge* 1, 3 ff; 11, 23–28. A. Russo in his edition of the *Hypotyposeon Pyrrhoneion* (Bari 1988, p. 65, note 27)

Anthropological doctrine 109

rightly refers not only to well-known Aristotelian sources but also to the Stoics. On this question, see also V. Pacioni, *L'unità teoretica* op. cit., p. 259.

21. N. Cipriani, *L'influsso di Varrone* op. cit., pp. 379–380.
22. I. Hadot, *Arts liberaux et Philosophie dans la pensée antique*, Paris 1984, p.189.
23. N. Cipriani, *Sulla fonte varroniana* op. cit., p. 208.
24. Aristotle, *De anima* II, 4, 415b, 18–19.
25. Aristotle, *Ethica nicomachea* VIII, 11, 1161a 32–1161b. Compare also C. Mazzarelli, *Introduzione ad Aristotele. Ethica nicomachea*, Milano 1993, p. 15, which maintains that Aristotle, in the second stage of elaborating his concept of the soul, as we find it described in the *Ethics*, stressed that the soul itself is the master of the body of which it makes use as a passive instrument.
26. I cannot agree with what E. Gilson writes on this point in *The Christian Philosophy* op. cit., p. 45: "We are sometimes surprised that he (Augustine) did not discuss or even notice, the metaphysical difficulties implied in such a definition. The reason is simply that the abstract problem of the man's metaphysical structure seemed to him an idle one. It is the moral problem of the sovereign good that interests him."
27. *beata v.* 2, 7.
28. *lib.arb.* I, 15, 32; *mor.* II, 9, 14–15.
29. *ord.* II, 8, 25; 20, 54, where an explicit reference is made to Varro and Pythagoras; *div. qu.* 83, 30; *civ.* XIX, 5
30. *civ.* XV, 3–4; XIX, 11.
31. *Gn. litt.* VIII, 9, 17.
32. *vera rel.* XLV, 83; see also *De quantitate animae* 33, 71 and *De bono coniugali* 16, 18.
33. *civ.* XIX, 3, 1; *conf.* X, 31, 43–44.
34. Cicero, *De finibus* V, 16, 45.
35. *div. qu.* 83, 30; *doctr. chr.* I, 22, 20–21; *ep.* 140, 2, 3–4; *trin.* X, 10, 13.
36. A. Carlini, *Perché credo*, Brescia 1952, pp. 133–134.
37. *ord.* II, 18, 47.
38. *Acad.* III, 17, 37.

39. Ibid., III, 10, 22 – 14, 31.
40. *beata v.* 2, 7.
41. *sol.* II, 1, 1.
42. F. Cayré, *Initiation à la philosophie de saint Augustin*, Paris 1947, pp. 186–188.
43. A. Guzzo writes in *S. Agostino dal «Contra Academicos» al «De vera religione»*, Torino 1957, p.54: "Everyone goes along with the Cartesian thinking *cogito, ergo sum*; but the Augustinian position is not that of Descartes. In common they have the declaration that it is not possible to speak of *knowing* what the senses reveal, e.g. whether we move or not; but this negation of scientific value to the mere *datum* of the senses was common to all, at least from Plato onwards. There is also in common the statement that one *knows* that one thinks, while one does not *know* that one moves. But while Descartes says that he knows he exists *in that* he knows that he thinks, Augustine says that he knows he exists, that he knows he lives and he knows that he thinks".
44. A. Carlini writes, in *Cattolicesimo e pensiero moderno*, Brescia, 1953, p. 110: "In Plotinus, too, the sense of interiority is greatly stressed, but it is not the interiority of the soul in itself, but rather the interiority, *in the soul*, of the true meaning and value which the things have outside of the soul."
45. R. Radice, *Oikeiosis. Ricerche sul fondamento del pensiero stoico e sulla sua genesi*, Milano 2000, p. 112.
46. A. Guzzo, *S. Agostino* op. cit., p. 50.
47. *sol.* II, 4, 4.
48. *Ibid.* II, 5, 8.
49. A. Guzzo, *S. Agostino* op. cit., p. 50.
50. *sol.* II, 4, 6.
51. Ibid., II, 2, 5–8.
52. Ibid., II, 5, 7.
53. Ibid.
54. Ibid.
55. Ibid., II, 5, 8.
56. Ibid., II, 7, 13.
57. Ibid., II, 8, 15.

58. Ibid.
59. Ibid., II, 8, 15.
60. Ibid., II, 9, 16.
61. Ibid., II, 10,18.
62. Ibid.
63. A. Guzzo, *Agostino* op. cit., p. 52.
64. For a further close examination of these concepts, see M. Malatesta, *The primary Logic* op. cit., pp. 51–73.
65. *sol.* II, 11, 19–21.
66. Ibid., II, 13, 24.
67. *an.quant.* 1, 2.
68. N. Cipriani, *Sulla fonte varroniana* op. cit., pp. 210–220.
69. *retr.* I, 8, 1.
70. *Gn.litt.* VII, 12, 18–19; 21, 27; X, 25, 41; 26–45.
71. E. L. Fortin, *Augustine's "De quantitate animae" or the spiritual Dimensions of human Existence*, in "De moribus ecclesiae catholicae et de moribus manichaeorum", "De quantitate animae" *di Agostino d'Ippona*, Roma 1991, pp. 136–138.
72. In this context it is stated that the soul is in the image of God; in a later moment Augustine states that the soul was created in the image of the Trinity.
73. E. L. Fortin, *Augustine's* op. cit., p. 150.
74. *conf.* VII, 1, 1.
75. *an. quant.* 4, 5.
76. Ibid., 4, 6.
77. Ibid., 5, 7; cf. G. O'Daly, *Augustine's philosophy* op.cit., pp. 22–23.
78. *an. quant.* 5, 9.
79. Ibid., 11, 18. The scheme of inference is correct, since the implication corresponds, i.e. the implication which has as its antecedent the logical product of the premises, and as a consequence the conclusion, proves to be a logical law or tautology. Cf. G. Balido, *Strutture logico-formali e analisi linguistiche di testi agostiniani*, Roma 1998, pp. 11–12.
80. *an. quant.* 14, 23–24.
81. Ibid., 15, 26.

82. E. L. Fortin, *Augustine's* op. cit., p. 154.
83. *an. quant.* 18, 31.
84. G. O'Daly, *Augustine's Philosophy* op. cit., pp. 24–25.
85. *an. quant.* 19, 33.
86. G. O'Daly, *Augustine's Philosophy* op. cit., pp. 25–26.
87. N. Cipriani, *L'influsso di Varrone* op. cit., p. 387.
88. *an. quant.* 13, 22.
89. Ibid., 22, 40.
90. Ibid., 30, 60.
91. G. O'Daly, *Augustine's Philosophy* op. cit., p. 26.
92. *an. quant.* 32, 65 ff.
93. Sextus Empiricus, *Adversus mathematicos* VIII, 2.
94. *mus.* VI, 17, 56.
95. R. Holte, *Béatitude* op. cit., pp. 251–259.
96. SVF II, 458–462; 714–716 ; see also G. Reale, *Storia* op. cit., pp. 380–381.
97. *mor.* II, 2, 2.
98. *div. qu.* 35.
99. N. Cipriani, *L'influsso di Varone* op. cit., pp. 373–374.
100. *mus.* VI, 14, 45; *sol.* I, 10, 17.
101. *vera rel.* LII, 101; *doctr. chr.* I, 25, 26: "So what human beings have to be instructed in is precisely the way in which we are to love ourselves so as to benefit from it. But to doubt whether we do love ourselves and wish to benefit from doing so is simply crazy. We also need to be instructed how to love our bodies, so as to care for them in an orderly and prudent manner. Because again, it is equally obvious that we do also love our bodies, and wish to have them hale and hearty. So then, you can, of course, love something more then the health and well-being of your body. We find, after all, that many people have willingly submitted to pain and the loss of some of their organs or limbs in order to obtain other benefits which they valued more highly. So it is no reason to say that people do not value the health and safety of their bodies, just because there is something they love more. Take the case of a miser, for instance; even though he loves money, he still buys himself bread, and when he does

this he gives away money that he loves so much and wants to get more of. But this is because he places a higher value on the welfare of his body, which is maintained by that bread. It would be a waste of time to discuss such a totally obvious point any further, though for all that the error of godless people so often obliges us to do so."

102. N. Cipriani, *Lo schema dei* tria vitia (voluptas, superbia, curiositas) *nel* "De vera religione": *antropologia soggiacente e fonti*, "Augustinianum", XXXVIII, 1998, pp. 166–168; cf. M. Pohlenz, *Die Stoa. Geschichte einer geistigen Bewegung*, Göttingen 1959, pp. 111–114; R. Radice, *Oikeiosis* op. cit., pp. 110–121.
103. *civ.* XIX, 4, 5.
104. *sol.* II, 10, 18.
105. *Acad.* I, 3, 8.
106. *ord.* I, 3, 6.
107. *lib. arb.* I, 11, 22; *vera rel.* XLIX, 94–95; *conf.* X, 35–54.
108. *conf.* X, 23, 33.
109. Ibid.
110. *vera rel.* XLV, 85.
111. ibid. XLVI, 87.
112. *mus.* VI, 13, 39; *civ.* XIX , 4, 2; cf. N. Cipriani, *Lo schema* op. cit., pp. 171–172.
113. *vera rel.* LIII, 102–103.
114. *mus.* VI, 14, 45; *Gn. adv. man.* I, 25, 43.
115. *civ.* XIX, 5.
116. *an. quant.* 33, 71 – 33, 72.
117. *civ.* XIX, 12, 2; cf. M. Pohlenz, *Die Stoa* op. cit., p. 200, which illustrates this natural trend in the Stoic philosopher Panetius.
118. *mor.* I, 11, 18.
119. *Acad.* III, 17, 37; cf. G. Reale, *Introduzione ad Aurelio Agostino. Natura del bene*, Milano 1995, pp. 17–18.

V

THEORY OF KNOWLEDGE

1. Sensible Perception

In the polemic against the Academics, Augustine finally clarified his criterion of truth. In the act of sensible perception, reason, reflecting upon itself, arrives at the knowledge of itself, and at that of the intelligible world. At the same time it is forced to recognize the existence of an external sensible reality and to lend assent to it. All modifications, produced on the senses through the action of external objects, although not supplying true knowledge in any absolute sense,[1] nevertheless attest with certainty to the existence of a multiplicity of sensible data.[2] Sensation, then, as simple appearing for what it is, is unfailing. It is the task of reason to intervene in order to correct the message which sensible objects deliver to the corporeal sphere of man, in which the sensory organs are located.[3]

In the *De quantitate animae* we find the first attempt to analyze the phenomenon of sense-perception as a psychosomatic process:

> I think that sensation is 'a bodily experience of which the soul is not unaware'.[4]

Sensory perception is a change brought about in the organ of a body owing to the action of an external agent.

In another definition, which is to be found in the same work, the active role of the soul in the act of perception is again pointed out:

> Surely, sensation is always a bodily experience of which the soul is not unaware, but this proposition

cannot be inverted, because there is the experience of the body in growing or shrinking that we know and of which the soul, therefore, is not unaware.[5]

The act of sensory perception implies on the one hand the existence of an external object which produces a physical impression in the sensory organ—in this first moment we have what is commonly called the feeling (*passio corporis*) —and on the other hand the soul which, becoming aware of the modification produced by the external object, intervenes on the body. This active character of the soul in the act of perception is stressed by an expression that recurs in various works: *sentire non est corporis sed animae per corpus*.[6]

Scholars are agreed in attributing the origins of this notion of sensory perception to Plotinus,[7] for whom the soul does not undergo any impression or modification through external objects; on the contrary the soul is active in the perceptive act, even though it ought to be acknowledged that such an act is *occasioned* (not operated) by a corporeal *passio*, which in itself is not unknown to the soul.[8] Without the soul there is only the corporeal impression or affection; with the concomitant intervention of the soul, the *passio corporis* becomes sensory perception so that reason may judge the quality of the things.

Beginning with the *De musica*, this psychosomatic process is interpreted through the notion of *intentio*, tension, concentration, which is an echo, though a de-materialised one, of the Stoic notion of *tónos*;[9]

> I think the body is animated by the soul only to the purpose of the doer. Nor do I think it is affected in any way by the body, but it acts *through* it and *in* it as something divinely subjected to its dominion. But at times it acts with ease, at times with difficulty, according as, proportionately to its merits, the corporeal nature yields more or less to it.[10]

Even though it does not depend on the body, the soul nevertheless possesses a tension, a desire of the body to which it tends to unite itself in order to govern it, animate it and defend it, by adapting its own specific action to that of the body. This adapting of the soul to the body is interpreted by the use of certain doctrines of the neo-Pythagorean philosophy. In fact, in the *De musica* a new element is added to the previous characteristics of sensory perception. This is not analysed only as an impartial process linked to the awareness and attention to the stimuli produced by external objects, but it is also conceived as a motor[11] of appetition and aversion, of correspondence (*congruentia*), of rhythm (*numerositas*) and of disaccord with external objects. For this reason a sensation is pleasurable and another one is painful.

This is a fundamental passage, in which the echo of neo-Pythagorean philosophy is evident:

> And so, when it fights the body's opposition and with difficulty throws the matter subjected to it into the ways of its operation, it becomes more attentive to the actions because of the difficulty. And this difficulty on account of the attention, when not unobserved, is called feeling, and this is named pain or trouble. But when what is taken in or touches it easily agrees, all that or as much as is necessary is protected into the course of its operation. And this action of the soul by which it joins its body to an outside body harmonizing with it, since it is accomplished more attentively because of an unusualness, is not unobserved, but because of the harmony is felt with pleasure.[12]

The pleasurable sensation is produced by the correspondence (*congruentia*) of the external agent with our corporeal organs, because of which we receive experience of pleasure (*delectatio*), of beauty, of harmony (*numerositas*); on the contrary the painful sensation is the result of a lack of correspondence, because of which we feel aversion and pain. It is not difficult to recognise some influence from neo-Pythagorean teaching in this conception of sensory perception, and indeed it can already be seen in the *De Ordine*, for which pleasure, beauty and harmony which we are able to experience are all sensible manifestations of rhythm, traces of certain numbers (*vestigia numerorum*). The importance of the role assumed by number in the interpretation of sensation is also documented by the subtle classification of the numbers, explored for the first time in the first verse of the well-known hymn of St Ambrose, *Deus creator omnium*.

By a rigorously technical and original method, Augustine classifies the various families of numbers and rhythms:

1) *numeri iudiciales*, which concern the capacity on the part of the senses to distinguish pleasing or displeasing, convenient or inconvenient rhythms;

2) *numeri progressores*, which are the rhythms produced when we declaim or recite a verse;

3) *numeri occursores*, which are rhythms of reaction perceived by means of the intervention of the soul for the purpose of maintaining the harmony of the body, which is acted upon by the external thing;

4) *numeri recordabiles*, rhythms deposited in the memory with which we reproduce sensations from the past without any external movement having to make our ear vibrate;

5) *numeri sonantes*, rhythms which resound outside us independently of whether they be perceived or not.[13]

This hierarchy of numbers or rhythms is established on the basis of a principle according to which the inferior does not act on the superior, the body on the soul; on the contrary, it is the soul which has command and which, through its tension or intention, tends to adapt its own action to that of the external agent which stimulates the body. It should not surprise us, then, that Augustine considers the rhythms felt (*occursores*) and remembered (*ricordabiles*) not to be products of those which resound (*sonantes*).[14] Neither Plotinus nor his disciple Porphyrius, as far as we know, taught such a decidedly Neopythagorean doctrine of sensory perception as this one, expounded in the sixth book of the *De musica*. We may suppose that Augustine himself attempted

Theory of knowledge

to bring the neo-Pythagorean tradition into harmony with the Neoplatonic one on this point.[15]

2. Phenomenology of Signs

After studying the notion of sensation, Augustine goes on to investigate the problems connected with the nature of signs.

As is well known, in the writings of Aristotle, from those dealing with philosophical problems to those dealing with Poetics, the syntactic and semantic dimensions of language are mentioned.[16] But the Stoics gave a more systematic exploration of the problems of semiotics. In elaborating the rational aspect between signs and the interpreters of signs they arrived at the relationship between the pragmatic and semantic dimensions, in addition to the syntactic one—and thus at the three-dimensional character of language.[17]

In Augustine's *De dialectica*,[18] a work which was once considered to be spurious, we can trace the motifs which bear witness to the assimilation of Aristotelian and Stoic themes used in this youthful treatise which would subsequently be reworked to approach a theory of linguistic signs. This not only has a psychological and communicational character, but also examines the relation between object language and metalanguage and the different levels of metalinguistics.[19] In the *De dialectica* we can find the correspondence between the *dicibile* and the Stoic *lektón*, and at the same time the break from the Stoic point of view, holding that the *verbum* is the expression in which sign and significance are merged.[20] Moving from the level of signification to that of designation, the double referential aspect of a word must also be stressed, which leads Augustine to distinguish the case in which the *verbum* is either a linguistic expression which mentions itself or a sign which mentions extra-linguistic entities, in which case the word assumes the name of *dictio*.[21] The scholastics were later on to speak in a similar way of *suppositio materialis* and of *suppositio formalis*. In this context, the distinction between categoregmatic or descriptive predicates and syncategoregmatic or non-descriptive predicates is by no means marginal. As is well known, these have an intra-linguistic function, giving rise to the sentence connectives of the logical functions.[22] Naturally, a correct and appropriate use of the logical tool, which is constantly applied in the writings of Augustine, not only reveals that the African has a profound knowledge of the argumentative techniques favoured by the classical world, but is also a fine and intelligent precursor of the use which such techniques were to have in more recent eras.[23] A clear knowledge of the nature and function of language is provided for us above all in *De magistro* and in *De doctrina christiana*, but there is no lack of interesting references in *De catachizandis rudibus*, and in *De fide rerurm quae non videntur*. We shall confine ourselves here to noting the structural points of the first two works. In *De magistro*, Augustine includes in the category of *signa* not only non verbal signs, such as military emblems, but also the expressions of spoken language;[24] he reaches the conclusion that all words are a sign, that not every sign is a word, and that between sign and word there is the relationship of genus to species, which in the earliest moment was attributed to the difference between word and name.[25] Thus a relationship is established among three terms *signum, verbum* and *nomen* in the following way:

> The set of the words *Verba* (V) has a lesser extension than that of the set of the *Signa* (S). Between the two sets, *Verba* (V) and *Nomina* (N), there is a bi-univocal correspondence: to every element of the set (V) there corresponds an element of the set (N), and vice-versa. The Set of the linguistic expressions known as *Nomina* (N) is a sub-set of the *Signa* (S). If we restrict the extension of the *Signa* (S), eliminating from this set the elements that belong to unarticulated language, we shall have a unique relationship of equivalence among *Signa, Verba* and *Nomina*.[26]

In the *De magistro*, Augustine makes an attempt to unveil the divine activity by offering us a form of semiotics which, on the one end is incapable of transmitting knowledge,[27] but on the other, does not preclude the function of a means of communication among human beings.[28]

In *De doctrina christiana*, in a linguistic perspective which considers dialectic as pertinent to the things concerning the reason,[29] Augustine sees "in the rational connections of thought, a dawning awareness of the rational connections placed by God in things".[30] The *signa* thus come into the more comprehensive sphere of the *res*, since they have, thanks to the fact that they belong to the latter, the characteristic of being perceptible by the senses. Even more interesting is the characteristic of "making reference to something else, to cause us to think, with their presence in the consciousness of those who perceive them, of something other than what they are".[31] Thus we arrive at the distinction between *signa naturalia* and *signa data*: the latter, as distinct from the former (concerning, for instance, smoke, footprints, expressions of the face), are linked to the intentionality which belongs exclusively to human beings, and thus from them derive what are defined as *verba visibilia*.

It is important to underline the primacy of the linguistic sign over the other signs, because of its metalinguistic capacities; Augustine has made a strenuous effort to help us understand that a complete semiological discourse must come within the broader examination of the system of signs constituted by the writings.[32] From this viewpoint, the theological argument is interwoven with the cultural one by a deeper and very conscious reading of the sacred texts; Augustine, in the last analysis, makes a distinction between disciplines which have as their object what man himself has elaborated (*res institutae ab hominibus*) and those which were not instituted by man (*res hominibus non institutae*) in which human action intervenes in a preordained plan by God (*res divinitus institutae*).[33]

We may conclude this brief reflection on the sign by repeating what is stated in the *De Magistero*: only God teaches the intelligible truths (which are at the basis of our knowledge of the sensible world) inwardly; human words can only stimulate, admonish, call us back to an effort at knowing, a pursuit that God will crown with reward.[34] In the *De doctrina christiana* the three guides to greater depth (philosophical, theological and cultural) lead the thought of Augustine to a semantic ontology capable of analogically interpreting the gap between creation and Creator from a Christological point of view in which the Incarnate Word, as Mediator, resolves the impotence of the human word.[35]

3. Imagination

In Epistle VII, addressed to Nebridius, there is mention of man's capacity to represent to himself both objects already seen and objects never seen. This possibility is identified with the imagination (*imaginatio*), by means of which we can re-activate the incorporeal images of perceived objects, deposited in our memories, or we can create new images, using the representations received from outside ourselves.[36]

In the *De musica*, the notions of *phantasia*, with which the images deriving from external objects are formed, and *phantasma*, with which the images of images are produced (*imaginum imagines*):

> Then whatever this memory contains from the motions of the mind brought to bear on the passions of the body are called *phantasiai* in Greek. And I don't find in Latin anything I should rather call them. And the life of opinion consists in having them instead of things known and things perceived, and such a life is at the very entrance of error. But these motions react with each other, and boil up, you might say, with various and conflicting winds of purpose, they generate one motion from another; not indeed those impressed from the senses and gotten from the reactions to the body's passions, but like images of images, to which we give the name *phantasmata*. For my father I have often seen I

Theory of knowledge

> know, in one way, and my grandfather I have never seen, another way, the first of these is a fantasy, the other phantasm. The first I find in my memory, the last in that motion of my mind born of those the memory has, but it is difficult both to find out and to explain how they are born. Yet, I think, if I had never seen human bodies, I could nowise imagine them by thinking with a visible form. But what I make from what I've seen, I make by memory. Yet it is one thing to find a fantasy in the memory and another to make a phantasm out of the memory. And a power of the soul can do all these things.[37]

The imagination, therefore, possesses the power to reproduce images in the memory as well as creating new representations.[38] An important role in this process is played by memory, which functions as an immense container in which the perceived images of all types are stored while waiting to be re-awoken.[39] Man possesses a certain power of control over the creative processes of the imagination, by means of reason and will.[40] In a passage from *De genesi ad litteram*, we have a summary of the various ways by which the *vis imaginativa* produces incorporeal images of material objects:

> I think it is sufficient now to demonstrate this one fact, namely, that there exists in us a spiritual nature in which the likenesses of bodily things are formed. This spiritual nature functions when we come into contact with a body by means of our bodily senses, and the image of it is immediately formed in our spirit and stored in our memory; or when we think of bodies previously known but now absent, in order to form from them a spiritual vision of those things that were already in our spirit even before we began to think of them; or when we behold likenesses of bodies which we do not know but whose existence we do not doubt, not as they are in themselves but as they happen to present themselves to us; or when we arbitrarily and fancifully think of other objects that do not exist or whose existence

is unknown to us; or when various forms of the likenesses of bodies come into our minds from any source whatever without our concurrence and against our will. Again, it is the spiritual nature in us that operates when we are about to perform some bodily action and we order beforehand the stages of it, first going through it all in thought; or when in an act itself, whether we are speaking or going through some bodily motion, all the movements of the body are anticipated through their likenesses in our spirit in order that they may be executed (for no syllable, however short, could be pronounced in its proper place unless previously planned in thought). It is the spiritual nature of the soul also that is affected when dreams come in sleep, either with or without a meaning.[41]

Augustine distinguishes eight ways by which we are able to form incorporeal images:

1) the act by which the soul produces images derived from the stimulus of perceived external objects, and by which they are preserved in the memory;

2) the act of recalling, by which we form a certain spiritual vision of objects which are no longer present to us as realities, but as known objects;

3) the act not produced by the activity of memory but by a kind of mental projection of new images, an operation by which we create the image of a body, which we do not know, but of whose existence we are certain;

4) an act of imagination similar to the previous one; the difference seems to reside in the fact that the image created is the product of a more casual and hypothetical activity of the imagination;

5) the fifth act of imagination seems to refer to the images which are simply present in our mind without our creating or willing them. Augustine is probably referring here to the interior experience mentioned in the *De Trinitate*, XV, 11, 20, where he recalls that man has the power to think the sounds of words and recite poems inwardly without moving his lips; such sounds, by means of incorporeal images which represent

Theory of knowledge 125

them, are present in the thought of those who scan the respective memoirs in silence;

6) the imaginative act through which, at the moment when we are planning to undertake a certain action, we conceive in advance the time and the way in which we intend to do it;

7) the act of precognition of the immediate future, which takes place actually during the execution of the previously conceived action; that is, in performing an action or pronouncing words, we anticipate by means of interior images what we wish to do or say in the immediately subsequent moment;

8) the act of imagination linked to the phenomenon of dreams, of which we have experience during our sleep.

4. Memory

In Augustine's works, we can find a constant interest in, and growing exploration of the theme of memory. We shall therefore examine the nature of this faculty diachronically, to show how Augustine came to a clear and final notion of memory after long reflection.

We find the first mention of memory in the *De Ordine*,[42] where a notion of memory linked exclusively to the sensible world comes in for criticism. Here, it is stressed that memory does not only play a role within the inferior functions of the human soul, but also occupies an important place in the cognitive context, as for example in the teaching of knowledge. In the *De Quantitate animae*,[43] and in the seventh *Epistula*,[44] the memory is conceived both as a capacity to retain images of an absent object, and as a power of mentally determining the distance of such an object. When penetrated by intelligence, it possesses a kind of particular spatial sense;[45] apart from the capacity to reach things past, it also has the property of recognising, through its recall, entities which still exist. Subsequently, Augustine was to broaden the context in which memory operates; it comes to be expanded from temporal realities to intelligible permanent ones.

A brief treatise on the nature of memory, defined as *vis animi*, is to be found in the *Confessiones*,[46] where he distances himself specifically from the Platonic theory of reminiscence, with the theory of *cogitatio*—a constructive activity of the mind, which pre-supposes the presence of intellectual notions in the memory.[47] Four kinds of content in the memory are distinguished. The first is constituted by the images of corporeal entities, introduced through the various sense organs, or by the fantasy creations of the imagination (X, 8, 12). The second, by the notions that we have all learned through teaching, such as the definitions of the *artes*, the distinctions, the relationships (*rationes*), the rules (*leges*) of numbers, and by the fundamental desire for happiness, for unity (X, 9, 16; 12, 9; 20, 29–21, 31). The third type of content is identified with certain acts of the past; for example how something has been learned (X, 13, 20); or how the ability to distinguish true from false has been learned, or how we have learned or forgotten something (X, 16, 24–25). The last kind can be identified with psychic experiences of the past, such as sentiments of joy or sorrow. Such contents are present in the memory in a variety of ways. The corporeal entities through their images (X, 8, 15; 17, 26); the intelligible entities and the past acts are present in and of themselves (X, 9, 16). But in the case of past psychic experiences, such as the sentiment of fear, terror, or joy (X, 14, 21), it is difficult to say how they come to be present in the memory, whether through images or in some other way.[48]

The faculty of memory is conceived not only as a depository of a multiplicity of images and intelligible entities, but also as an instrument for unifying the whole personal experience, and the awareness that the subject has of him/herself (X, 8, 14–15),[49] to the point of identifying the memory itself with the mind, and with the subject which shows awareness:

> Great is the power of memory; its deep and boundless multiplicity is something fearful, O my God! And this is the mind, and I am this myself.[50]

Theory of knowledge

This identification takes place at the level of the human subject where the mind (*mens*) discovers the reasons (*rationes*) of numbers, the rules (*leges*) by which it judges, giving order to the data of concrete experience, which in Augustine epistemology are described as playing the role of *admonitio*.[51] Solignac suggests[52] that memory is here conceived as the means by which the human mind participates in the eternal *rationes*. Indeed, it comes to be conceived as the mind in its outpouring, in its source, in the point at which the native desire for happiness and truth arises, the desire by which we are urged on to search for our ultimate origin.

> Indeed, the happy life is joy arising from Truth, O God; Thou art 'my light', the salvation of my countenance, o my God. This happy life all men desire; this life, which alone is happy, all men desire; the joy arising from truth all men desire. I have been acquainted with many men who wish to deceive, but not one who wished to be deceived. Where, then did they get their knowledge of this happy life, unless where they got their knowledge of truth, too? For they love the latter, also, since they do not wish to be deceived. And, when they love the happy life, which is nothing other than joy arising from truth, they certainly love truth, also. Nor would they love it, unless some knowledge of it were in their memory.[53]

In the *De Trinitate*, the reflection on memory is one of the key points in the passage from anthropology to theology. On the one hand, Augustine enquires—as far as it is possible for the human mind to do so—into the theological mystery in the light of human psychology. On the other hand he attempts to understand man in the light of the Trinitarian mystery, coming to perceive in the human subject the image of the Trinity for which he provides this analogical image: *memoria, intelligentia, voluntas*.[54] Augustine distinguishes *memoria, intelligentia, voluntas sui* (X), and *memoria, intelligentia, voluntas Dei* (XIV–XV).[55]

For a brief description of the developments that the notion of memory takes on in this context we shall confine ourselves to illustrating certain essential passages taken from Books X, XIV, and XV of the *De Trinitate*.

Augustine underlines that none can love something completely unknown.[56] Thus anyone who seeks to look more deeply into what he does not know, witnesses to a love for something which in the past he has already known, and about which he wishes to know what he is still ignorant of.[57] The human mind (*mens*) knows what it is to know, and loving to know, desires also to know itself, because it does *not* know itself. However it would not have the desire to know itself if it had not, in some way, in fact known itself:

> (...) therefore, it knows itself. Thus, when it seeks to know itself, it already knows itself, it already knows that it is seeking itself. Therefore, it already knows itself. Hence, it cannot be altogether ignorant of itself, since it certainly knows itself, insofar as it knows that it does not know itself. But if it does not know that it does not know itself, then it does not seek itself in order to know itself. And therefore, the very fact that it seeks itself clearly shows that it is more known than unknown to itself. For it knows itself as seeking and not knowing, while it seeks to know itself.[58]

The mind knows itself because it knows three things about itself; it knows that it understands, exists and lives.[59] Ignorance of the self is thus self-forgetfulness, and knowledge of the self is nothing but memory itself. Augustine makes an original distinction: the soul knows itself (*se nosse*) even if it does not actually and intentionally think of itself (*se cogitare*). When it thinks of itself, it remembers itself.[60] The intimate structure of the *mens* is made up of memory, intellect and love of oneself;[61] to primaeval primitive memory, intelligence and will are immanent.[62] The first place belongs to memory, as the *mens* in its source.[63] Augustine here perceives a significant, even though inadequate, image of the Trinity.

> (...) although the memory of man, and particularly that which beasts do not have, namely, that in which intelligible things are so contained that they do not come into it through the senses of the body, has, in proportion to its own small measure in this image of the Trinity, a likeness, incomparably unequal, of course, but yet a likeness of whatever kind it may be to the Father; and similarly, although the understanding of man, which is formed from the memory by the attention of thought, when that which is known is spoken—it is a word of the heart and belongs to no language—has in its great unlikeness some likeness to the Son; and although the love of man which proceeds from knowledge and combines the memory and the understanding, as though common to the parent and the offspring—whence it is understood to be neither the parent nor the offspring—has in this image some likeness, although very unequal, to the Holy Spirit, yet we do not find, that, as in this image of the Trinity, these three are not the one man, but belong to the one man, so in the highest Trinity itself, whose image this is, are those three of one God, but they are the one God, and there are three Persons, not one.[64]

5. Rational Knowledge

The human soul is not only capable of paying attention to modifications which external objects bring about on the sensory organs, and of forming *similitudines corporales* which the faculty of memory preserves within itself, but it also possesses the capacity of judging sensible phenomena. This capacity is identified with the faculty of *ratio*, of which the following definition is given in the *De Ordine*:

> Reason is a mental operation capable of distinguishing and connecting the things that are learned.[65]

The reason is a faculty of the *mens*, and has the function of discerning, defining and distinguishing phenomena, and assembling the laws which unite them. In *De Quantitate animae* the notion of *ratio* is taken further by Augustine, who replies in this way to his interlocutor, Evodius:

> (...) because a little while ago you said that I ought to agree with you that we have knowledge before reason, on the ground that reason rests upon the knowledge of something in leading us to something unknown. But now we have found that when this leading is done, it is not to be called reason, for the sound mind is not always reasoning, even though it always has reason. Quite properly, this process is called *ratiocinatio*. So that reason, you might say, is the sight of the mind (*mentis aspectus*), but reasoning is reason's search (*rationis inquisition*), that is, the actual moving of the sight of the mind over the things that are to be seen.[66]

Ratio is defined as a sight of the mind, a permanent function distinct from the act of reasoning. Reasoning is an enquiry conducted by the reason, a movement of the mind's gazing on the objects to be examined.[67] In this movement, the reason is guided by objective rules,[68] on the basis of which it judges the sensible data. That is, it applies known principles to external objects. These rules are present in the *mens* as immutable common truths; they are not the personal property of the individual reason, even though each individual human being may perceive them with his or her own reason.

The faculty of reason is above all a power for forming judgments.[69] Through rational activity, we understand the reason why the oar seems broken in the water, while in fact it is intact, and why the eyes experience this situation; in fact the vision is capable of confirming only the objectivity of the phenomenon, and cannot give a judgment about the data relating to phenomena.[70] Through the reason, we are freed from the deceits and illusions of the senses. One who reasons takes note of objective data, and judges them. The judgment implies the addition of an *aliquid*, so that a comparison can be established. This *aliquid* does not originate from experience, which is the sphere of sensible data, nor from the reason, which although it is a mutable reality, judges according to immutable and essential principles; it is the condition of judgment, the rule which, on the one hand, precedes experience, and on the other hand is superior to reason itself.[71] In the passage from the one form of knowledge to the other, from association to the distinction of sensible data, the reason discovers the relationship among the particular phenomena, and at the same time reveals the tendency towards truth and unity within itself.

In the second book of the *De Ordine*[72] Augustine describes the process of the discursive faculty of the *mens*, that is, of the reason, directed at ordering sensible data in the light of rules or principles. The prime step of the activity of reason is the invention of language. Augustine places here, to use the language of contemporary semiotics, the pragmatic, syntactic and semantic dimensions of language. Man has understood, from the origins of his development, that it is necessary to impose names—significant sounds—on things, which will serve to identify them. In fact words are characterized by their semantic value. By qualifying the *res*, the language, or articulated sound, comes to form a privileged vehicle for social communication. Reason, realising the insufficiency of language to meet with distant or absent people, sees the need to create alphabetic signs (*litterae*) and thus invents letters, syllables and numbers. With the invention of writing and calculation, we are at the beginnings of grammar.[73] Man develops his rational capacity, and his skill (*ars*) through experience (*quae notatur experiendo*, as he says in *De vera religione* XXX, 54) and through the reasoning (*quae ratiocinando indagatur*, as he says in *De vera religione* XXX, 54). At the same time, as we find in the *De ordine* II, 12–35, man gives origin to the *artes in faciendo*, the *artes in dicendo* and the *artes in delectando*. In operating, he gives himself a practical aim, a purpose, an *utilitas*: thus we have the *artes in faciendo*, which are subdivided into *artes utiliter operandi*, or *vulgares*, to follow Varro's terminology, which concern the level of the *necessitates naturae*, and the *artes bene vivendi*, (*De Civitate Dei* XIX, 1, 2 and ff). With the *artes bene vivendi*, we are at the beginnings of morality; man at this point poses the problem of himself and his behaviour. He comes to realise that he must order his actions for good. Overcoming the sphere of 'mere doing', that is, of the *artes in factis*, we come to the *artes in dicendo*, used by man to dialogue, persuade and teach. Reason arrives at the creation of grammar, rhetoric and dialectic. After the *artes in dicendo* follow the *artes in delectando*, or *artes bene contemplandi*, which are music, geometry, astronomy and mathematics. We should underline that in speaking of music or the science of sounds, Augustine enriches the notion about semiotics which has found the greatest depths of expression in the philosophy of the Stoic school. Stoic semiotics can in fact be summed up as a philosophy of articulated language. Augustinian semiotics, like that of modern times, is, in contrast, inclusive of all signs, of which those of articulated language are only a part, though the most important part. Reason, at this point in its journey, discovers musical language, made up of sign-sounds of three kinds: the articulated musical language which is expressed in sign-sounds that are words; the musical language which is expressed in sign-sounds produced by wind instruments, and the musical language which is expressed in sign-sounds produced by percussion. The first is proper to singers, the second to instruments such as the flute, the third to those such as the zither and lyre.[74] Reason also discovers mimetic language, such as dance, and figurative language such as architecture.[75] We are on the threshold of philosophy here, by which mankind questions itself on its own ultimate origin.

N. Cipriani has observed that this scheme of the liberal arts derives from the work of Antiochus of Ascalon, or of Philo Larissa, or Posidonius and that it reached Augustine through the works of Varro.[76]

Theory of knowledge

6. Role and Function of Dialectic

Dialectic at the time of Augustine was a miscellany, in which all the elements of dialectic of Platonic origin, all the themes of Aristotle's *Organon* and all the semiotics, psychology and formal logic of the Megaro-Stoic school were mingled. In the *De Ordine*[77] Augustine describes dialectic as the science of sciences (*disciplina disciplinarum*). Why, we may ask, is this privileged role ascribed to this science rather than to metaphysics? The reply will seem obvious only if we reflect on the fact that in the *later ancient world*, alongside the tripartite division originating with the Stoics, namely logic, physics and ethics, the Academic/Stoic division was also making its influence felt—in this case grammar, dialectic and rhetoric—(see Antiochus of Ascalon and Varro), in addition to the quadripartite division of music, geometry, astronomy and arithmetic.

While the object of dialectic is not that of metaphysics, it nevertheless remains true that it was dialectic which was to become the organ of metaphysics. It is important to keep in mind that the rational proof of the existence of God in the second book of the *De libero arbitrio* is conducted, as we shall see, by argumentative tools provided by dialectic, and the same thing can be found true for a great part of the work *De diversis quaestionibus octaginta tribus*. Augustine adds new functions to those ascribed to dialectic in late antiquity. First, dialectic has a teaching function – it teaches us how to teach (*docet docere*), and teaches us how to learn (*docet discere*). Furthermore:

> In it, reason itself exhibits itself, and reveals its own nature, its desires, its powers[78]

E. Kant places the issue on a quite different level, but it is not hard to find the analogy between the functions that Kant ascribes to transcendental logic and those which Augustine attributes to dialectic. For the philosopher of Königsberg, transcendental logic is the science which determines the origin (*Ursprung*), the context (*Umfang*) and the objective validity (*objektive Gültigkeit*) of the concepts which can be referred *a priori* to objects of experience. For Augustine dialectic is the science of the essence of reason (*quae ratio sit*) of the intentions of reason (*quid ratio velit*) and of the powers of reasons (quid ratio valeat). We should mention in passing that while the transcendental dialect of Kant limits the powers of reason, that of Augustine strengthens them to the very threshold of infinity.

But the functions of dialectic do not end here. For Augustine it is still fervently the science of self-knowledge (*scit scire*): not only has it the aim of rendering man conscious, but it also has the capacity to do so (*sola scientes facere non solum vult, sed etiam potest*).[79] To these characteristics, attributed to dialectic for the first time in human thought, are added those that were traditionally attributed to this science. We have seen in Chapter 3 of this book how Augustine used Stoic logic to face the problem of uncertainty; in the second book of the *De doctrina christiana* he again makes use of Stoic theory. They had discovered that an argument is conclusive when the connection (συνεμένον) which arises out of the link between the premises, and ends in the conclusion, is sound (υγιες).[80] They had also seen that among conclusive arguments, some are true and others are not. The true ones are those in which not only is the connection resulting between premises and conclusion sound, but in which the conclusion is true and the link between the premises is true.[81]

Augustine provides three examples:

1. If there is no resurrection of the dead, neither has Christ risen. But Christ has risen; therefore, there is a resurrection of the dead.

2. If a snail is an animal, it has a voice; but the snail has no voice; therefore, the snail is not an animal.

3. If that man is just, he is good; but he is not just; therefore he is not good.[82]

As far as the first example is concerned, Augustine observes:

Theory of knowledge 135

> In the cited passage, where resurrection is mentioned, both the structure of the reasoning and the conclusion deduced from it are true.

Regarding the second example, he observes:

> This conclusion is false, but once a false antecedent is admitted, the connection that leads to such a conclusion is true. Therefore the truth of a proposition has value in itself, while the truth of a reasoning, is based on that which the one, with whom one reasons, believes or admits.

Concerning the third example, he observes:

> Therefore, even if all these things are true, the norm with which the conclusion is arrived at, however, is not true. In fact, when a consequent is removed the antecedent also is necessarily removed, but when an antecedent is removed, the consequent also is not necessarily removed.[83]

M. Malatesta synthesizes it in this way: "The second of these three arguments is formally correct, but its first premise is materially false and the argument is therefore invalid; the third argument is formally incorrect because it is possible to deduce the negation of the consequent from the negation of its antecedent. All this leads to an important conclusion of Augustine: It is one thing to know the rules governing the logical relationships (i.e. the rules guaranteeing formal correctness), and another to know the truth of statements ("aliud est nosse regulas connexionum, aliud sententiarum veritatem": *doc. Chr.* 2, 34, 52)".[84]

In short, there are formally correct and valid arguments (ex. 1); formally correct and non-valid arguments (ex. 2), and non-formally correct arguments (ex. 3). Augustine's use of Stoic logic is all too apparent.[85]

7. Intellectual Knowledge and the Nature of Illumination

Judgment is the qualifying function of reason, which at the same time implies rules which are the foundation of true knowledge. Human reason is capable of formulating four kinds of judgment: cognitive, aesthetic, moral and ontological,[86] which render man capable of true knowledge. This judgment activity is rendered possible by the illumination of truth, which is the interior object of the *mens*, not capable of reduction to any sensible external datum. Reason is thus able to have norms available to it through which it can judge, and by which it is judged, because these norms are *given* to reason and not produced by it.

In distinction from the rational knowledge that applies rules to sensible data, there is also an intellectual knowledge in man.[87] While reason implies a presence which is reflective of truth, the intellect on the other hand enjoys an immediate presence of truth, an objective presence of truth with respect to the *mens*; a sort of interior quality which excludes the immanence of truth itself on the one hand and implies its transcendence over the intellect on the other.[88]

To understand the nature of intellectual knowledge, an activity distinct from the discursive one of reason, we have to examine two basic problems: the first concerns the nature of the ideas which form the objective content of the intellect, and the second concerns the theory of *illumination*.

The distinction between *ratio* and *intellectus* is a basic presupposition of Augustine's gnoseology. The intellect is a faculty superior to the reason: it is the principle of understanding, the true eye of the soul.[89] If the right use of the reason is the foundation for science, and renders true judgments possible and builds up discourse, the right use of the intellect, illuminated by the superior light, is a condition for the intuitive understanding of the intelligible world. In the *Soliloquia*,[90] the intellect is defined as *visio*, while reason, seen in action, is described as *aspectus*. With the intellect man intuits the universal ideas, present to the mind as an intelligible object; these are not, however, innate, but they are always present, even when man is absent from them.[91]

On this question, let us look here at a passage from the *De diversis quaestionibus*.

Hence in Latin we can call the ideas either "forms" *(formae)*, or "species," *(species)*, which are literal translations of the word. But if we call them "reasons" *(rationes)*, we obviously depart from a literal translation of the term, for "reasons" *(rationes)* in Greek are called *logoi*, not "ideas" *(ideae)*. Yet, nonetheless, if anyone wants to use "reason" *(ratio)*, he will not stray from the thing in question, for in fact the ideas are certain original and principal forms of things, i.e., reasons, fixed and unchangeable, which are not themselves formed and, being thus eternal and existing always in the same state, are contained in the Divine Intelligence. And though they themselves neither come into being nor pass away, nevertheless, everything which can come into being and pass away and everything which does come into being and pass away is said to be formed in accord with these ideas. However, every soul but the rational is denied the power to contemplate these ideas. This the rational soul can do by that part of itself wherein its excellence, i.e., by the mind and reason, as if by a certain inner and intelligible countenance, indeed, an eye, of its own. But if these reasons of all things to be created or (already) created are contained in the Divine Mind, and if there can be in the Divine Mind nothing except what is eternal and unchangeable, and if these original and principal reasons are what Plato terms ideas, then not only are they ideas, but they are themselves true because they are eternal and because they remain ever the same and unchangeable. It is by participation in these that whatever is exists in whatever manner it does exist. Now among the things which have been created by God, the rational soul is the most excellent of all, and it is closest to God when it is pure. And in the measure that it has clung to him in love, in that measure, imbued in some way and illumined by him with light, intelligible light, the soul discerns—not with physical eyes, but with its own highest part in which lies its excellence, i.e., with its intelligence—those reasons whose vision

> brings to it full blessedness. These reasons (*rationes*), as was said, may be called ideas, or forms, or species, or reasons; and while it is the privilege of many to name them what they wish, it is the privilege of very few to see them in their reality.[92]

Augustine calls these ideas by many different names — immutable forms, eternal truths, eternal reasons, exemplary causes, paradigms according to which things are shaped. In the *De libero arbitrio* he lists several of these ideas: the numbers and the laws that govern them (II, 8, 23), the moral laws (II, 10, 28), the laws of beauty (II, 16, 41); the laws of logic. In the natural order, the main operation of the intellect is the formation of the *interior* or *mental word*,[93] which is transmitted through exterior language — the latter changeable from one country or language to another. We do not see the ideas directly, but we possess an image or reflection of them for participation: an analogical representation.[94] For this reason, we do not see the truth in itself, but truths, which are as fragments of truths — *index veritatis*.[95] These ideas, impressed in the *mens*, refer back necessarily to the eternal forms, so that the intellect which intuitively perceives them, is made a participant of truth.

How can we know the forms which constitute the actual object of intellectual knowledge? Augustine advances the theory of *illumination* as the instrument for apprehending intelligible truths, and as a normal and natural illustration of the Truth granted to every human mind, even though not all humans become aware of it in reflective fashion.[96] This theory is the product, at one and the same time, of a re-thinking of Platonic and Neoplatonic gnoseology, and a reflection on the *Holy Scriptures*. We find many traces of this theory in Augustine's works.[97] We shall take a look at two texts in particular.

The first is taken from the *De Trinitate*, in which Augustine criticises the Platonic theory of reminiscence as expounded in the Menon. Plato tells the story of a slave who, when questioned on certain points of geometry, replied as a master of that science. According to the Greek philosopher, this fact witnesses that the boy must have attained his scientific knowledge in a previous existence. If it were a matter of recall of truths learnt earlier, very few, says Augustine, would have been able to reply to the questions inherent in geometry, since very few would, in any prior existence, have been skilled in it, since the world is so poor in men who devote themselves to such studies. Without going in to the validity of the argument put forward by Augustine, we need only stress the following words:

> But we ought rather to believe that the nature of the intellectual mind (*mens*) is so formed as to see those things which, according to the disposition of the Creator, are subjoined to intelligible things in the natural order, in a sort of incorporeal light of its own kind (*in quadam luce sui generis incorporea*), as the eye of the flesh sees the things that lie about it in this corporeal light, of which light it is made to be receptive and to which it is adapted.[98]

Since this passage has been the subject of a variety of interpretations, we should seek first to untie the knot caused by Augustine's use of the expression: *sui generis*.[99] From a grammatical point of view, this expression may refer either to the term *mens*, or to the term *lux*. If we accept the first hypothesis, we have the following translation: "the intellect sees intelligible realities in a certain incorporeal light of its own actual nature"—i.e. incorporeal like that of the soul. But if we accept the second hypothesis, the translation will be: "the intellect sees intelligible realities in a special light (or sort of light) of a particular kind (or a special incorporeal light)". The first interpretation was favoured by Thomas Aquinas (Q.d. *De spiritualibus creaturis*, art. 10), and he went on to identify Augustine's doctrine of illumination with that of the *lumen intellectus agentis*. The light which allows us to understand intelligible truths would be an illuminatory power possessed by the human soul. God illuminates, but indirectly, through the activity of the *intellectus agens*, which would itself be the light that renders sensible fantasms intelligible in action. This interpretation was accepted by many Thomists during the last century, notably by Ch. Boyer.

The second hypothesis proposed has been supported by R. Jolivet, and above all by M. F. Sciacca and F. Piemontese, and it is their understanding of the problem that we shall follow.[100] According to the interpretation by the latter two writers, the light of truth is not to be identified with a *subjective power*, possessed by the subject as a faculty of his own; the light to which Augustine refers is not conceived as a faculty of the thinking subject but as an objective presence which can be found in all minds. A sort of created light, a gift from God, of a special kind: i.e. incorporeal, not to be identified with the intellectual faculty; an objective light, made by God to be part of the mind, and thus 'special' in this particular sense. Thus we have a question of a light which is not God Himself, but nonetheless, *proceeds from* God. It is an entity made so that it can be adapted and joined to the human intellect. Through it we can intuit intelligible realities. It is not a 'supernatural' light, but a 'natural' one; i. e. one adapted to the human intellect. The nature of the mind has been formed in such a way that it is connected and subjected to intelligible entities. The human intellect is thus subordinated to intelligible truths, images of the eternal truth. In another passage from the *De Trinitate*, the nature of *illumination* understood as objective and created light, an image present in us and before us of the uncreated Divine Light, is found even more clearly stated, as stress is also laid on the function which rules play in the formation of judgments.

> For hence it is that even the godless think of eternity, and rightly condemn and rightly praise many things in the moral conduct of men. By what rules, pray, do they judge these things if not by those in which they see how each one ought to live, even though they themselves do not live in the same manner? Where do they see them? For they do not see them in their own nature, since these things are doubtless in the mind, and their minds are admittedly changeable;

> but it sees these rules as unchangeable, whoever can see even this in them; nor does it see them in any state *(habitus)* of their mind, since these rules are the rules of justice, but their minds are admittedly unjust. Where are these rules written in which even the unjust man recognizes what is just, and in which he perceives that he ought to have what he does not have? Where, then, are they written except in the book of that light which is called Truth? From thence every just law is transcribed and transferred to the heart of the man who works justice, not by wandering to it, but being as it were impressed upon it, just as the image from the ring passes over into the wax, and yet does not leave the ring.[101]

Augustine holds that our intellect possesses an objective, created light, an image of the uncreated Light. Through it, everyone can perceive the forms, the absolute and external rules by which to make judgments of a cognitive, moral, aesthetic or metaphysical kind. These forms do not have their basis either in a subjective nature *(in sua natura)*—our mind is mutable, the rules are immutable—nor in a stable disposition of the mind *(in abitu mentis)*—the moral rules are rules of justice, whereas our mind is at times unjust—but in the Light which is the Truth itself. Such ideas, or 'laws' are contained in the divine book of the Truth, whence they are revealed to humankind, almost, as it were, being moved into the human mind, but not in the sense that they migrate into it *(non migrando)*. In other words, it is not that the law which is in God is offered as a gift to the intellect to the extent of possessing it, and seeing it in itself as it is in God, but in the sense that an image of this same divine rule is impressed *(imprimendo)* in the human mind: an analogous image to the form that passes from the ring to the wax. The divine Idea imprints the image of itself in the human mind without losing anything of itself. This, in fact, is the notion of *participatio*.[102] Such a light permits an analogical vision of the Idea, so that the human mind, by participating *per speculum* in the divine Idea, comes to possess the guarantee of the truthfulness of the judgments of reason.

We shall end this chapter with some remarks intended not so much to review the history of studies on this theme, as to stress some positive points agreed on by the critical writers.

In the 1930s and on into the 1950s, the problem concerning *illumination* in Augustine's works was the subject of a new and wide debate. Most scholars were agreed in excluding an ontological interpretation of *illumination*. The neo-scholastic school, especially in the person of Ch. Boyer, took up again the theory according to which the *illumination* of which Augustine speaks does not differ from the notion of abstraction in the Aristotelian/Thomist tradition. M. F. Sciacca responded to Boyer by maintaining that the true problem which the notion of *illumination* tries to resolve is that of the truth of judgments, and not that of the formation of concepts, which is the problem dealt with by Aristotelian abstraction. Since Gilson also followed this line of interpretation, rejecting the ontological and Thomist interpretation, he held that Augustinianism is a doctrine in which thought, capable of directly reading the intelligible in the image, must no longer concern itself with anything other than knowing what the real source of truth is.[103] He added that the action of *illumination* on thought is summed up in its purely regulatory, normative and formal role, without involving any content. The function of *illumination* would thus be that of conferring on reason the capacity to judge the truth of certain ideas, and to formulate judgments. This interpretation by Gilson, as G. O'Daly[104] has stressed, does not give enough idea of the breadth of Augustine's conception, to which there can be no doubt that an ontological dimension *is* applicable. *Illumination*, in fact, is an attempt to explain mental contents, i.e. the access of the intellect to ideas, and to rules, and is not simply a formal explanation of the capacity for judgment.

It seems to me that we can state, with the support of the texts cited above, that according to Augustine, intelligible truths are conferred on the human mind in a light which, emanating directly from God, is created, objective and formative of the intellect itself—an analogical image of the absolute, subsistent Truth.[105] The knowledge of intelligible truths which this illumination permits is natural, but of an analogical nature; in fact it is not the Ideas in themselves that we know but the images of the Ideas. The light of truth present in the intellect is a sort of analogical representation of the Truth itself, a created participation of the Divine Truth. What the intellect participates in is an objective Light of truth, not the ideas in their eternal being and distinction. This light is an indeterminate, objective, enigmatic presence, from which certain ideas spring from time to time. From it arises an innate formative attitude, which renders the intellect capable of seeing the intelligible behind the appeal of corporeal affections, and renders the reason capable of making cognitive, moral and ontological judgments.

Notes

1. *div. qu.* 9: "(...) non est constitutum iudicium veritatis in sensibus".
2. *ep.* XIII, 4: "nemo de illo corpore utrum sit intelligere potest, nisi cui sensus quidquam de illo nuntiarit".
3. M. F. Sciacca, *S. Agostino* op. cit., p. 158.
4. *an. quant.* 23, 41; cf. V. J. Bourke, *Augustine's Quest of Wisdom*, Milwakee (Wisconsin) 1945, pp. 111–112.
5. Ibid. 25, 48; cf. G. O'Daly, *Augustine's Philosophy* op. cit., p. 86; H. Rohmer, *Intentionalité des sensations chez St. Augustin*, in *Augustinus Magister* I, 1955, p. 492; K. Svoboda, *L'esthétique* op. cit., pp. 80–81; E. Gilson, *The Christian Philosophy* op. cit., pp. 56–65.
6. *an. quant.* 23, 41; *Gn. litt.* III, 5, 7; XII, 11, 23.
7. Plotinus, *Enneads* IV, 4, 19; VI, 21.
8. T. Manferdini, *Comunicazione ed estetica in S. Agostino*, Bologna 1995, p. 146.
9. G. O'Daly, *Augustine's Philosophy* op. cit., p. 85.

10. *mus.* VI, 5, 9; *Gn. litt.* XII, 12, 25.
11. G. O'Daly, *Augustine's Philosophy* op. cit., p. 86.
12. *mus.* VI, 5, 9; 16, 38; *vera rel.* XLII, 79.
13. *mus.* V, 6, 16; cf. M. F. Sciacca, *S. Agostino* op. cit., p. 166; U. Pizzani, *Il sesto libro*, in "De musica" *di Agostino d'Ippona*, Palermo 1990, p. 70.
14. *mus.* VI, 5, 8: "non ergo, cum audimus, fiunt in anima numeri ab iis quos in sonis cognoscimus".
15. N. Cipriani, *Lo schema* op. cit., p. 164.
16. Aristotle, *De Interpretatione* 1–5 and *Poetica* 20; *Physica* 263b, 13; *Metaphysica* 993a, 17; 996b, 8.
17. Sextus Empiricus, *Adversus mathematicos* VIII, 11–12. Cf. B. Mates, *Stoic Logic*, Los Angeles 1973; cf. M. Malatesta, *The Primary Logic* op. cit., pp. 15–29.
18. Aurelius Augustinus, *De dialectica, translated with introduction and notes by B. Darrell Jackson*, Dodrecht-Boston 1975; J. Pépin, *Saint Augustin et la dialetique*, Villanova (Pennsylvania) 1976.
19. G. Balido, *Strutture logico-formali* op. cit., pp. 27–29.
20. G. Manetti, *Le teorie del segno nell'antichità classica*, Milano 1987, p. 227.
21. Ibid., p. 228.
22. M. Malatesta, *The Primary Logic* op. cit., pp. 43–49.
23. G. Balido, *Strutture logico-formali* op. cit., p. 5.
24. G. Manetti, *Le teorie del segno* op. cit., p. 226.
25. G. Balido, *Strutture logico-formali* op. cit., p. 32.
26. Ibid., pp. 33–34.
27. *mag.* 13, 42.
28. E. Riverso, *Introduzione a Sant'Agostino, Il maestro*, Roma 1990, p. 79; F. J. Crosson, *Show and Tell: the Concept of Teaching in St. Augustine's "De magistro"*, in "De magistro" *di Agostino di Ippona*, Palermo 1993, pp. 13–65. According to Crosson the investigation carried out in *De magistro* shows that the two forms of teaching cannot be combined: the one, understood in the primary sense, that is teaching with the goal of making something present; the other, understood in the divine sense with the goal of making us understand

Theory of knowledge

eternal truths, that is teaching which leads to happy life, a goal which cannot be pursued without the intervention of a power greater than our own. One can affirm, in light of this close examination, that while human teaching uses a language with its own strengths and weaknesses, the teaching of the interior Teacher becomes a metalinguistic foundation capable of clarifying the opacity which words manifest.

29. E. Riverso, *Introduzione* op. cit., p. 64.
30. Ibid., p. 65.
31. U. Pizzani, *Il secondo libro del "De doctrina christiana"*, in "De doctrina christiana" *di Agostino d'Ippona*, Roma 1995, pp. 41–42.
32. Ibid., p. 46.
33. Ibid., p. 63.
34. *mag.* 14, 46; cf. E. Riverso, *Introduzione* op. cit., p. 118.
35. L. Alici, *Il primo libro del "De doctrina christiana"*, in "De doctrina christiana" *di Agostino d'Ippona*, Roma 1995, pp. 11–37.
36. *ep.* VII, 3; *trin.* VII, 9; X, 17; XI, 5, 8.
37. *mus.* VI, 11, 32.
38. G. O'Daly, *Augustine's Philosophy* op. cit., pp. 106–120.
39. L. Hölscher, *The Reality of The Mind. Saint Augustine's Philosophical Arguments for the Human Soul as a Spiritual Substance*, London/New York 1986, p. 58.
40. *mus.* VI, 32; *ep.* VII, 6.
41. *Gn. litt.* XII, 23, 49. The text used here is taken from *Ancient Christian Writers, St. Augustine, The Literal Meaning of Genesis*, Newman Press, New York, N.Y./Ramsey N.J., 1982. The importance of the quoted text has escaped scholars and was first pointed at by L. Hölscher, *The Reality of the Mind* op. cit., pp. 45–57.
42. *ord.* II, 2, 6–7.
43. *an. quant.* 5, 7; 33, 71.
44. *ep.* VII, 2.
45. M. F. Sciacca, *S. Agostino* op. cit., pp. 254–255.
46. *conf.* X, 8, 12–27, 38.

47. A. Solignac, *Le livre X des Confessions*, in "Le Confessioni" *di Agostino d'Ippona*, Palermo 1987, p. 20.
48. L. Hölscher, *The Reality of Mind* op. cit., p. 62–63.
49. A. Solignac, *Le livre* op. cit., pp. 20–21.
50. *conf.* X, 17, 26.
51. Ibid., X, 10, 17.
52. A. Solignac, *Le livre* op. cit., p. 21.
53. *conf.* X, 23, 33.
54. *trin.* XV, 3, 5.
55. A. Trapè, *Introduzione* a S. Agostino, *La Trinità*, Roma 1973, p. XL.
56. *trin.* X, 1, 1.
57. Ibid., X, 1, 3.
58. Ibid., X, 3, 5.
59. Ibid., X, 10, 13.
60. Ibid., X, 11, 17–18; 12, 19; XIV, 5, 7–8.
61. Ibid., XIV, 14, 19.
62. Ibid., XV, 21, 41.
63. A. Solignac, *Le livre* op. cit., p. 23.
64. *trin.* XV, 23, 43.
65. *ord.* II, 11, 30; cf. V. Pacioni, *L'unità teoretica* op. cit., pp. 256–260.
66. *an. quant.* 27, 53.
67. L. J. Van der Linden, Ratio *et* Intellectus *dans les premiers écrits de s. Augustin*, "Augustiniana", VII, 1957, pp. 26–27.
68. *lib. arb.* II, X, 28–29.
69. *conf.* VII, 17, 23.
70. *vera rel.* XXIX, 53; cf. L. Hölscher, *The Reality of Mind* op. cit., pp.100–103.
71. *vera rel.* XXXI, 58; cf. O. Grassi, *Prefazione* a "La vera religione", in Aurelio Agostino *Il filosofo e la fede*, Milano 1989, p. 149.
72. *ord.* II, 12, 35–15, 43; cf. V. Pacioni, *L'unità teoretica* op. cit., pp. 271–301.
73. Ibid., II, 12, 35.

74. Ibid., II, 14, 39.
75. Ibid., II, 12, 34.
76. N. Cipriani, *Sulla fonte varroniana* op. cit., pp. 203–224.
77. *ord.* II, 13, 38.
78. Ibid.
79. Ibid.
80. Sextus Empiricus, *Hypotyposeon Pyrrhoneion* II, 137.
81. Ibid., II, 138.
82. *doctr. chr.* II, 33, 51.
83. Ibid.
84. M. Malatesta, *Dialectic*, in *Augustine through the Ages. An Encyclopedia*, Grand Rapids (Michigan) 1999.
85. For a more exhaustive treatment of the topic we refer you to the following essays: J. Pépin, *Saint Augustin et la dialectique*, Villanova (Pennsylvania) 1976; G. Balido, *Regole e leggi logiche in alcuni passi del "De doctrina christiana" di Agostino*, in "De doctrina Christiana" *di Agostino d'Ippona*, Roma 1995, pp. 121–131.
86. *vera rel.* XXXII, 59 – XXXVI, 67.
87. *Gn. litt.* XII, 7, 16; *trin.* XII, 15, 25.
88. M. F. Sciacca, *Filosofia e Metafisica*, Milano 1961, p. 125.
89. *ord.* II, 2, 5.
90. *sol.* I, 6, 13.
91. M. F. Sciacca, *Filosofia* op. cit., p. 113.
92. *div. qu.*, 46, 2.
93. *trin.* IX, 7, 12; XIV, 14, 24; cf. E. Gilson, *The Christian Philosophy* op. cit., p. 296; L. Alici, *Il linguaggio come segno e come testimonianza. Una rilettura di Agostino*, Roma 1976, pp. 59–60.
94. *trin.* XIV, 15, 21; XV, 23, 44.
95. *ord.* II, 15, 43.
96. L. Hölscher, *The Reality of Mind* op. cit., p. 107.
97. *Acad.* III, 6, 13; *beata v.* IV, 35; *imm. an.* 10, 17; *mag.* 11, 38; *lib. arb.* II, 9, 27; *vera rel.* XXXIX, 72; *conf.* VII, 17, 2–3.
98. *trin.* XII, 15, 24.

99. Here we would promote the interpretation of the text by F. M. Sciacca and F. Piemontese, who have done an in-depth study on *illumination*.
100. R. Jolivet, *Dieu soleil des esprits. La doctrine augustinienne de l'illumination*, Paris 1934, pp. 149–165; see also M. F. Sciacca, *S. Agostino* op. cit., pp. 224–243; F. Piemontese, *La Veritas agostiniana e l'agostinismo perenne*, Milano 1963, pp. 67–77.
101. *trin.* XIV, 15, 21.
102. F. Piemontese, *La Veritas agostiniana* op. cit., pp. 75–76.
103. E. Gilson, *The Christian Philosophy* op. cit., pp. 85–86.
104. G. O'Daly, *Augustine's Philosophy* op. cit., pp. 206–207.
105. R. Jolivet, *Dieu soleil* op. cit., pp. 149–165; M. F. Sciacca, *S. Agostino* op. cit., p. 223; F. Piemontese, *La Veritas agostiniana* op. cit., pp. 113–123.

VI

FREE WILL AND THE MORAL PROBLEM

1. Rational and Free Judgement of Will

Augustine is the first Western thinker to have dealt systematically with the notion of free will. He achieved this by starting from a threefold speculation: the first concerned the origin of evil, in dispute with Plotinus and the Manicheans (*De libero arbitrio*), the second involved the nature of the interior conflict within the will, which divides between *velle* and *nolle* (*Confessiones*); in this he was inspired by his reading of St Paul; the third was on the function of mediation which the will fulfills in the psychological process between the *mens* and *notitia sui* (*De Trinitate*). The notion of free will is also the result of Augustine's profound enquiry into the doctrine of the *oikeiosis*, and of the *prima naturae*, belonging to the Academic/Peripatetic tradition. Traces of the conception of a free will can be found in the *De quantitate animae*, in the *De vera religione*, in the *Confessiones* and above all in the *De Trinitate*.

In every living being there exist original appetites (*appetites*), such as the tendency to self-preservation, procreation and action, referred to by Augustine as *voluntates communes*, forming a constitutive part of all living beings whether rational or otherwise. The first meaning in the broad sense of *voluntas* thus coincides with the notion of appetites, or more precisely with the tendency to action (*appetitus ad agendum*). The merit of having pointed out for the first time this aspect of *voluntas* in the broad sense belongs to N. Abbagnano: "the will has sometimes been identified with the principle of action in general, in other words with appetition. The first to expound this general concept of the will was St Augustine".[1]

In the fourteenth book of *De Civitate Dei*, when investigating the nature of the passions, Augustine observes:

> The will is in all of these affections; indeed, they are nothing else but inclinations of the will.[2]

The will is thus identified, among original tendencies, especially with *appetitus ad agendum*, which the Greeks called *ormé*. Man is equipped with a cognitive faculties, such as sense and reason, and a principle which urges him to action. This point of view is borrowed from the *De officiis* and the *De finibus* of Cicero who after investigating the tendencies to pleasure and to knowledge, had shown the *appetitus ad agendum* which drives men towards multiple activities of the cognitive, moral and civil type. Augustine, however, goes beyond that and further analyses this notion of will. In the fifth book of the *De Civitate Dei* he observes that appetite, sense and memory are present in all animal beings, whereas in the rational being the mind, the intelligence, and the will are added to these three qualities.[3] The will discussed in this text is a specific power (*vis*) of being rational, or a faculty provided with free will (*liberum voluntatis arbitrium*). If will in the broad sense is determined *ad unum*, will is also understood in the strict sense as a capacity for self-determination; i.e. of willing or not willing a certain thing.

This second notion as a specific faculty of the human being is defined by Augustine, in *De Libero arbitrio*, *vis animi*, as a middle good of which the subject may make good or bad use. It is the condition of human morality, a concept developed in the first chapter of the third book of *De Libero arbitrio*.

When the discussion between Augustine and Evodius is resumed in the above work, two particular problems are dealt with. Evodius asks what the origins are of that movement through which the soul detaches itself from

Free will and the moral problem

immutable good and turns to changeable goods, and if this movement is natural, necessitated or voluntary. Distinct replies are given to the two hypotheses. Augustine observes that the movement by which the soul detaches itself from immutable good in order to turn to changeable goods, truly belongs to the soul as, for example, the movement of the fall of a stone belongs truly to the stone. He adds that nevertheless there exists a qualitative difference between the two movements: that of the stone is natural, determined by physical laws, while that of the soul is voluntary, in the sense that it depends on us. It is in our power (*in nostra potestate*). While the *appetitus* is a movement directed towards external objects, and determined *ad unum*, that of the free will is capable of deciding of itself what it wishes to do, without any compulsion (*cogente nullo*).[4] Evodius agrees:

> There is nothing I perceive so surely and intimately as the fact that I have a will which moves me to find delight in anything. But if this power which enables me to will or not to will is not mine, then I cannot readily find anything to call my own. So if I do wrong by my will, to what can I impute the act, if not to myself? Since it is the good God who made me, and I can do good only by my will, it is clear enough that the good God gave it to me for this purpose.
>
> But if the movement by which the will can turn in different directions were not voluntary and subject to our control, a man ought not to be praised or blamed when, so to speak, he turns the hinge of his will in the opposite directions of higher and lower goods. And there would be no need at all to admonish him to neglect things temporal and to strive for the possessions of the eternal, or to try to lead a good rather than a bad life. But anyone who would think that man should not be so admonished, should be banished from the company of men.[5]

After describing the nature of the will as a faculty with which the moral act is brought back to its source, and having asserted that the cause of evil lies in a judgment and decision of the will itself, Augustine illustrates the dynamic of the psychological process from which the free act actually arises: reason determines the deliberation (*consilium*), develops the judgment (*arbitrium*) by a choice (*electio*) and urges us on to consent (*assensus, approbatio*) so as to guide our will towards good or evil.

Augustine goes on to study the relation existing between the cognitive act and that voluntary act, especially in the ninth book of *De Trinitate*. He perceived in the triad *mens, notitia sui* and *voluntas* the image of the Trinity itself in the human soul. In his controversy against Pelagius, Augustine goes a step further studying the nature of the will, passing from a descriptive level to a more strictly historical one. He examines the will as a faculty of human nature considered in general, and the will as a faculty possessed by man in his present historical condition. He asks whether freedom has preserved its full integrity over the span of human history, and concludes that the present state of man is different from that preceding the original Fall. Because of the suffering of difficulty (*difficultas*) and the blindness of ignorance (*ignorantia*),[6] the will which man currently possesses does not have the same force for good as it had from the beginning.

2. Nature of the Passions

An anthropological view like that of Augustine, which excludes any form of anti-corporeal dualism cannot fail to look into the nature of human passions, and also to compare itself with the schools which have developed particular teachings in this matter. In Books IX and XI of *De civitate Dei*, Augustine inquires into the nature of the passions, and compares his views especially with those of the Platonists and Stoics. In this issue too, Augustine's thought is in some ways in debt to the classical tradition, but is also innovative in some points which are certainly not marginal. Terms and definitions concerning human passions

Free will and the moral problem 153

are accepted from ancient philosophy. He lists[7] many Latin terms corresponding to the Greek term *páthe: perturbatio, affectio, affectus*, taken from Cicero[8] and the neologism *passio* taken from Apuleius;[9] in *De Civitate Dei* VIII, 17, he also mentions the definition of passion taken from Cicero:[10] "perturbation of the human soul contrary to human reason", and recognizes, also following the Latin writer, that there are four passions: *cupiditas, laetitia, timor* and *tristitia*, and that from these arise the immorality of certain types of human behavior.[11] In discussing the constituent nature of these passions, Augustine states in the first place that he is not in agreement with the Platonists, who perceive the roots of passions in the nature of the body itself:

> Nevertheless, they think that our souls are so influenced by 'the earthly limbs and mortal members' of our bodies that from these arise the diseases of desires and fears, of joy and sadness.[12]

According to Augustine, the soul is not only conditioned by the body in desire, fear and joy as well as affliction, but can also be stimulated from within itself. Referring to the Platonists, he maintains that there is no reason to blame the nature of the flesh for our sins and vices. This would be an insult to the Creator, because the body is, in its own way, a good thing.

Similarly, he takes his distance from the Stoics who interpreted the passions as the fruit of erroneous judgments of the reason, or irrational impulses of the soul produced by erroneous opinions. Indeed, these philosophers taught the ideal of imperturbability (*apátheia*) according to which a wise man achieves the elimination of every passion already in the present condition. Augustine, however, observes that the immunity of the mind from every impulse contrary to reason is not possible, even if desirable in this life.[13]

On the nature of the passions, Augustine makes further remarks consistent with his anthropology. He reduces the four passions to two; on other occasions, following the Stoics, he reduces them solely to the impulse of *libido, cupiditas* or *amor*. These disturbances of the soul are forms or acts of will whose nature is appetition and consent or adversion and rejection.[14] Desire (*cupiditas*) and joy (*laetitia*) are will itself converging with the objects we desire; fear (*metus*) and sadness (*tristitia*) are will in the divergence from objects we do not desire. An idea is introduced which is new with respect to the Stoic conception. The passions can be good emotions of the soul if the will is directed towards true good or bad if the will is oriented to loving an inferior good, excluding the supreme Good:

> The affection of the upright will, then, is good love and that of a perverse will is evil love. Thus, love yearning to possess the object loved, is desire and love delighting in the object possessed is joy; its avoidance of what is abhorrent is fear and its sufferance of a present evil is sadness. Further, all such emotions are evil only if man's love is evil; they are good if man's love is good.[15]

Against the Stoic idea of *impassibilitas*, according to which a wise man reaches the point of feeling no passion, Augustine points out that emotions and passions must not be considered bad or immoral when they are in conformity with correct reason.[16] His reflection concludes with a series of remarks on sexual desire and the functioning of the sex organs to emphasize the complexity of the interaction among sense perception, body and intellect.

3. Prima naturae and Doctrine of Tria vitia

In the presentation of anthropological doctrine, Augustine's use of the original tendencies or *prima naturae*, taught by Varro, was emphasized. Traces of the anthropological model that Augustine will explore later can be found in the *De immortalitate animae*.[17] Reference is made here to a threefold tendency of which the human soul is composed, the tendency to know (*appetitus sentiendi-sciendi*), to act (*appetitus agendi*), and to live (*appetitus vivendi*), which is the lowest level and which corresponds to the concept

Free will and the moral problem

of *oikeiosis* of which the Stoics spoke. The use of Varro's anthropological model comes out more clearly in *De moribus ecclesiae catholicae*, in *De quantitate animae*, in *De musica*, and, above all in *De vera religione* and in *Confessiones*. In these writings.[18] Augustine explores in depth the natural tendency towards health of the body, or the quietness, an *appetitus* which is none other than a determination of the *oikeiosis*, or *amor sui*, the tendency of every living being to safeguard itself and ensure its safety, of which the Stoics[19] had spoken; he is concerned then, with the tendency or natural desire to act with ease (*facilitas actionis*),[20] by which man wishes to be *invictus* and *liber*, finally with the natural desire to know the truth (*appetitus noscendi*).[21]

Augustine adopts the doctrine of Varro but makes significant contributions, especially from the point of view of ethics. He maintains that in the dynamics of the three natural tendencies disorder has crept in, such that in the present historical condition the orientation of each *appetitus* toward its own *finis* is often deviated toward other disorderly *fines*. Desire addressed to one's own health and integrity often becomes the seeking after pleasure (*voluptas*). The desire to act with ease turns into the desire to dominate and get the better of others (*superbia*). The natural desire to know truth becomes curiosity (*curiositas*). These forms of deviation (*vitia*) from the *prima naturae*, in some ways already observed by Cicero in his distinction between *studiosus* and *curiosus*[22] and the remark about children who compete and struggle to stand out,[23] are explored in depth by Augustine both from the ethical and anthropological points of view. The three quotations that follow clearly illustrate the evolution in Augustine's thought concerning the pagan philosophers.

The degeneration of the *appetitus* for health and safety of the body to the mere pleasure seeking (*voluptas*) is described in the *Confessiones*:

> There is another 'evil of the day': would that it were sufficient unto it. For, we repair the daily running down of the body by eating and drinking, until

> Thou dost destroy both food and stomach, when Thou wilt extinguish my need with a wonderful fullness and clothe this corruptible body with an immortal incorruption.
>
> Now, indeed, the need is sweet to me, yet I fight against this sweetness, lest I be taken over. I wage a daily battle 'in fastings', often bringing my body into subjection, yet my sufferings are banished by sensual pleasure. For, hunger and thirst are sufferings of a sort; they burn and kill like a fever, unless the remedy of food comes to the rescue. Since this is at hand, as a result of the consolation of Thy gifts, among which earth, water and sky minister to our weakness, our disability is called delight.
>
> Thou hast taught me this: that I should partake of foods as if they were medicines. But I reach the condition of peaceful satisfaction, passing from the annoyance of need; I am beset in this very transition by the snare of concupiscence. The transition itself is a sensual delight, yet there is no other way of transition than that which necessity forces us to pass over. Since health is the reason for eating and drinking, perilous enjoyment joins its company like a lackey and often strives to get in front so as to become the reason for that act which I claim, and wish, to do only for the sake of health.
>
> Now, the measure is not the same for each, since what is sufficient for health is not enough for enjoyment. It often becomes uncertain whether necessary concern for the body seeks still more sustenance, or whether, urged by the treacherous lust for pleasure, the gratification of greed has begun.
>
> The foolish soul grows joyous at this uncertainty and makes ready the protection of an excuse based on this fact; it rejoices that what is enough for healthful moderation is not evident, and so it may conceal the business of sensuality under the pretext of health.[24]

The *appetitus* that orients man toward true liberty and moral excellence is described in *De vera religione*. This can, however, turn into the desire to subjugate others arrogantly:

We want to be unconquered and rightly so, for the nature of our mind is unconquerable though only in so far as we are subject to God in whose image we are made. But his commandments had to be observed, and if they were obeyed no one would overcome us. But now while the woman to whose words we basely consented is subject to the pains of childbirth, we labour on the ground and are disgracefully overcome by anything that can trouble or disturb us. We do not want to be overcome by men.[25]

How the *appetitus* to know truth can turn into the unsavoury desire of *curiositas* is explored in the *Confessiones*.

To this, another kind of temptation joins company, one dangerous in many ways. For, over and above the concupiscence of the flesh which finds a place in the enjoyment of all sensations and pleasures, to which they who put themselves far from Thee become slaves unto their perdition, there is present in the soul through the same bodily senses a certain vain and curious desire — cloaked under the name of knowledge and science — not for fleshly enjoyment, but for gaining personal experience through the flesh. Because this consists in the craving to know, and the eyes are the chief agents for knowing among the senses, it has been called concupiscence of the eyes in holy Scripture.

Indeed, the proper function of the eyes is to see. We also use this word in reference to the other senses, when we direct them toward the act of knowing. Indeed, we do not say: 'Hear how it gleams,' or 'smell how it glitters,' or 'taste how it shines,' or 'feel how it glows' — 'see' is the proper word in all these cases. Thus, we say not only: 'See how it lights up,' which the eyes alone can perceive, but also: 'See how it sounds; see how it smells; see how it tastes; see how hard it is.'

That is why the general experience of the senses, as has been said, is called concupiscence of the eyes, for even the other senses appropriate to themselves, by way of analogy, the function of seeing, where the eyes hold first rank, whenever they seek out any object of knowledge.

Now, from this, one can more clearly perceive what there is of pleasure and of curiosity in the functioning of the senses. Pleasure eagerly pursues beautiful, melodious, sweet-smelling, attractive-tasting, soft things, but curiosity even seeks the contraries to these, for the sake of trying them, not to undergo any discomfort, but because of a lust for experience and knowledge.

What pleasure is there in seeing a macerated corpse, at which you would stand in horror? Yet, if one is lying around anywhere, people rush to it only to become sad and pale. They are also afraid to see such a thing in their sleep, as if anyone had forced them to see it while awake or some rumor of its beauty had attracted them!

The same holds true for the other senses; it is too long to go over them all. Because of this diseased craving certain monsters are exhibited in shows. From this craving comes the tendency to examine closely the hidden things of nature outside of us; although knowledge of them is of no value, men crave for nothing but to know them. The same craving is responsible if, having in view that same end of perverted science, men use magical arts in their investigations. And it is from the same cause that, in religion itself, God is put on trial, through a demand for signs and wonders, when these are wanted, not for any saving purpose, but simply for the sake of personal experience.[26]

All sins, evil deeds (*flagitia*) and unjust actions (*facinora*) are traced back by Augustine to these three deviations from the primary tendencies that constitute human nature:

> These are the capital forms of iniquity, which sprout in rank abundance from the lust for domination, for observation, or for sensation—either from one or two of these, or from all together. Thus does one live evilly in opposition to the three and seven, the

'psaltery of ten strings', Thy Decalogue, O highest and most sweet God.[27]

Finally, following the Holy Scriptures,[28] Augustine identifies the three *vitia* with the three concupiscences (*concupiscentia carnis, concupiscentia oculorum, superbia vitae*) which John the Evangelist speaks of (I Gv 2, 17) and the three temptations of Christ in the desert. He subsequently develops these notions further arriving at a more general definition of *concupiscentia* e *libido*.Both the Christian faith and important ideas from Cicero and Varro led Augustine, from the beginning of his conversion on, to free himself of his Manichean and platonic pessimism and develop a new anthropological and ethical position. According to the anthropological model taught by Antiochus of Ascalon and acquired from the writings of Varro and Cicero, nature moves the human being on a physical and biological level to ensure his preservation, freeing himself from pain and death, on a cognitive level to know truth, freeing himself from ignorance and, finally, stimulates him to communicate through language, create friendships and peace with his fellow creatures, promote liberty and personal fulfilment, freeing him of humiliation and disdain.

In 388–389, Augustine began to correct this model, exploring the scheme of the three *vitia* and pointing out that the *appetitus* of human nature are, because of sin, subject to deviations. The new vision of anthropology and ethics was likely developed and inspired by St. Ambrose, and by reappraisal of the doctrine of the Ancient Academy in the light of the first Letter of St. John.

4. The uti/frui Distinction

To understand the *uti/frui* distinction on which the Augustinian conception of ethics is based, two remarks of extreme importance should be recalled: the former concerns anthropology and the latter the nature of good things. On the subject of anthropology we have pointed out that human life consists of three degrees of being subordinated to one another: the first is vegetative life, the second, rational and social activity, and the third, intellectual and contemplative capacity. *Ordo naturae* requires that the rational level govern the biological one and the intellectual level preside over rational and social activity.[29] The various *appetitus* or *amores* must be regulated in order that the various degrees of being may be respected, without descending to the level of the baser ones and, at the same time, mortification of the higher ones. In other words the human being must orient *amor sui* toward *amor Dei*,[30] without, however, abandoning the physical dimensions and social aspects as the Neoplatonists had taught.

In his second remark, concerning the nature and function of natural goods, Augustine distinguishes among three orders of goods: the highest ones (*magna*), which are the virtues for which one lives righteously; the middle ones (*media*), which are the mental faculties indispensable to action, but which can be used for good or evil; finally, the lowest ones (*minima*) which are corporeal goods.[31] There is a long list of this third type of goods which we possess to safeguard our being, society and peace; among these are the body and those which are called its goods, such as good health, acute senses, strength and beauty. Then comes the political liberty of free men desired by those who want to be freed of their masters; followed by parents, brothers and sisters, the spouse, children, relatives, family, friends and all those who have been united for some reason. There is also the city where one lives, usually considered a mother, then honours, praise and popularity. Money occupies the last place and the term includes all our legitimate property and what we have the power to sell and buy.[32] Gold and silver are not to be blamed for the evil use of property by misers, of food by gluttons, of wine by the drunken, of feminine beauty by libertines or adulteresses, and so on.

The first discussion of the *uti/frui* distinction is in the thirtieth *quaestio* of *De diversis quaestionibus*:

> There is the same difference between the terms honorable and useful as between the terms enjoyable and useful. For although it can be maintained (though requiring some subtlety) that everything honorable is useful and everything useful is honorable, nevertheless, since the term honorable more appropriately and usually means "that which is sought for its own sake," and the term useful, "that which is directed to something else," we now speak in terms of this distinction, while safeguarding, of course, the fact that the word honorable and the word useful are in no way opposed to one another. For these two terms are sometimes thought to be mutually exclusive, but this is an uninformed opinion of the crowd. Therefore we are said to enjoy that from which we derive pleasure. We use that which we order toward something else from which we expect to derive pleasure. Consequently every human perversion (also called vice) consists in the desire to use what ought to be enjoyed and to enjoy what ought to be used. In turn, good order (also called virtue) consists in the desire to enjoy what ought to be enjoyed and to use what ought to be used.[33]

The source of the *uti/frui* distinction is the theory concerning the *honestum-utile* which the Stoics spoke of. Cicero's *De officiis*, which Augustine knew well, deals with *honestum* in the first book, *utile* in the second and the possible conflict between the two in the third. Augustine points out that the good in itself (*honestum*) and the useful good (*utile*) are two distinct orders, but they are not opposites. The difference between the two is that goods in themselves are to be enjoyed, where as useful ones are to be used. Man, a rational being, is capable of observing this distinction. So if an irrational animal enjoys food and any corporeal satisfaction whatsoever, an animal possessing reason makes use of every good in reference to a more noble one to be enjoyed.

In *De doctrina christiana*, the *uti/frui* distinction is further clarified after an important remark, semiotic in nature, is made:

> There are, then, some things which are to be enjoyed, others which are to be used, others which are enjoyed and used. Those which are to be enjoyed make us happy. Those which are to be used help us as we strive for happiness, in a certain sense sustain us, so that we are able to arrive at and cling to those things which make us happy. But, if we who enjoy and use things, living as we do in the midst of both classes of things, strive to enjoy the things which we have supposed to use, we find our progress impeded and even now and then turned aside. As a result, fettered by affection for a lesser goods, we are either retarded from gaining those things which we are to enjoy or we are even drawn away entirely from them.[34]

The *uti/frui* distinction takes on a broader meaning in this text. While the *uti/frui* distinction implied only two types of goods in *De diversis quaestionibus* this implies three. According to Augustine there are things to be enjoyed, others to be used, then a third type of goods to be enjoyed and used at the same time. The first order of goods, identified with the Holy Trinity itself, is a source of happiness. The second, identified with temporal goods, is an aid speeding one on the path to happiness. The third type of goods is identified with the human being who finds himself amidst things which are enjoyed and those which are used. There is no doubt that by this third type Augustine means some type of enjoyment among human beings,[35] but it is not clear whether the value of *uti* has an instrumental or only partly instrumental role. The instrumental aspect is implied in the image of the trip used in the subsequent paragraph of *De doctrina christiana* in which he writes:

> (…) suppose, then, we were travellers in a foreign land, who could not live in contentment except in our own native country, and if, unhappy because of

> that travelling abroad and desirous of ending our wretchedness, we planned to return home, it would be necessary to use some means of transportation, either by land or sea (…).[36]

Immediately thereafter, Augustine introduces the idea that our final destiny is not an impersonal entity, but personal and one of the community, that is, a Trinity of Persons.[37] Speaking of love for one's own kind seems to be a retraction of the concession made according to which human beings may in some way be objects of enjoyment. He repeats that human beings must be loved *propter aliud*:

> Consequently, in all these things the only ones which are to be enjoyed are those which we have mentioned as eternal and unchangeable. The other things are to be used that we may be able to arrive at a complete enjoyment of the former. We who enjoy and use other things are things ourselves. Man is a noble being created to the image and likeness of God, not in so far as he is housed in a mortal body, but in that he is superior to brute beasts because of the gift of a rational soul. Hence, the great question is: whether men ought to enjoy themselves or merely use themselves, or whether they may do both. We have been commanded to love one another, but the question is: whether man is to be loved by men for his own sake or for another reason. If he is loved for his own sake, we are enjoying him; if he is loved for another reason, we are using him. But, it seems to me that he should be loved for another reason. For, if a thing is to be loved for itself, we find in it the happiness of life, the hope of which consoles us in the present time, although we do not yet possess the reality. Yet, 'cursed is the man who places his hope in man.' (…) Therefore, if you ought to love yourself, not for your own sake, but on account of Him who is the most fitting object of your love, no other man should be angered if you love him also for the sake of God.[38]

Something subtle and new can be perceived in these words. Love for one's neighbour, which must be experienced *propter aliud*, is conceived as arising from the same ultimate goal that concerns all men, therefore love for the same destiny generates a common feeling. Earlier, Augustine had spoken of the ultimate goal of our fruition, which has a social dimension (Trinity of Persons). Now he speaks of the ultimate aim as a common destiny toward which those who love one another must look. He compares the actions of those who love God to the way in which a fan of a particular actor applauds that actor in the theatre. Here the love of one's neighbour is interpreted as a sort of social relation based entirely on love and desire for God. The shared love of God is the foundation for a communal enjoyment:

> Nevertheless, we ought to desire that they all love God within us, and all the assistance which we either give them or receive from them must be directed toward that one purpose. In the theatres, places of wickedness, if a man has a fondness for some actor and enjoys his acting as a great, or even as the greatest, good, he likes all who share this fondness with him, not on their own account, but because of the one whom they like in common. They more ardent in his own affection for that actor, they more he strives in every possible way to have more people like him, and he is all the more anxious to show him off to more people. When he sees anyone somewhat unenthusiastic, he stirs him up as much as he can by his praise of the actor. If he chances upon someone who opposes him, he is greatly vexed at his dislike for the object of his affections and strives in every way he can to remove the feeling. How should we act who are united by the love of God, the enjoyment of whom constitutes our happy life, from whom all who love Him receive their existence and their love of Him, of whom we have no fear at all that, once known, He could fail to satisfy anyone? He wishes to be loved, not for any benefit to Himself, but that He may grant to those who love Him an everlasting reward, that is, Himself whom they love.[39]

Free will and the moral problem

Clearly, Augustine intends here to attenuate the instrumental nature of the *uti* category, since enjoyment is insisted upon in *societate dilectionis Dei*.[40]

In paragraphs thirty four and thirty five of the first book of *De doctrina christiana* Augustine compares the love of God and one's neighbour with God's love for human beings, which is a love of use, with which he intends to convey a benefit and a reward. At this point the *uti* category is once again called into question. Whereas God derives no advantage from the beings he loves, human beings derive advantages from one another in some way. Love of one's neighbor and attention directed toward the same goal promote the common well-being and, at the same time, give rise to the enjoyment of God and of the other. This is the benefit, the reward from *caritas* over *cupiditas*. If man tends toward the supreme Good in a condition of mutability, that is precariousness, in search of a more secure transcendent mooring, God, on the contrary, reaches forth to man out of pure generosity. This absolute goodness relieves the *uti* relation of any suspicion of instrumentality. It is man who benefits from this behavior.[41]

In paragraph thirty seven of this work Augustine explains what is meant by enjoyment of a human relationship in God:

> When you enjoy a man in God, you enjoy God rather than the man. For you enjoy Him by whom you are made happy and you will rejoice that you have come to Him in whom you place your hope. Accordingly, Paul said to Philemon: 'Yes, indeed, brother! May I enjoy thee in the Lord!' If he had not added 'in the Lord' and had said only 'May I enjoy thee,' he would have placed in him his hope of happiness. Yet, 'to enjoy' is very close to saying 'to use with delight.' When that which is loved is close at hand, it is inevitable, also, that it bring pleasure with it. It you pass beyond this pleasure and refer it to that end where you are to remain for ever, you are using it; it would not be correct, but an error, to say you are enjoying it. It you cling to it

> and place the cause of all your joy in it as a permanent abode, then you ought with truth and correctness to be said to enjoy it. And this we must not do, except in regard to the holy Trinity, the greatest and unchangeable good.[42]

As O'Connor[43] observes, Augustine seems to suggest that enjoyment is a sort of "definitive use", which lends an instrumental touch to the love directed toward God and would be used by human beings for love and for the happiness which God grants them.

In *De civitate Dei*[44] and *De Trinitate*[45] the *uti/frui* distinction is applied in the same way as in the texts quoted above. Human nature is driven by two opposing impulses which are *charitas* and *cupiditas*. Human beings must love one another according to the orderly love of charity with the desire oriented towards God. Only thus can enjoyment have full meaning. If love for another excludes love of God, it becomes *cupiditas*.

In *De Trinitate*, investigating the nature and function of the faculty of memory, Augustine studies the structure of the human mind to discover the image of the Trinity in us. The *uti/frui* distinction reappears in Augustine's attempt to explore the relationships among *memoria, notitia sui* and *voluntas*, this time in reference to the faculty of will. We underscore the latter reference because, as will be seen, the instrumental meaning of *uti* is further defined. Three passages already noted by O'Connor[46] will be discussed. The first:

> In two of these three, therefore, in the memory and the understanding, the knowledge and science of many things are contained, and the will enables us to enjoy or use them. For we enjoy the things that we know when the will rests by rejoicing in them for their own sake; but we use things by referring them to something else which we are to enjoy. Neither is the life of man vicious nor culpable in any other way than in enjoying things badly and in using them badly.[47]

Free will and the moral problem

Augustine observes that we come to know some things, whereas we can enjoy and make use of them through will. Here the *uti/frui* distinction is transposed to within the faculty of will itself. When the latter enjoys the object which intelligence knows and in which the *propter se* resides enjoying it, we have the experience of enjoyment. On the contrary, when will uses the object going beyond this *propter aliud*, we have the experience of use. The vice comes to light when love is disordered, hence we enjoy goods in disorderly fashion (*male frui*) and use them in disorderly fashion (*male uti*).

The second passage:

> (...) a mind that loves fervently is only to be praised when that which it loves deserves to be fervently loved.
>
> When we speak, therefore, of these three, talent, learning, and use, our judgment upon the first of these three depends upon what a man can do in his memory and understanding and will. In the second we consider what each one has in his memory and understanding, and at what point he has arrived by his loving will. But the third one, use, lies in the will which disposes of those things that are contained in the memory and the understanding, whether it refers them to something else, or rests satisfied in them as an end. For to use is to take up something into the power of the will, but to enjoy is to use with the joy, not of hope, but of the actual thing. Therefore, everyone who enjoys, uses, for he takes up something into the power of the will and finds pleasure in it as an end. But not everyone who uses, enjoys, if he has sought after that which he takes up into the power of the will, not on account of the thing itself, but on account of something else.[48]

The third passage:

> (...) these things which have been created are not known by God because they have been made; rather they have been made, even though changeable, because they are known unchangeably by Him.

> This ineffable embrace of the Father and the Image is, therefore, not without pleasure, without love, or without joy. Consequently, this love, this delight, this happiness, or this blessedness, if indeed it can be worthily expressed by any human word, is briefly defined as Use by Hilary.[49]

Augustine alludes to the relationships between the Persons of the Trinity in this text. The notion of use, stripped of the instrumental sense, is carried within God himself.

This brief analysis of the *uti/frui* leads to several general conclusions.

The *uti* category can take on two meanings: a primary one with an instrumental meaning, and a derived one, without the dimension of instrumentality. All the nuances of the *uti* category that we have identified, contribute to a true understanding of Augustine's ethics. In order to achieve an orderly love, man must respect the order of goods. When he upsets this order, he experiences a disorderly love, which, aimed exclusively at enjoyment in itself, comes to exclude the ultimate goal from the horizon of existence.[50]

The criterion of the moral order depends on the *uti/frui* distinction. Eternal goods must be the object of enjoyment, temporal ones must be the object of use,[51] with the moderation of whoever makes use of them and not the affection of whoever loves them.[52] The *uti/frui* principle certainly gives rise to a demanding moral doctrine, because it is based on a hierarchical conception of beings. However, it is not based on a dualistic anthropological conception. The latter takes distances itself from Neoplatonism, because, for one thing, of its insistence upon social engagement. It also distances itself from Manichaean gnosis, insisting as it does on the goodness of temporal things. Finally, it distances itself from Stoicism, because it identifies the supreme Good with the transcendent Being. We must then emphasize that the Augustinian moral doctrine, rigorous in its creation and formulation, does not take on the utilitarian character that is present the historical conception of

Free will and the moral problem 169

Cicero's ethics. Augustine makes use of the Stoic *uti/frui* notion but he rethinks the contents. For the African, as for Cicero, human beings come under the category of "things of which use is to be made". Cicero, however, teaches: "(…) the task of virtue is to reconcile the soul of men and induce them to favour what is useful to them",[53] in order "(…) to encourage the cooperation of others so that it turns to our advantage".[54] Augustine, on the contrary, teaches: "man makes use of his friends to exchange benefits, of his enemies to practice patience; he makes use of those who have money to do charity; he makes use of everybody to be benevolent".[55]

The *uti/frui* distinction is certainly the underlying theme in Augustinian ethical thought. An analysis of the texts on that subject leads to the conclusion that this doctrine of ethics cannot be accused either of egocentrism or of opportunism as A. Nygren has insinuated,[56] especially if one keeps in mind the new ideas concerning anthropology that Augustine introduced on the subject just after his conversion to Christianity.

5. Eternal and natural Law

For Augustine, ethical rectitude has two sources: the first comes from the personal conscience, while the second comes from eternal law, the definition of which was provided for us in the work *Contra Faustum*:

> The eternal law is the divine reason or will of God that orders us to preserve the natural order and forbids to perturb it.[57]

This originates in God himself.[58] It is universal and immutable in nature and orders us to maintain the *ordo naturae* that distinguishes each being. To eternal law, to which all creatures must be subject, corresponds, as a reflection, natural law from which prescriptions arise with which positive laws must be in conformity.[59] All created beings are good and man must respect their hierarchy: corporeal entities must be subordinate to spiritual ones, inferior to superior, temporal to eternal,⁶⁰ *ut omnia sint ordinatissima*.⁶¹ Man lives virtuously when he recognizes eternal law as making up the natural order. Several universal rules are pointed out in *De libero arbitrio* which preside over cognitive and practical activities. These rules, accessible to anyone, are conferred on free will so that the latter can be properly oriented.⁶² As Augustine reminds Evodius, these concern justice, prudence, temperance and fortitude:

> Will you not also admit that these statements have an absolute truth which is present and common to you as well as to me, and to all who see it, namely we ought to 'live justly', 'the less perfect should be subordinated to the more perfect', 'like things should be equally esteemed', 'each one should be given his due'? (...) Can you deny that 'something incorrupt is better than the corrupt', 'the eternal better than the temporal', 'the inviolable better than what is subject to injury'? (...) Can anyone say, therefore, that this truth belongs to him alone when its changeless character is there to be seen by all who have the power to behold it? (...) Who, again, is there to deny that the soul should turn from what is corrupt to the incorrupt, and should love, not the corrupt, but the incorrupt? Or how can anyone, once he acknowledges that something is true, fail to understand its changeless character or to see that it is present to all alike who are able to behold it?⁶³

Acceptance by reason and will of those rules is the way to attain the supreme good: *hoc enim natura expetit*.⁶⁴ The notion of natural law is imprinted in the human spirit:

> Therefore, by way of this ineffable and sublime management of things which is the work of Divine Providence, natural law is transcribed, as it were, upon the rational soul so that in the conduct of this life and in their earthly ways men might preserve semblances of the workings of God.⁶⁵

Augustine accepted the truth of the combination *nomos* and *physis* in reference to the divine *logos* of which the Sto-

Free will and the moral problem 171

ics spoke.[66] In his view the divine *logos* comes to coincide with the transcendent reality which constitutes the basis of natural law. This is the prerequisite of the moral order (*ordo vitae*), of the cultural order (*ordo studiorum*) and of the civil order (*ordo civitatis*). No evil act can destroy the law written in the heart of man;[67] everyone can be aware of this, even if not in the same way, since the present human condition is marked by *ignorantia, infirmitas* and *difficultas*.

There are determined rules guiding the course of nature (*leges naturales*) according to which the vital human spirit (*spiritus vitae*) carries within itself tendencies that free will can only subdue but not destroy at its roots.[68] Man is urged to obey natural law which is provided as an aid, so that his constituting tendencies will not be deviated. Augustine teaches that God himself, in so far as he is the father and governs all beings and, at the same time, the mother because he takes care of them,[69] enlightens man so that he will be able to submit his senses to reason and reason to Him.[70]

The ethical doctrine, presented here in its basic principles, is the work of a man converted to Christianity and deeply immersed in classical culture. Augustine had come to know the pagan moral doctrines from Varro, Cicero, and Seneca, from whom he had learned, as he recalls in *De doctrina christiana*,[71] "highly useful moral precepts". Even though he left behind no general treatise on ethics, aside from *De moribus Ecclesiae Catholicae et de moribus Manichaerum*, which is a reply to the Manichaen accusations against the Catholic Church and a criticism of the moral point of view of the Manichaeism, nonetheless, there remain various moral works on the various states of life, virtues and vices. It is not by chance that Augustine has been recognized as the one who laid the foundations for Christian moral science.[72]

Notes

1. N. Abbagnano, *Volontà*, in *Dizionario di filosofia*, Torino 1980, p. 925.
2. *civ.* XIV, 6; *trin.* XIII, 3, 6–4, 7.
3. *civ.* V, 11.
4. *duab. an.* 10, 14.
5. *lib. arb.* III, 1, 3; *vera rel.* XIV, 27.
6. *lib. arb.* III, XVIII, 52.
7. *civ.* IX, 4, 1.
8. Cicero, *Tuscolanae disputationes* III, 4, 7; IV, 5, 10.
9. Apuleius, *De Deo Socratis* 12.
10. Cicero, *Tuscolanae disputationes* III, 24; IV, 9, 22.
11. *civ.* XIV, 5.
12. Ibid.
13. Ibid. XIV, 9; cf. G. Reale, *Storia* op. cit., pp. 423–428.
14. *civ.* XIV, 6; cf. J. Brachtendorf, *Cicero and Augustine on the Passions*, "Revue des Études Augustiniennes", XLIII, 1997, pp. 289–308.
15. *civ.* XIV, 7, 2.
16. Ibid., XIV, 9, 3.
17. *imm. an.* 13, 20.
18. *vera rel.* 52, 101; 53, 103; *mus.* VI, 14, 45.
19. N. Cipriani, *Lo schema dei* tria vitia op. cit., pp. 165–166.
20. *vera rel.* 45, 85; 52, 101; 53, 103.
21. *conf.* X, 35, 54.
22. Cicero, *De finibus bonorum et malorum* V, 17, 48–49.
23. Ibid., V, 22, 61–62.
24. *conf.* X, 31, 43–44.
25. *vera rel.* 45, 85.
26. *conf.* X, 35, 54–55.
27. Ibid., III, 8, 16.
28. I Jo. 2, 17; cf. N. Cipriani, *Il modello antropologico nel libro I delle* Confessioni, in *Le* Confessioni *di Agostino (402–2002): bilancio e prospettive*, Roma 2003, pp. 426–433.

29. *civ.* V,11; *c. Faust.* 22, 27.
30. *doctr. chr.* II, 22, 21; II, 26, 27.
31. *lib. arb.* II, 19, 50.
32. Ibid., I, 15, 32.
33. *div. qu.* 30.
34. *doctr. chr.* I, 3, 3.
35. W. R. O'Connor, *The* uti/frui. *Distinction in Augustine's Ethics* "Augustinian Studies", XIV, 1983, p. 52; see also R. Holte, *Béatitude* op. cit., pp. 200–206.
36. *doctr. chr.* I, 4.
37. Ibid., I, 5.
38. *doctr. chr.* I, 22, 20–22, 21.
39. Ibid., I, 29, 30; cf. W. R. O'Connor, *The* uti/frui. *Distinction* op. cit., p. 53.
40. L. Alici, *Il primo libro* op. cit., pp. 25–27.
41. *doctr. chr.* I, 34–35.
42. Ibid., I, 33, 37.
43. W. R. O' Connor, *The* uti/frui. *Distinction* op. cit., p. 54.
44. *civ.* XI, 25.
45. *trin.* IX, 13; XI, 25.
46. W. R. O'Connor, *The* uti/frui. *Distinction* op. cit, p. 56.
47. *trin.* X, 10, 13.
48. Ibid., X, 11, 17.
49. Ibid., VI, 10, 11.
50. *doct. chr.* III, 10, 16.
51. *s.* XXXVI, 5, 5.
52. *mor.* I, 21, 39.
53. Cicero, *De officiis* 2, 5, 17.
54. Ibid., 2, 6, 20.
55. *vera rel.* XLVII, 91.
56. A. Nygren, *Eros und Agape*, Berlin 1955, *passim*.
57. *c. Faust.* 22, 27; *civ.* XIX, 6, 22.
58. *ord.* II, 8, 25; cf. P. Brezzi, *I fondamenti filosofici del diritto e dello Stato in S. Agostino*, in *Sant'Agostino e le grandi correnti della filosofia contemporanea*, Roma 1955, pp. 195–201.

59. *lib. arb.*, I, 6, 15; *civ.* XIX, 13, 1.
60. *lib. arb.* I, 15, 32; *Gn. litt.* VIII, 23, 44.
61. *lib. arb.* I, 6, 15.
62. Ibid., I, 13, 29.
63. Ibid., II, 10, 28.
64. *civ.* XIV, 25.
65. *div. qu.* 53, 2.
66. M. Pohlenz, *Die Stoa* op. cit., pp. 132–134.
67. *conf.* II, 4, 9.
68. *Gn. litt.* IX, 18, 32.
69. *en. Ps.* XXVI, 18.
70. B. Roland-Gosselin, *La morale de Saint Augustin*, Paris 1925, p. 48.
71. *doctr. chr.* II, 40, 60
72. Th. Deman, *Le traitement scientifique de la morale chrétienne selon S. Augustin*, Montréal–Paris 1957, pp. 123–125; see also J. Mausbach, *Die Ethik des hl. Augustinus*, Freiburg 1909, 2 voll. and B. Roland-Gosselin, *La morale* op. cit..

VII

NATURE AND EXISTENCE OF GOD

1. Metaphysical Notion of God

In *Confessiones*, Augustine recalls that before he converted to Christianity and came into contact with Neoplatonism he had embraced the materialistic vision of the Manichean gnosticism. According to this doctrine the ultimate origin of reality lies in two opposing material substances, good and evil. Both are infinite although to differing degrees: the evil mass is more limited and the good is more extensive.[1] He later abandoned that conception. Although he had come to believe that God was incorruptible, immutable, inviolable, he remained convinced that divine reality had to be conceived of as something corporeal.

> (...) I was forced to think, not in terms of the shape of a human body, but of some corporeal being in local space, either spread out in the world or even infinitely diffused outside the world, applying this concept even to that incorruptible, inviolable, and immutable thing which I set above the corruptible, violable, and mutable.[2]

Augustine's reading of Neoplatonic books enabled him to move from the material to the spiritual conception of God. The discovery that ontological reality has a hierarchical structure was a determining factor. It was through Plato that he realized that all reality is structured in a hierarchical order: the levels of intelligible and perceivable reality. In Neoplatonism he discovered a similar hierarchical structure, headed by the One, which Plotinus had enriched with new components from Greek philosophy. Through Porphyrius, Augustine discovered a theodicy in which the One of Plotinus encountered that of the Being in Aristotle. Having converted and yet aware of the tension arising form contact between Neoplatonic metaphysics and Christian faith, Augustine was able to rework some aspects of Neoplatonism that were not in conflict with the Christian view of reality, finding original solutions.[3] Out of this came a new theodicy which, especially because of the introduction of the notion of *creatio ex nihilo*, changed the framework and scope of Platonism. These metaphysical concepts, subjected to acute analysis and enhanced with fresh intuitions, converge in the new Augustinian notion of God.

Having made these historical and critical observations, let us analyze the nature of the notion of God; then, we shall illustrate Augustine's proof of the existence of God.

One of the first metaphysical notions with which the idea of God is introduced is that of the Supreme Measure (*summus Modus*).

> The truth, however, receives its being through a supreme measure from which it emanates and into which it is converted when perfected. However, no other measure is imposed upon the supreme measure. For, if the supreme measure exists through the supreme measure (*modus per summum Modum*), it is measure through itself.
>
> Of course, the supreme measure also must be a true measure (*verus Modus*). But, just as the truth is engendered through measure, so measure is recognized in truth. Thus, neither has truth ever been without measure, nor measure without truth.
>
> Who is the Son of God? It has been said: The Truth. Who is it that has no father? Who other than the supreme measure? Whoever attains the supreme measure, through the Truth, is happy.[4]

Augustine defined God as Measure without measure,[5] excluding the idea of a measure, a limit imposed by another. The form and order of temporal beings arise from this Supreme Measure, as an act of creation.[6]

The Supreme Measure is also called the Supreme Good (*summum Bonum*).[7] It is an eternal and immutable Good above which nothing else exists.[8] All things are its work and participate in its goodness albeit in a condition of mutability and precariousness. There is one sole Good, simple and immutable, in which being and having identify with one another.[9] It has caused all other realities that are not simple but mutable to be called into being.

God, Supreme Measure, Supreme Good, is, finally, called One (*Unum*), a supreme unity, without extension. It does not have a part here and another there, or one now and one afterwards, because God is One in an absolute sense.[10] Every finite being is not only a good, but, because of the Original One, possesses a unity of its own. Stone is stone since all its parts are composed in a unity; a tree would not be a tree if it did not have oneness; an animal would not exist if its members were to be separated from the unity; what do friends desire if not unity? People are a nation because they consider harmful all dissent over the principles that constitute them. Human passion itself causes great pleasure because bodies love one another and unite… and why is pain woeful? … because it tends to divide what is one.[11] The original One breathed into living beings an aspiration toward unity (*appetitus unitatis*):[12]

> To be truly formed is to be brought into a unity. For what is supremely one is the principle of all form.[13]

The One is the principle based on which all that exists is unity. True things are true because they exist and they exist since they are similar to the One, the form of all things that are.[14]

Plato was the first to conceive Measure as being at the summit of reality. By Measure he meant the Absolute, which includes within itself the good and the beautiful. These are the basis of proportion and order in things.[15]

In *Leges*,[16] arguing against Protagoras, the Greek philosopher wrote that not man but God is the Measure of all things. In *Respublica* we find the definition of God as Supreme Good.[17]

As far as the idea of God as One is concerned, Augustinian thought comes close to that of Plotinus.[18]

The notion of God as the Supreme Measure, the Supreme Good, the Originating One, was combined by Augustine with that of the Supreme Being of Aristotelian origin. In *De moribus*[19] this definition of God was given: "We must love God (...) of whom I will not say anything but that He is the very Being" (*Deum ergo diligere debemus ... quod nihil aliud dicam esse nisi Idipsum esse*). Here we should quote a passage from *De vera religione* in which integration with Aristotelian thought is clear:

> But you say, Why do they become defective? Because they are mutable. Why are they mutable? Because they have not supreme existence. And why so? Because they are inferior to him who made them. Who made them? He who supremely is. Who is he? God, the immutable Trinity, made them through his supreme wisdom and preserves them by his supreme loving-kindness. Why did he make them? In order that they might exist. Existence as such is good, and supreme existence is the chief good.[20]

He then identifies being, living and thinking in God:

> (...) in God, being is not one thing and living another, as though He could be and not be living. Nor in God is it one thing to live and another to understand, as though He could live without understanding. Nor in Him is it one thing to know and another to be blessed, as though He could know and not be blessed. For, in God, to live, to know, to be blessed are one and the same as to be.[21]

Augustine could not find a definition more pregnant with meaning than this: *Idipsum esse*, meaning that God is eternal, not subject to mutation because He is responsible for

Nature and existence of God

the fullness of being.[22] The Gnostic-Manichaean dualism has been overcome:

> For that must be said to be in the highest sense of the word which remains always the same, is identical with itself throughout and cannot be corrupted or altered in any part, and which is not subject to time, nor different now from what it used to be. This is being in its truest sense. For the word *being* signifies a nature which subsists in itself and is altogether changeless. And this can be said of no other being than God, to whom there is absolutely nothing that is contrary, for the contrary of being is non-being.[23]

Plato is the source of the notion of God as the Supreme Measure and Supreme Good; Plotinus, that of God as One.

How does Augustine arrive at the Aristotelian notion of God as pure Being, integrated with the notion of One, since Plato and Plotinus place the One above Being? It is Porphyrius who inspires the Augustinian conception of God as One and as Being: indeed mediation between henology and ontology is clearly supported by Porphyry in his comment on the *Parmenides* of Plato reported in an anonymous writing that P. Hadot has shown to be the work of a disciple of Plotinus.[24] Regarding this issue it is useful to quote a passage already pointed out by G. Reale[25] in his Introduction to *De natura boni*:

> See now if Plato does not seem to mean this, that is that the One which is above substance and the existing thing, is neither existing thing nor substance, neither substance nor activity, but rather acts and He himself is pure action; thus He himself is *the Being which is prior to the Existing Thing*; participating in this Being, then, the second One possesses a derived being, and this is the participation of the existing thing. It follows that Being is dual: the first pre-exists the Existing Thing, the second is what is produced by the One which is above and beyond; and the One is absolutely the Being in itself.[26]

Porphyrius' idea of God as One, a true Being which conceives himself, is a metaphysical model which Augustine felt appropriate to use from the start of his philosophical production. It must be recalled that Augustine was familiar with the notion of God, the Supreme Being, as this was already being taught in the *Scriptures* (*Exodus* 3, 14) even before Plato.

Thus, he develops his metaphysics under the influence of the Pagan philosophers, Platonists above all, acknowledged to be those closest to him (*propinquiores*).[27]

But some remarks should be made here concerning Platonic theology. In the eighth book of *De civitate Dei*, after listing the numerous intuitions of Platonic philosophers about the transcendence of God, Augustine maintains that Platonic theology can, on the one hand, be considered positive and fruitful, but on the other, marred by a principle that all Platonists, starting from their master, have shared in its entirety:

> God does not mingle with mankind (*nullus Deus miscetur homini*).[28]

Because of that principle Platonists have been forced to accept the need for demonological mediation, hence idolatry. Augustine points out that the unacceptability of this principle lies in the dualistic conception that opposes the supreme goodness of God to the evil nature of matter, from which the divinity keeps its distance, without intervening in or communicating with the lives of human beings. The Platonists filled the gap between God and human beings with the mediation of demons, ascribing to them a impetratory and vaticinatory function.[29] Augustine criticizes the incongruence and incoherence of such mediation, pointing out that man needs a divine mediator, different from the one conceived by Pagan philosophers. He also condemns their metaphysical principle involving the unbridgeable gap between the goodness of God and the evil of matter. In books eleven and twelve of *De civitate Dei* Platonic theology is confuted and the principle of the *creatio ex nihilo* is introduced. The act of creation and metaphysical structure of the created cannot be identified with the deployment of the One, mentioned by Plotinus, nor with the action of the demiurge of which Plato spoke.[30]

2. "Sicut creator ita moderator"

Concerning Augustinian doctrine pertaining to the notion of *creatio ex nihilo* the meaning taken on by the terms *production, procreation, creation* in this context must be explained. The meaning of the term human production is explained in the *Confessiones*: when humans shape an object, they impress a form on pre-existing matter.

> A human artificer (*homo artifex*) imposes the form (*species*) on something already existing and in possession of being, for instance, on earth, on stone, on wood, on gold, or anything whatever of that sort.[31]

The act of production must be distinguished from that of procreation, since the latter is an operation in which the substance of what is generated comes from the same substance as the one that procreates. Thus, if a human procreates a child or builds a house, the child and the house both come from him (*ex ipso*); but the child is "by him" (*de ipso*), hence it is procreated. The house, on the contrary, is "of earth and wood" (*de terra et ligno*), and so it is produced. The act of procreation presupposes an identity of substance[32] between the procreator and the procreated. The act of creation is to be distinguished from the two preceding concepts: it cannot be derived from experience, but it can be intuited through reason and is, in any case, a revealed fact, an operation from nothing (*ex nihilo*), that does not presuppose pre-existing matter. The result does not come from the substance of the one who operates but from an act that brings into existence in its entire nature what absolutely did not exist previously, either in terms of matter or form. The *creatio ex nihilo*, which Augustine frequently speaks of, is thus an absolute beginning which, when it occurs, establishes the difference between the *Idipsum esse* and the existing thing which received the existence.³³ It is also to be distinguished from the idea, described in *Timaeus*, concerning the creation of the world by the demiurge, which does not procreate the cosmos out of itself, but shapes the world using a pre-existing and disorderly matter.

As Augustine developed his doctrine, he had to face two problems dating back to Neoplatonist philosophy: the first concerned the nature and origin of formless matter, considered eternal by the Platonists; the second concerned the mutation assumed to have been caused by the *creatio ex nihilo* in the divine will itself.³⁴

Augustine dwelt at length on the explanation of the idea of unshaped matter and eventually arrived at the definition of *capacitas formarum*, a principle inherent in the mutability of material entities, almost but not precisely a nothing; in other words a *nihil aliquid*, an *est non est*.

> But I wanted to know, not merely to suspect; and, if my voice and writing were to confess to Thee all that Thou hast opened up for me concerning this question, who among my readers would stay with it long enough to grasp it? Yet, my heart shall not cease, despite this, to give honour to Thee and to sing Thy praises concerning these things which it is not adequate to put into words.
>
> The mutability, then, of mutable things is itself capable of receiving all the forms into which mutable things are changed. And what is this? Is it mind? Is it body? Is it a species of mind or of body? If one could say: 'nothing—thing' and 'is—is not,' I should say it is thus; yet, it would have to have some kind of being, in order to be able to receive these visible and organized forms.³⁵

Matter cannot be without a form. It precedes it, but not in time, rather as a condition at the origin, just as a sound produces a song.

> Thus, material is prior to that from which it is made, not prior in the sense that it produces it actively, for its part here is passive instead, nor prior by a

period of time. For, we do not emit formless sounds in prior time, without the song, and then arrange and fashion them into the form of a song in a later period of time, as wood is used in making a box, or silver is fashioning a dish. Of course, such kinds of matter precede even in time the forms of the things made from them.

But in a song, it is not that way. When it is sung, its sound is heard, not as first sounding in a formless way and then being formed into the song. Whatever thing sounded at first in whatever way has passed away, and you cannot find any part of it that you might pick up and put together by means of art. So, the song has its being in its sound; the sound of it is its material. And this receives a form so that the song may exist. Hence, as I was saying, the material in the act of sounding is prior to the form of the act of singing: not prior as through the power to make it, for sound is not the artificer of the act of singing, but it is supplied as a subject, from the body of the singer, to his soul, as that from which he may make the song. Nor is it prior in time, for it is uttered together with the song. Nor is it prior in choice, for the sound is not preferable to the song, since the song is not only a sound, but also a beautifully formed sound. But, it is prior in origin, because the song is not formed so that the sound may exist; rather, the sound is formed so that the song may exist. With this example, let him who can, understand that the matter of things is first made and called heaven and earth, because from it heaven and earth have been made. But, it was not made first in time, because it was the very forms of things that gave rise to periods of time. This matter was formless and now it is observed along with periods of time (...).[36]

Thus God created matter and form together:

But we must not suppose that unformed matter is prior in time to the things that are formed; both the

> thing made and the matter from which it was made were created together.³⁷

So, for example, the voice is the matter of the words and words denote the voice that has been formed. A speaker, however, does not previously produce a formless voice that he could subsequently determine and form to make up words. Similarly, God did not create formless matter first, then, through a second operation, shaping it following the order of the various natures, since He created shaped matter.³⁸

As far as the second objection is concerned, Augustine maintains that the act of creation does not involve any change of will and decision in God and it is opposed to the conception of eternity of the world taught by classical philosophy. The will by which God created and governed beings is not new in Him, but immutable and eternal. To explain this doctrine Augustine distinguishes four modalities of priority of one reality over another: according to eternity, according to time, according to choice, according to origin. According to eternity, God precedes things; according to time, the flower precedes the fruit; according to value, the fruit precedes the flower; according to origin the sound precedes the song. The first and last of the mentioned priorities are extremely difficult to understand, the second and third very easy.³⁹ God does not precede times in reference to one time, but precedes them all, absolutely. He precedes them with his eternal 'now' through which all our days pass.⁴⁰ Creation is, therefore, an absolute act, distinct from that of procreation and from any artisan's model of production. As such it is opposed to the Greek philosophical conception of the eternity of time.

The subject is taken up again with the intention of disputing the Neoplatonists who, convinced of the eternity of the world, maintained that creation in time would mean a change in God:

> Whatever is affected suffers a change and whatever suffers a change is mutable. Hence, one can no more

think of God in His leisure suffering from indolence, inactivity, or inertia any more than we can think of Him suffering from labor, effort, or eagerness in His work. For He knows how to rest while He acts and to act while He rests. To every new work whatsoever He applies not a new but an eternal design. Nor does regret for any former inactivity prompt Him to create what had not been created before.

When His 'former' leisure and 'subsequent' activity is mentioned, and I do not know how man can understand this, surely, the time reference is not to Him, but to things which 'formerly' did not exist but 'subsequently' did, for in Him there is no 'subsequent' choice which modifies or rejects a 'former' resolution. It is by one and the same, eternal, and unchangeable will that He brought it about that His created works should 'formerly' not exist so long as they had no existence and should 'subsequently' exist from the moment they began to be.[41]

Change is in creatures, not in God who is immutable. A relation may arise without change in any of the terms to which the relation refers: *in nobis ergo fit aliqua mutatio (...) in illo autem nulla*.[42] Not only the world, but time, as well, began with the act of creation.

> Of course, they (Platonists) may admit that it is silly to imagine infinite space since there is no such thing as space beyond the cosmos. In that case, let this be the answer: it is silly for them to excogitate a past time during which God was unoccupied, for the simple reason that there was no such thing as time before the universe was made.
>
> The distinguishing mark between time and eternity is that the former does not exist without some movement and change, while in the latter there is no change at all. Obviously, then, there could have been no time had not a creature been made whose movement would effect some change. It is because the parts of this motion and change cannot be simultaneous, since one part must follow another, that, in these shorter or longer intervals of duration, time

> begins. Now, (since) God, in whose eternity there is absolutely no change, is the *Creator* and *Ruler* of time ... I do not see how we can say that He created the world after a space of time had elapsed unless we admit, also, that previously some creature had existed whose movements would mark the course of time.
>
> Again, sacred and infallible Scripture tells us that in the beginning God created heaven and earth in order. Now, unless this meant that nothing had been made before, it would have been stated that whatever else God had made before was created in the beginning... Undoubtedly, then, the world was made not in time but together with time (*procul dubio non est mundus factus in tempore, sed cum tempore*).[43]

An important distinction is made with the expression 'not *in* time but *with* time'. Creation *in* time cannot be spoken of, since there cannot be time before the mutable creature exists; but creation *with* time must be spoken of since time presupposes becoming. Eternity excludes it. God, therefore is *existendi et, ut dicam, essendi auctor*.[44]

Augustine acknowledges that the Platonists should be admired for having intuited the threefold order which binds the creature to the creator: God is the cause of the created universe, a truth that enlightens the mind, a source that makes man happy. They did not, however, arrive at the true notion of creation, since they were still convinced of the pre-existence of matter and eternity in the world.[45]

The act of creation, according to Augustine, places the difference between the created being and the Supreme Being. As an image, the created being realizes in itself the resemblance with the principle because it participates in the being even if in a limited way[46] while remaining mutable and temporal.[47] God conferred on formless matter a stable mode of existence through the form,[48] which is participation in the eternal ideas of God. By virtue of that act, matter is realized in a completed reality. The result of the act of creation is that the structure of every created being has the following triad: measure (*modus*), form (*species*), order (*ordo*).[49] Various lexical variations of this can be found throughout the works of Augustine: *unus, numerus, ordo*,[50] or *mensura, numerus, ordo*,[51] from Platonic philosophy[52] and from the *Scriptures*.[53]

The first component or perfection of the created being is measure (*modus*), which means end, limit, that which marks boundaries, determines, identifies every finite being. *Modus* coincides with the deployment of unity in multiplicity. A second property of the created being is given by the form (*species*), which in Augustinian philosophy means beauty, but can also mean number. Number confers on every created being its own form:

> Look at the heavens and the earth and the sea, and at all the things they contain. Whether these shine from above or crawl on the earth below, or fly or swim, they all have forms because they possess number. Take away number from them, and they are nothing. What then, is the source of their existence but that same source from which number derives, since, in fact, they enjoy existence only insofar as they are possessed of number?[54]

Numbers constitute the premise for clearly determined form making the existing thing knowable. They possess that function since they coincide with the paradigmatic, atemporal forms in the divine mind of the created being. They are identical to ideas.[55] Form in the created being is synonym of beauty,[56] harmony, correspondence, proper proposition of the parts.[57] The third perfection of the created being is *ordo*, the subject studied in *De ordine*. The word *ordo*, which at times is used as a synonym of beauty (*pulchritudo*),[58] has two meanings: *ordo* as a principle through which all the things God has established are conveyed;[59] *ordo* as arrangement of like and unlike things whereby each of them is assigned its proper place (*parium dispariumque rerum sua cuique loca tribuens dispositio*).[60] The first definition shows the tendency existing in every being to achieve the goal for which it is destined. The second underlines the condition experienced by a being in conformity with the divine plan. The concept of weight (*pondus*) used at times as a synonym of *ordo* refers to the first meaning of *ordo*.[61] Augustine developed a polysemantic notion of *ordo*, as Aristotle had done with the concept of being.[62] For Aristotle, being can be expressed in many ways, and similarly for Augustine *ordo* can be expressed in many ways. It is surprising that Augustine succeeds in recognizing in the personal God the source of *ordo* present in all things, while not neglecting any of the many meanings of this polysemantic term.

The basic characteristic of the reality created is mutability (*quae mutatio in omni creatura sive possibilitate inest etiamsi desit effectu*),[63] but not all creatures change in the same way. Some change with space and time, others only with time. Only God is immutable and eternal.[64] The structure of created beings is made up of three goods (*tria bona*) recalled, the imprints of Him who is the Supreme Measure (*summa misura*), the Supreme Number (*summus numerus*), the Supreme Order (*summus ordo*).[65]

The act of creation took place in one sole instant, without any time interval, even if all beings were not created in the same way. Many beings were complete, others only potentially (*potentialiter*) or in embryo (*seminaliter*). All the beings that were born or appeared throughout the centuries were created at the beginning of time, even if only in their *rationes seminales* or *causales* which, as latent embryos, develop in time through the incessant and mysterious action of God.[66] The doctrine of the *rationes seminales* is illustrated in *De genesi ad litteram* within the conception of nature described earlier. If human nature is a dynamic principle of *appetitus*, living nature in general is a dynamic principle of force or capacity (*occulta quaedam vis*).[67] Augustine defines that dynamism using expressions from the Stoics: *rationes seminales*,[68] *causae primordiales*,[69] *primordia seminum*.[70] From the beginning the world was pregnant (*gravidus*) with seeds, with *causae primordiales* containing as latent realities all those beings that would mature later following the established time order.⁷¹ As for their nature, seminal reasons are moist seeds belonging to the fourth element which is water. These have been created and spread by God since the beginning of creation (*in ictu condendi*),⁷² with a powerful internal dynamism, provided with highly effective numbers carrying with them energies, constituent virtues instilled in the created reality.⁷³ Seminal reasons are made up of elements that have an essence (*qualitas*) and a force (*vis*) such that a grain of wheat produces wheat and not beans, a human creates another human and not an animal of a different species. We can then state, in agreement with the Augustinian texts, that seminal reason is a more remote and hidden cause of the seed itself, which is already destined to produce a certain vegetable, a certain animal, a certain human. Seminal reason is an arrangement, a virtue introduced into things from the very first instant of the act of creation, so that the first individual of any of the species that we observe today is created through the divine power and environmental conditions at a determined time.

> In the seed, then, there was invisibly present all that would develop in time into a tree. And in this same way we must picture the world, when God made all things together, as having had all things together which were made in it and with it when day was made. This includes not only heaven with sun, moon, and stars, whose splendor remains unchanged as they move in a circular motion; and earth and the deep waters, which are in almost unceasing motion, and which, placed below the sky, make up the lower part of the world; but it includes also the beings which water and earth produced in potency (*potentialiter*) and in their causes (*causaliter*) before they came forth in the course of time as they have become known to us in the works which God even now produces.⁷⁴

Even if the natural process is hidden from us, it is not subject to chance nor to blind necessity but, on the contrary, is guided and governed within by divine Providence.⁷⁵

Augustine denies that there can exist any form of creative evolution, which would involve the creation of new beings not present at the beginning. Furthermore, he excludes any possible form of transformism.[76]

With the concept of *creatio ex nihilo* a notion of divine Providence is formulated, which is different from what was taught by Stoicism and Plotinus. Earlier we showed this difference in reference to the notion of *ordinatio iudiciaria*. Here we will merely add a few considerations regarding the action of divine Providence in temporal realities. The provident action of God on created realities takes place without interruption, such that creatures would cease to exist if it came to an end. The *dispositio temporalis* of Providence takes care of both the *ordo rerum* of each being and the *ordo universitatis*.[77] Providence, writes Augustine in *De vera religione*,[78] takes care of each person almost privately (*quasi privatim*), but also of the entire human race in a way that could be called public (*tamquam publice*). What God does *privatim* is known only by the individual acted upon. What is done in favor of the human race is discovered through history and prophecies. In *De genesi ad litteram*,[79] Augustine maintains that the provident God continues his presence in universal history through his *administratio*. He provides this care of beings in a natural and voluntary way, through the hidden laws of nature and the proper use that humans make of will and intelligence. In *De ordine* he had taken his distance from the Plotinian conception of Providence for ontological reasons. In *De civitate Dei* he criticized the theological conception of Cicero for moral reasons. Cicero denied divine foreknowledge to defend human freedom, but, according to Augustine, it is madness to admit the existence of God and deny him the foreknowledge of future events:[80] God knows all things before they occur, without this excluding the freedom of human determination.

> However, our main point is that, from the fact that to God the order of all causes is certain, there is no logical deduction that there is no power in the choice of our will. The fact is that our choices fall

within the order of the causes which is known for certain to God and is contained in His foreknowledge—for, human choices are the causes of human acts. It follows that He who foreknows the causes of all things could not be unaware that our choices were among those causes which were foreknown as the causes of our acts.[81]

3. Proof of the Existence of God

The argument for the existence of God follows a more elaborate procedure in the second book of *De libero arbitrio*.[82] The human being is the point of departure for reflection and is understood to be a finite reality, endowed with thought, capable of knowledge, will and judgment: a being that claims total intelligibility and seeks after its ultimate origin.

The proof is carried out in three phases: the passing from the certainty of being to that of living and knowing (II, 3, 7); the progression starting from sensation and through internal sense arriving at reason (II, 3, 8 – 6, 13); the overcoming of reason (II, 6, 14–15, 39). This third movement in turn takes place in three stages: the existence and nature of numerical truths (II, 8, 20–24); the existence and nature of moral rules (II, 9, 24–10, 29); the subsisting truth, source of the universal rules present in the mind (II, 11, 30–15, 39).[83]

Starting from the most evident truths, Augustine turns to his interlocutor Evodius:

> I will ask you whether you yourself exist. Possibly, you are afraid of being mistaken by this kind of a question when actually, you could not be mistaken at all if you did not exist.[84]

The return to the critical point of view marks the beginning of the discussion on the existence of God. In *Contra academicos* the problems of certainty and consent had been solved and the principle of self-awareness discovered. Human reason is certain that it possesses a logical structure through which the correspondence of external reality and its cognitive activity can be acknowledged. In *De libero arbitrio* the content and environment of self awareness are enhanced. Humans are sure that they know and they *know* that they are involved in a reality that is more vast than their ability to think. Furthermore they have the certainty of their own existence as an objective reality that comes before any reasoning process, any doubt or deception that reason can fall prey to. From that first certainty a second can be deduced. Still addressing Evodius, Augustine observes:

> Then, since it is evident that you exist, and that this could not be so unless you were living, then the fact that you are living is also evident.[85]

Only a being which is a living being at the same time can possess the certainty of existing. Evodius agrees with his teacher who suggests a third step: humans could not know that they exist, live, if at the same time they did not have the ability to know. To the degree to which their rational faculty is active, humans are aware that they exist, live and know. Of these three things, existing, living and knowing, the stone, for example, has only existence. The animal has existence and living and, finally, they who know using their intellect not only have existence and living but also the certainty thereof. Whoever possesses these qualities at the same time is certainly superior to those who lack two or one of these.[86] Indeed, what lives also exists: but it cannot be concluded from this that it can know intellectually. Such is the life of the animal. What simply exists does not, therefore, possess living and the ability to know. We can say that a corpse exists, but not that it lives. What does not have life does not have the faculty of knowledge. Differently from the stone and the animal, man possesses all three of the aforementioned qualities. It is reasonable that to demonstrate the existence of God starting from finite reality it is advisable to favor as a starting point finite reality, which exists, lives and thinks; a finite reality then, capable of reflecting on itself and on the outside world.

Nature and existence of God

The first level of knowledge is determined in humans by the sensory perception through which it is possible to perceive physical reality. But within the sensory perception there are various degrees of sensation and perceiving. Augustine and Evodius carry on a subtle discussion of corporeal senses which is not without its interest and originality in comparison with the study of the nature of sensation previously performed.[87] The argumentation proceeds with the goal of identifying a criterion for the superiority in rank of one being over another. The functions of the sensory organs are examined, those of internal feeling and reason, as well as the relationship existing among the various objects of sensory perception and rational knowledge.[88] Each of the five senses with which humans are endowed has its own object of sensation: for sight it is color; for hearing it is sound; for smell it is an odor; for taste it is that which is tasted; for touch, that which is soft or hard, smooth or rough. Some senses however, especially sight and touch, have common objects such as largeness, smallness, roundness. These can be perceived both by sight and touch.

There is also an interior sense to which the five external senses refer all things. The sense with which an animal sees is something different from the one by which it is attracted or from which it is repelled by what it perceives through sight. With the internal sense, animals perceive the utility or danger of an external object. It cannot be identified with sight, hearing, smell, taste, or touch, but with something that presides over all the senses. The internal sense is a force different from reason, which is capable of distinguishing the object from the sensory organ that perceives it, and this, in turn, from the internal sense itself. Augustine argues:

> These points are clear: corporeal qualities are perceived by the bodily senses; one and the same sense cannot perceive itself; the inner sense perceives that corporeal qualities are perceived by the bodily sense and also the bodily sense itself; all these things of

sense, as well as reason itself, are known by reason and come under the heading of knowledge.[89]

Knowledge, which presides over existing and living, is broken down into three new degrees in a hierarchy: the external sense, the internal sense and reason.[90] On what criterion is the hierarchy based? How are these orders of cognitive power subordinated to one another? All that the bodily sense reaches with the eyes or with another bodily organ concerns only the existence level; the sense is above the external object perceived because it belongs to the order of living that presupposes that of existing. The difficulty arises when one wants to know why the internal sense that belongs to the same order of living reality of the external sense must be considered superior to the latter.[91] If it is stated that the internal sense perceives the external one, we still have not found the criterion (*regula*) that will enable us to deduce with certainty that every being that senses is better than that which is sensed. When one supports the principle that every knowing subject is superior to the object known, one is obliged to assume, for example, that humans are better than wisdom since they know it, and this is false.[92] The true criterion by which it can be maintained, without the danger of going astray, that the interior sense is superior to the external one is the following: the former guides and judges the latter. It is the internal sense by which even the soul of an animal is advised, which orders, for example the sense of sight, to look at the object or to draw back, or it induces it to be more careful. It functions as a moderator and judge of the external sense. This is the principle that Augustine underlines:

> There can be no doubt in anyone's mind that what judges is better than what is judged.[93]

This rule must be applied to the relationship existing between reason and internal sense. Reason guides our investigation, distinguishes the external sense from the object, the internal sense from the external one, judges the superiority of the external sense over the object and the internal sense over the external one. It is, so to speak, the head and the eye of the soul. If, as we have pointed out earlier, the *iudiciales* rhythms are at the top of the hierarchy of rhythms, and they judge the quality of unpleasant or pleasurable rhythms, disapprove or approve, this is possible because there is a faculty in us whose function is to judge, to distinguish, to classify perceivable external and internal reality. It is superior to the things judged. There is nothing nobler than this in the nature of human beings.[94] If nothing superior to reason exists in human nature, it is necessary to inquire into the possibility of transcending reason itself to find the existence of a superior reality. This is what Augustine asks of Evodius:

> (...) if you should find that there is nothing above our reason but an eternal and changeless reality, would you hesitate to say that this is God? You notice how bodies are subject to change, and it is clear that the living principle animating the body is not free from change but passes through various states. And reason itself is clearly shown to be changeable, seeing that at one time it endeavors to reach the truth, and at another time it does not, sometimes it arrives at the truth, sometimes it does not. If reason sees something eternal and changeless not by any bodily organ, neither by touch nor taste nor smell nor hearing nor sight, nor by any sense inferior to it, but sees this of itself, and sees at the same time its own inferiority, it will have to acknowledge that this being is its God.[95]

Having said that he will call God that to which nothing superior is found, Evodius agrees with Augustine on the necessity of continuing the investigation that has been undertaken.

The discussion about the nature of feeling is resumed. If the investigation into sense perception has shed light on the hierarchical superiority of one form of knowing over another—for example, the internal sense is superior to the external one because it moderates, judges the activity of the latter, just as reason is superior because it judges the activity of the former—it now becomes necessary to analyze the properties of the objects of the various types of knowing. The two participants in the dialogue agree that they individually possess exterior senses, an interior sense, and reason; they also agree that there are objects that each one of us perceives individually and others that we perceive together at the same time. A cup of honey, for example, cannot be tasted by both at the same time. On the contrary, a melody can be listened to and enjoyed at the same moment by several people. Hence there are individual and common perceptible objects in sensory perception:

> We are to understand by individual and, so to speak, private property, that which is identified with each one of us and which each one alone can perceive within himself as belonging properly to his own nature. By common and, so to speak, public, we understand that which is experienced by all who perceive something, without any deterioration or change in the thing itself.[96]

The reflection on the private and common character of the objects of the sensory perceptions is the starting point for an original investigation into the transcendent nature of common rational facts.[97] This character belongs to the *ordo numerorum* and the principles of wisdom. Augustine asks Evodius if all rational subjects see things in common, each with his own mind, something visible, of which all are aware, and which is not transformed by how it is used by those aware of it, such as food or drink, but which remains whole and unsullied. Without hesitating, Evodius replies:

I see there are many, but it is sufficient to single out one of them, the nature and truth of number (*ratio et veritas numeri*) which are present to all who make use of reason. Everyone engaged in computing (*computator*) them strives to grasp their nature with his own reason and intelligence (…).[98]

Human reason is capable of understanding the nature of the number and the laws governing numerical relations

Nature and existence of God 197

such as division, addition and subtraction. These truths are incorruptible and eternal, present to those who use their rational faculty. Even if we first perceive numbers with our bodily senses, nonetheless, it is with reason, enlightened by an interior light unknown to the bodily sense, that we arrive at the laws governing numerical relationships.[99]

Rule of numbers, with their immutable and incorruptible nature, recall rules (*regulae*) of wisdom. Wisdom is the truth in which the Supreme Good is to be seen and possessed. It is unique and common to all, as the Supreme Good is unique. Augustine helps Evodius to understand this idea suggesting to him an analogy from cosmic reality:

> It does not follow, does it, that wisdom itself is not something one and common to all alike, simply because those goods which they see and choose in the light of this wisdom are many and varied? If you think it does, you could also doubt that the sunlight is something one, since the objects we see in it are many and varied. From among these objects each one freely chooses something to enjoy through his sense of sight. One man likes to look at a mountain height and finds delight in such a view; another, at the level expanse of a meadow; another, at the slope of a valley; another, at the green forest; another, at the undulating surface of the sea; another gathers in all or several of these at once for the sheer delight of looking at them.
>
> The things which men see in the light of the sun and which they choose for their enjoyment are many and varied, yet there is the one sunlight in which each viewer sees and takes hold of an object for his enjoyment. Similarly, the goods are many and varied from which each one chooses what he wants, and it is by contemplating and taking hold of this object of his choice that each one really and truly makes this the highest good wherein to find his enjoyment. It is still possible that the light of wisdom itself, in which these things are seen and grasped, may be one and shared by all alike who are wise.[100]

Wisdom is the sole truth which all rational beings have in common. The notion of this (*notio sapientiae*) is impressed on our minds. This seal of truth in us is revealed to be as structure of rules through which it is possible to form judgments. If at first the investigation had dwelled on the various forms of knowledge and had reached the certain conclusion that those who judge are better than what is being judged, this is now transposed onto nature and the truth of judgments. Thus, the properties of the rules by which judgments are made must be analyzed and the origin of this investigated. In every era, human beings have recognized interior rules of truth, which are true and evident as the rules of numbers and dialectics. A brief list follows of original things known to the minds of everyone: all humans wish to arrive at the truth and achieve happiness; one must live according to justice, subordinate the worst to the best, place things which are equal on the same level, give each one what he deserves, recognize that the uncorrupt is better than the corrupt, the eternal is better than the temporal, the inviolable better than the violable. One must love not corruption, but the incorruptible. No one doubts that existence not shaken by adversity is better than that which is overwhelmed by temporal adversities.[101] Anyone who lives a life enlightened by judgments formulated in the light of these principles can be considered wise.[102] It must be emphasized that these rules are not empty functions of reason or products of the conscience, but immutable truths present in the minds of everyone.[103]

Augustine goes on to point out that the interior rules of the truth of numbers and wisdom are consubstantial. To aid in an understanding of how these truths, albeit manifesting themselves in different functions, have something in common ontologically speaking, an analogy is put forth coming from the natural world:

> Light and heat are perceived coexistent, so to speak, in the one fire and cannot be separated from each other. Yet the heat reaches objects placed near it, while the light is spread even over a larger area. In

like manner, the power of understanding, present in wisdom, warms what is near it, such as rational souls, whereas, for things farther removed, such as bodies, it does not reach them with the warmth of its wisdom, but permeates them with the light of number.[104]

Being immutable, the interior rules of truth are superior to reason, which, differently from them, is changeable. They do not come from the corporeal world,[105] nor do they belong to the nature of our mind. They transcend reason even if they are present as an *aliquid tertium* within it.[106] We judge things on the basis of these rules of truth, but no one among us judges the rules. When we assert sentences, moral or numerical truths for example, seven plus three are ten, no one claims that it should be so, but simply acknowledges that it is so. They do not make corrections as examiners, but delight in the discovering of that truth (*non examinator corrigit, sed tantum laetatur inventor*).[107]

Finally, Augustine explains the final step: the identification of the numerical and moral truths with Truth, which reveals itself as an immutable reality to all those who acknowledge it and on its basis judge reality. Numerical and moral rules are immutable truths since an immutable Truth exists,[108] which includes all things that are immutably true:

> But if this truth were of equal standing with our minds, it would itself also be changeable. At times our minds see more of it, at other times less, thereby acknowledging that they are subject to change. But the truth which abides in itself, does not increase or decrease by our seeing more or less of it, but, remaining whole or inviolable, its light brings delight to those who have turned to it, and punishes with blindness those who have turned from it.
>
> And what of the fact that we judge about our own minds in the light of this truth, though we are unable to judge at all about the truth itself? We say that our mind does not understand as well as it ought, or that it understands as much as it ought.

> But the mind's understanding should be in proportion to its ability to be drawn more closely and to cling to the unchangeable truth. Consequently, if truth is neither inferior nor equal to our minds, it has to be higher (*superior*) and more excellent (*excellentior*).[109]

All that we touch, taste and smell are similar to this Truth, but those which we hear and see are even more similar, since every word is perceived in its entirety by those who hear it and by everyone at the same time. Every form that appears before one's eyes, is seen by that one, and, at the same time by the other. However, these entities are similar to the Truth in a distant manner. No word resounds in its entirety all at once, since it is drawn out in time and part of it is heard first and another part afterwards. Every visible form expands, so to speak, in space and is not in its entirety everywhere. Our mind, incorporeal and immortal, superior to the corporeal things we see and touch, is capable of attaining the immutable rules. It is, however, only an image of Truth which is simply present. It does not pass with time, nor does it move from one place to another. It is very close to all those who love it, as a secret light which, at the same time, is open to all (*secretum et publicum lumen*). It admonishes externally, teaches internally. No one judges it and no one judges well without it.[110]

With this reflection on the nature of Truth and its transcendence, Augustine feels that he has come to the end of the demonstration of the existence of a reality superior to reason and endowed with divine attributes. Once the existence of transcendent Truth has been demonstrated, it has been proven that God exists. The conclusion is to be found in an inference with which Evodius agrees totally:

> (…) if there is anything more excellent, then this is God; if not, then truth itself is God. In either case, you cannot deny that God exists, which was the question we proposed to examine in our discussion (*Si enim est aliquid excellentius, ille potius Deus est; si autem non est, iam ipsa veritas Deus est. Sive ergo illud*

> sit sive non sit, Deum tamen esse negare non poteris; quae nobis erat ad tractandum et disserendum quaestio costituta).[111]

The teacher and the pupil agree that the rational proof of the existence of God, which they have achieved, is a form of knowledge that is certain, although still quite tenuous; it is enough, however, to enable them to continue their investigation.

Notes

1. *conf.* V, 10, 20.
2. Ibid., VII, 1, 1; cf. N. Cipriani, *Dio nel pensiero di S. Agostino*, in *Dio nei padri della Chiesa*, Roma 1996, p. 258.
3. *Acad.* III, 20, 43.
4. *beata v.* 4, 34.
5. *Gn. litt.*IV, 3, 8.
6. *nat. b.* 3; 22.
7. *sol.* I, 1, 6; *mor.* II, 1, 1; *lib. arb.* II, 13, 36; *vera rel.* XVIII, 34–36.
8. *duab. an.* 8, 10.
9. *civ.* XI, 10, 1.
10. *vera rel.* XLIII, 81.
11. *ord.* II, 18, 48.
12. *lib. arb.* III, 23, 69.
13. *Gn. litt. imp.*10, 32.
14. *vera rel.* XXXVI, 66.
15. M. Pohlenz, *Der hellenische Mensch*, Göttingen, 1947; it. tr. *L'uomo greco*, Firenze 1986, p. 422.
16. Plato, *Leges* 716 c4–5; *Protagoras* 357 b.
17. Plato, *Respublica* VI, 508 a–b.
18. Plotinus, *Enneads* V, 4, 1, 6; V, 5, 13, 6.
19. *mor.* I, 14, 24.
20. *vera rel.* XVIII, 35.
21. *civ.* VIII, 6.
22. *en. Ps.* 121, 5; cf. Ch. Boyer, *Sant'Agostino filosofo*, Bologna 1965, pp. 61–65.

23. *mor.* II, 1, 1
24. Porphyrius, *Commentario al* Parmenide *di Platone. Saggio introduttivo, testo con apparati critici e note di commento a cura di* P. Hadot (1968), Milano 1993.
25. G. Reale, *Introduzione ad* Aurelio Agostino. *Natura del Bene*, Milano 1995, p. 76.
26. Porphyrius, *Commentario* op. cit., p. 91.
27. *civ.* VIII, 9.
28. Ibid., VIII, 20; IX, 16, 1.
29. Ibid., IX, 1; cf. Plato, *Symposium* 202e; Apuleius, *De deo Socratis* 5–6.
30. We must point out that we are not at all convinced by the interpretation given by G. Madec, *Connaissance de Dieu et action de grâces. Essais sur les citations de l'Ép. Aux Romains, I, 18–25, dans l'oevre de saint Augustin*, "Recherches Augustiniennes", II, 1962, p. 275—a highly rigorous and original scholar, however, who has made numerous contributions to Augustinian literature—of the comparison made by Augustine with the Platonists in Book VIII of *De civitate Dei*: "Cette théologie platonicienne est si proche de l'enseignement chrétien qu'Augustin n'hésite pas à la prendre à son compte (*nobiscum sentiunt*, écrit-il). C'est au point que l'on a pu voir dans cet exposé de philosophie platonicienne que donne Augustin au début du livre VIII du *De civitate Dei* "une synthèse de philosophie chrétienne". The same opinion is expressed by G. Madec in *Saint Augustin et la philosophie. Notes critiques*, Paris 1996, p. 120. We believe that a careful reading of Book VIII reveals an agreement (VIII, 10), but also a disagreement (VIII, 13; 20) whith Augustine in reference to Platonic theology. A recent study published by G. Fidelibus, *Ragione, religione, città. Una rilettura filosofica del libro VIII del "De civitate Dei" di Sant'Agostino*, Teramo 2002, focuses on an idea similar to ours.
31. *conf.* XI, 5, 7.
32. *nat. b.* 27; cf. G. Reale, *Introduzione ad* Aurelio Agostino op. cit., p. 23.
33. W. Beierwaltes, *Agostino e il Neoplatonism cristiano*, Milano 1995, p. 140.

34. A.Trapé, *La nozione del mutabile e dell'immutabile secondo sant'Agostino*, Roma 1959, pp. 53–54.
35. *conf.* XII, 6, 6.
36. Ibid., XII, 29, 40.
37. *Gn. litt.* I, 15, 29.
38. Ibid., I, 15, 29; Ch. Boyer, *Sant'Agostino* op. cit., p.76.
39. *conf.* XII, 29, 40.
40. Ibid., XI, 10, 12–13; cf. A. Trapé, *La nozione del mutabile* op. cit., p. 53.
41. *civ.* XII, 17, 2.
42. *trin.* V, 16, 17.
43. *civ.* XI, 5–6.
44. *mor.* II, 4, 6.
45. G. Reale, *Introduzione ad* Aurelio Agostino op. cit., pp.25–27.
46. In *De Trinitate* VII, 6,12, Augustine develops the notion of *dissimilis similitudo*.
47. *Gn. litt. imp.* III, 8.
48. *Gn. litt.* V, 5, 13–14.
49. *lib. arb.* III, 12, 35; *nat. b.* 3; *civ.* V, 11; XI, 45.
50. *mus.* VI, 17, 56.
51. *Gn. adv. Man.* I, 16, 21; *lib. arb.* II, 20, 54.
52. Plato, *Timaeus* I, 374, 27.
53. *Sapientia* 11, 21; cf G. Reale, *Introduzione ad* Aurelio Agostino op. cit., pp. 52–53; W. Beierwaltes, *Agostino* op. cit., pp. 144–157.
54. *lib. arb.* II, 16, 42; *mus.* VI, 17, 57; *Gn. litt.* IV, 3, 7.
55. W. Beierwaltes, *Agostino* op. cit., p. 149.
56. *vera rel.* XX, 40.
57. *ord.* II, 11, 33.
58. Ibid., I, 2, 4; 7, 18.
59. Ibid., I, 16 , 28; cf. V. Pacioni, *L'unità teoretica* op. cit., p. 147.
60. *civ.* XIX, 13.
61. *conf.* XIII, 9, 10; *c. Faust.* XXI, 6.
62. Aristotle, *Metaphysica* Γ, 1300b, 5; cf. V. Pacioni, *L'unità teoretica* op. cit., p. 14.

63. *Gn. litt.* IV, 1, 1.
64. *trin.* VI, 6, 8–9, 10.
65. *Gn. adv. man.* 1, 16, 26.
66. *Gn. litt.* V, 23, 45; V, 7, 20; cf. E. Gilson, *The Christian Philosophy* op. cit., pp. 205–209; Ch. Boyer, *Sant'Agostino* op. cit., pp. 76–81.
67. *Gn. litt.* VI, 10, 17; IX, 17, 32.
68. Ibid., VI, 10, 17.
69. Ibid.
70. Ibid., V, 7, 20.
71. *trin.* III, 9, 16.
72. *Gn. litt.* V, 7, 20; cf. E. Gilson, *The Christian Philosophy* op. cit., pp. 206–208.
73. *Gn. litt.* V, 14.
74. Ibid., V, 23, 45. The text used here is taken from *Ancient Christian Writers, St. Augustine, The Literal Meaning of Genesis*, Newman Press, New York, N.Y./Ramsey N.J., 1982. Cf. Ch. Boyer, *Sant'Agostino* op. cit., pp. 79–80.
75. *Gn. litt.* VIII, 26, 48.
76. Ibid., V, 23, 46; cf. E. Gilson, *The Christian Philosophy* op. cit., p. 207.
77. *ord.* I, 1, 1.
78. *vera rel.* XXV, 46.
79. *Gn. litt.* VIII, 9, 17.
80. *civ.* V, 9, 1.
81. Ibid., V, 9, 3.
82. The subject of the existence of God is also dealt with in *quaestio* LIV of *De diversis quaestionibus* LXXXIII and in chapters XXX–XXXII of *De vera religione*.
83. F. De Capitani, *Il "De libero arbitrio" di S. Agostino. Studio introduttivo, testo, traduzione e commento*, Milano 1987, p. 118.
84. *lib. arb.* II, 3, 7.
85. Ibid.
86. Ibid. II, 3, 7.
87. *an. quant.* 33, 71; *mus.* 6, 5, 8 ff.
88. *lib. arb.* II, 3, 8; 4, 10.

Nature and existence of God

89. Ibid., II, 4, 10.
90. Ibid.; cf. E. Gilson, *The Christian Philosophy* op. cit., p. 14.
91. *lib. arb.* II, 5, 12. For the Greek doctrinal origins of the Augustinian theory of the *internal sense*, see F. De Capitani, "De libero arbitrio" op. cit., pp. 120–121.
92. *lib. arb.* II, 5, 12.
93. Ibid.
94. Ibid., II, 6, 13.
95. Ibid., II, 6, 14.
96. *lib. arb.* II, 7, 19.
97. F. Cayré, *Initiation à la philosophie de saint Augustin*, Paris 1947, p. 121.
98. *lib. arb.* II, 8, 20.
99. Ibid., II, 8, 23. Here Augustine has in mind the same distinction of *intelligible number and quantitative number* as that found in *ep.* III, 2.
100. *lib. arb.* II, 9, 27.
101. Ibid., II, 10, 28.
102. Ibid., II, 12, 33.
103. Ibid., II, 10, 29.
104. Ibid., II, 11, 32.
105. Ibid., II, 8, 23–24.
106. Ibid., II, 12, 33–34.
107. Ibid.
108. F. De Capitani, il "De libero arbitrio" op. cit., p. 121.
109. *lib. arb.* II, 12, 34.
110. Ibid., II, 14, 38.
111. Ibid., II, 15, 39. It is easy to see that Augustine shows a rational proof of the existence of God using a scheme of inference coming from Stoic logic (the *constructive dilemma*) to prove a metaphysical thesis which, however, has nothing to do with the Stoic physical and mathematical conception.

VIII

"ORDO SAECULORUM": TIME AND HISTORY

1. Nature of Time

Augustine's reflection on time does not begin with the eleventh book of *Confessiones*, as many scholars have maintained, but with the work *De Genesi ad litteram imperfectus liber*. Augustine deals here with the nature of time and the act of creation. He defends the contents of the Book of *Genesis* from the attack of the Manichaeans and, at the same time, takes note of a theory regarding the creation of the angels, put forth by Ambrose of Milan. Interpreting the verse of *Genesis* 1,1, *In principio Deus fecit coelum et terram*, the latter states: "The world is not coeternal with God; it was created and began to exist, while it had not existed before; the Word of God, on the contrary was at the beginning and was always (...)". He adds: "But angels, dominations and powers, if all began to exist at a given moment, however they already existed when this world was created";[1] thus "(...) time began with the existence of this world, not before the world".[2]

Ambrose maintained that angels had been created by God before the world. At the same time, he had the creation of time coincide with the creation of this world, since he linked the notion of time to the movement of the bodies. In *De Genesi ad litteram imperfectus liber* Augustine observes the strangeness of that interpretation which he rejects, and writes:

> But if we say that they (the angels) were made at the start of time, so that time began with them, we have

to say that it is false that time began with heaven and earth, as some claim.³

If the angels had been created before this world, it must be assumed that the existence of time precedes the creation of heaven and earth. In actual fact, creatures already existed whose incorporeal motions caused the flow of time. Time must, then, have existed alongside those creatures as in the case of the soul, which can move with its own thoughts.⁴ If we maintain, as Ambrose did, that angels were created before time, we must conclude that they are coeternal with God. Augustine realizes the incongruence of this theory and goes beyond the concept of time linked to the movement of bodies. He connects this concept with that of the mutability of corporeal and incorporeal beings. Time is the succession of movement of all created entities, whether these are sensible or spiritual. Before writing *Confessiones* Augustine had already arrived at the discovery of a broader and more positive notion of time, as a natural condition in which all created beings, corporeal or incorporeal, moved.

In the eleventh book of *Confessiones* the investigation into the nature of time is dealt with systematically. There is a premise, in the form of an objection that some pagan philosophers made about the notion of *creatio ex nihilo*:

> Now, are those people not full of the 'old Enemy' who ask us; 'What did God do before He made heaven and earth?' 'For, if He were idle,' they say, 'and did not work, why did He not remain so, always and forever, just as before He had abstained constantly from working? For, if any new motion sprang up in God, and a new will to establish the world of creatures, which He had never before established, how, then, is it a true eternity when a will-act, which did not exist, arises? The will of God is not a creature, but is prior to creation, since nothing would be created if the will of the Creator did not precede it. So, His will pertains to the very substance of God. And if anything arose in the sub-

stance of God, which did not exist before, that substance is not truthfully called eternal. But, if God's will that creation should exist were eternal, why, then, is creation not also eternal?'.[5]

Augustine is probably thinking of the Neoplatonists who, in their defence of the postulates of Greek cosmology, rejected the idea that the world had had a temporal beginning. They maintained that the world emanates out of necessity from the One, which is not subject to any change or mutation. If the One is eternal, likewise the Intellect, the Soul of the world, and the cosmos are eternal. The introduction of the notion of *creatio ex nihilo* would have meant, for these philosophers, a change in the will and design of God himself.[6] There is no point in wondering what God did before creating the universe: worldliness and mutability are the characteristics of the entities created. They involve a first and a then, a time sequence that does not exist in eternal God. The temporal and changeable character of things began with creation. Moreover, the eternal immutability of God does not prevent one from creating new things with one sole eternal and immutable will. For a new relationship to exist like the one between the Creator and the creature a change in both is not needed: change in just one of them is sufficient.[7]

This point having been made, the investigation into the nature of time begins. It proceeds in three phases.

In the first, the cosmic concept of time is analyzed. As we have seen, it had already been treated in *De Genesi ad litteram imperfectus liber*. Time, according to a theory taught by Aristotle above all, is defined as the "measure of movement according to a first and a then".[8] Asked "What is time?" Augustine confesses that he is incapable of providing a conceptual definition, although he is certain that it is a basic component of our personal experience:

> If no one asks me, I know; but if I want to explain it to a questioner, I do not know.[9]

This fact of experience indicates an incontestable characteristic of time: mutability. We observe time as a movement which excludes any form of simultaneity. We are sure that if nothing took place, a past time would not exist. If nothing came along, future time would not exist. If there were nothing, a present time would not exist. But past and future time do not have consistency. The first does not exist anymore and the second does not exist yet. As for the present, if it should always remain such and never became past, there would no longer be any time, just eternity.[10] The present, too, like the future and the past, shows itself to be, so to speak, deconstructed in its consistency and thus elusive.[11] We can therefore truthfully state that time exists in so far as it tends toward non being (*nisi quia tendit non esse*). Augustine makes a subtle distinction, however: if the past and future are without consistency, the present has an existence even if only apparent. It is pure becoming, it is what "will not exist", since it passes away. The present is not denied, but the realm of its existence is circumscribed.[12]

The qualitative property of time, that is duration, is analyzed in paragraph eighteen. A long and a short time are spoken of, albeit only in relation to the past and the future. We call past time long if, for example, it goes back ten years. We call a future long if, for example, it goes to ten years later. Past time is brief if it is five days prior; the future, if it is five days thereafter. But the past cannot be called long, since it is no longer anything. The future cannot be called long, if it does not exist yet. Therefore, it is impossible to speak of a long or a brief duration for that which does not exist.[13] But the present does not have duration, either. It is a stretch of time which furtively slips from the future to the past, and does not have the slightest duration. Whatever duration it had would be dividable into past and future. But the present has no extension (*spatium*).[14] The present time has only the function of establishing the limit between the past and the future, hence an entity that is necessary but is without extension (*spatium*). Although the long or short duration of time belongs to our daily experience, it turns out to be something indecipherable. If the present, like the past and the future, does not have duration, then the attempt to measure time is bound to fail. Augustine observes that we find ourselves involved in a phenomenon which, on the one hand is familiar and habitual, on the other, obscure like the most intricate of enigmas.[15]

The first phase of reflection on the nature of time concludes in the twenty first paragraph, with the realization that this cannot be understood through speculation because of its indeterminable nature.

Augustine then goes on to investigate Plotinus' hypothesis of time as *distentio*. His reasoning begins as follows: only the present exists, stripped of the past and the future, an instant without dimensions, an ungraspable reality, with a purely apparent existence, although time, as our individual experience shows, is a sure fact, made up of past, present, and future. At times we foresee the future, just as we narrate events from the past. Now, however, what is no longer cannot be seen, nor could past events be related if we did not, somehow, see them. A future event cannot be foreseen if, somehow, it has not already been seen as a present event, just as anyone who relates a past event would certainly not be telling the truth if, somehow, he or she did not see it in his or her mind (*animus*).

> Therefore, both future things and past things do exist (*sunt ergo et futura et praeterita*).[16]

The future and the past exist, but they have a strange consistency:

> Or, do they also exist, but, when the present comes out of the future, does it proceed from something secret, and, when the past comes about from the present, does it recede into something hidden?[17]

If, however, the present and past exist, it is necessary to find out where they are. Since they cannot exist within a spatial entity, one must seek out an *act* which probably confers ontological consistency on them.[18] Augustine confesses that he knows that the future and the past can exist solely as present. When, for example, we relate events in the past, events in themselves are not extracted from the memory, but the words suggested by their images, as if they were traces of these impressed upon our minds by their passing through our senses.

> In fact, my boyhood, which is not now in existence, is in past time, which does not now exist; but, when I recall and tell about it, I see its image in present time, for it is still in my memory.[19]

As far as the future is concerned, we know that we premeditate future actions at times, but what is present is not the action (*actio*), because it is future, but the act of premeditation (*praemeditatio*), the causes, the signs of future things. Then, the consistency of time can be recovered, although it is fractioned into its three moments, in the present dimension. Augustine suggests that it might be more appropriate to consider a present made up of the memory of the past, a present consisting of the vision of the present, a present which is expectation of the future, rather than consider three distinct times. The three qualities of time exist somehow in the soul.[20] The past, present and future become three acts of the mind, distinct but related to one another. It is the mind that awaits (*expectat*), that is attentive (*adtendit*), that remembers (*meminit*). The present tension (*praesens intentio*) of the mind changes the future into the past through a process that has not fallen into a process of nullification, but a sort of distension of the consciousness (*distentio animi*)[21] through which the non-yet becomes waiting, the no-longer becomes memory, and the present instant becomes vision. It is important to note that Augustine, at this point, proposes that definition of time almost hesitatingly. In this second phase of the investigation, time is conceived of as an attention of the consciousness, a flow which does not coincide with a succession of empirical and spatial elements. Change and movement come to constitute the objective characteristics of time, whereas the soul, in so far as it is a spiritual substance, is the subjective condition.

Augustine wonders if that conception of time is capable of recovering the qualitative and quantitative properties of temporality, which, as we have seen, seem to dissolve in the cosmic conception. It seems that on this interior level, time possesses a certain duration, which is, in some way, measurable. That hypothesis is verified from an analysis of the first verse the Ambrose's hymn *Deus creator omnium*, in which eight syllables, long and short, alternate. The four short ones, that are: the first, third, fifth and seventh, are simple in comparison to the four long ones: the second, fourth, sixth and eighth. The latter last twice as long as the former. As our senses reveal, we measure the long syllable based on the short one, hearing that the long one has a duration twice as long as the short one. But when one syllable resounds after the other, if the first is short, and the long comes afterwards, how is it possible to withhold the short one and apply it to the long one to measure it and discover that it lasts twice as long, since the long one does not begin to resound until the short one has stopped doing so? How is it possible to measure the long syllable when it is present, when I can measure it only when it is finished? When it is finished, however, it has passed. What, then, am I measuring? Where is the short syllable I use for measuring? Where is the long one I have to measure? Both have sounded and both have disappeared. They are no longer. Yet I measure and state confidently, to the extent that we can trust our sensory experiences, that one syllable is simple and the other is double, in a spatial, temporal extension, of course (*spatium*). I can state this because they are past and finite. Thus I do not measure the syllables in themselves, which no longer exist, but an impression (*affectio*) which has been produced and which lasts in my memory. Thus the future, which does not exist, is not a long period of time, but a long future is the long awaiting of a future; the past, which does not exist, is not a long time, but a long past is the long memory of the past.[22] If I prepare to sing a chant I know, before beginning, my expectation extends over the entire chant. Once I have begun, my memory extends out over what I capture and consign to the past. The vital energy of my activity is directed toward memory for what I have recited and in expectation of what I shall recite. However, my attention (*adtentio*) is present. Due to this the future becomes the past as that action is carried out. The wait is shortened by that much and the memory is lengthened, until the wait ceases altogether, when the action has ended and passed on, in its entirety, to memory.[23] Thus my present tension (*praesens intentio*) gathers the past and the future in a single act. Here ends the second phase of the investigation into the nature of time.

In paragraph thirty nine Augustine abandons Plotinus' idea of time as *distentio*, and introduces the idea of time as *extensio*:

> (...) behold my life is but a distraction (*distentio*); and Thy right hand has held me up, 'in my Lord the Son of man, the Mediator between Thee as One and us as many, in many ways and by many means, so that through Him I may lay hold of that for which He has laid hold of me, and that I may be gathered in from the days of old and follow the One. Forgetting what is behind, not straining outward (*distentus*) to things which will come and pass away, but straining forward (*extentus*) to what is before, not according to distraction (*distentio*), but with mental concentration (*intentio*), I press on toward the prize of my heavenly calling, (...).[24]

This text and the reference in the notes suggest that Augustine borrowed the term *extensio* from St. Paul (*Phil.*, 3, 13-14). The notion of *intentio-extensio*, taken to define the time phenomenon in a new way, is seen in opposition to that of *distentio* supported by Plotinus. It becomes a positive term as opposed to the negative notion of *distentio*.[25] The reflection on time to be found in paragraph thirty nine, takes on a decidedly different meaning. As G. O'Daly has rightly said, the scriptural term is turned into a technical one to put forth a new idea. "Distension" of the soul becomes the *intentio-extensio* of human awareness reaching into the future, involvement in the present, and memory of the past. When humans reach out toward things which are before them, that is, toward eternal things, toward the Truth, time acquires a qualitatively new dimension, which turns becoming into history, re-establishing the connection between past, present and future. On the contrary, when the soul is dissipated in the multiplicity of things, the connection with the One which is Truth becomes lost. Time, already broken up as an empirical experience, is dissipated as a psychological and historical experience. Augustine thus forcefully points out that extension, not distension must be assumed (*Ecce extensionem: numquam distentionem*).[26]

At this point, the most characteristic features of the step taken by Augustine in the way of conceiving time should be summarized. According to Plotinus, the soul is eternal since it pre-exists the union with the body. For some necessity or due to some daring, it fell into the body and, finding itself in the becoming, was in a situation of scission, division, separation; a condition which is not natural for the soul. Taking care of the body, the soul dissipates into multiplicity and ends up forgetting its origin. Coinciding with this situation of the fallen soul, time comes to assume a totally negative character.[27] For Augustine, on the contrary, the soul and body are created by God. The condition of the human composition is, by its very nature, contingent and mutable; and time, created by God, is the natural, positive condition of this composition. Thus it is at the beginning. Later, with the original fall, as a consequence of bad use which humans made of free will, time, originally a positive condition, became negative because of the loss of contact with its origin. Time turned into *distentio* and since then humans have lived in the *saeculum* which is the time of death. This disorientation came about not because humans reside in the body, as the Neoplatonists taught, but because they had moved away from God as a result of a sin. When the relationship with the One and the Truth is re-established, time regains a positive character and *distentio* turns into *intentio-exstensio*. This broader notion of time, open to the three historical dimensions of present, past and future, is, for Augustine the basis of history.[28]

2. Time as a historical Process

Augustine discovered time as a historical process through a notion suggested by Saint Paul and unknown to the Greek philosophers. The latter conceived of history in terms of a purely circular motion, where everything circulates and everything returns, without a beginning, without an end, repeating itself in cycles. The time of history takes the place of the time of nature, through a mysterious divine design. Humans are immersed in temporality but they move toward the future. Departing from the notion of time as *extensio*, Augustine discovers the value of personal and public history, in the multi-dimensionality of the past, present and future. The perception of the past, the present and the awaiting on behalf of the individual is personal history, to which the *Confessiones* bear witness. Perception of the past, present and awaiting on behalf of the human race is public history, to which *De civitate Dei* bears witness.[29] This understanding of personal and public history is possible through knowledge (*scientia*) of temporal things, and wisdom (*sapientia*) which enlightens the human intellect.

Presenting his view of history, Augustine makes some critical remarks about Cicero. The latter denied that the work of Divine Providence could influence the lives of humans, because a Providence that foresees future things and acts accordingly would be in conflict with human freedom. Hence their lives cannot be governed by Divine Providence. The problem had already been treated in the third book of *De libero arbitrio*, but it was in *De civitate Dei* that Augustine, criticizing Cicero, provided an exhaustive explanation of the relationship between divine foreknowledge and human freedom. Cicero believed that, if all future events are foreseen, they will occur as foreseen. If they thus occur, it means that the order of things is pre-established by God who is aware of it beforehand. But if the order of things is determined, the order of the causes is also determined, since an effect can come to pass only on the condition that it is preceded by an efficient cause. Hence, if the order of causes by which all that exists is produced is determined, it follows that all events necessarily come to pass. It is clear, however, that if that were true, nothing would be in our power and free will could not exist.[30] Augustine's response to Cicero's conception is original. It is true that nothing happens without an efficient cause, but not every efficient cause coincides with the blind will of fate. He makes a distinction between three types of causes: fortuitous cause (*fortuita*), natural cause (*naturalis*), and voluntary cause (*voluntaria*). Only voluntary cause is an efficient one. A second distinction is then proposed. A voluntary cause exists that does everything but is not made, and a voluntary cause that does because it has the freedom to operate, but which has been made since it has been granted the power to operate.[31] Here, it is clear that Augustine has in mind the distinction of will as a faculty received by God and as an exercise of that faculty:

> From this we conclude that the only efficient causes of all things are voluntary causes, that is to say, causes of the same nature as the spirit or breath of life (...). The Spirit of Life, which gives life to all and is the Creator of all matter and of every created spirit is God, a Spirit, indeed, but uncreated. In His will is the supreme power which helps the good choices of created spirits, judges the evil ones, and orders all of them, giving powers to some and not to others.
>
> As He is the Creator of all natures, so is He the giver of all powers—though He is not the maker of all choices. Evil choices are not from Him, for they are contrary to the nature which is from Him (...). Thus, God is the Cause of all things—a cause that makes but is not made. Other causes make, but they

are themselves made—for example, all created spirits and, especially, rational spirits. Material causes which are rather passive than active are not to be included among efficient causes, for their power is limited to what the wills of spirits work through them. It does not follow, therefore, that the order of causes, known for certain though it is in the foreknowing mind of God, brings it about that there is no power in our will, since our choices themselves have an important place in the order of causes.[32]

From the ontological point of view God conserves the faculty of human will leaving humans the freedom to use it in one way or another. It must therefore be concluded that the divine foreknowledge and the free will of humans can co-exist. Free will is not prevented even though it had been known previously.

The Neoplatonic theory of cyclical time is critically analyzed in the twelfth book of *De civitate Dei*. According to this theory, human beings are destined to undergo the same suffering, the same trials, and the same joys in a periodic cycle. Augustine demolishes the wheel of fate showing that every event in history is something unrepeatable and decisive.[33] He writes:

> It was this controversy that led the natural philosophers to believe that the only way they could or should solve it was by a theory of periodic cycles of time according to which there always has been and will be a continual renewal and repetition in the order of nature, because the coming and passing ages revolve as on a wheel. These philosophers were not sure whether a single permanent world passes through these revolutions or whether, at fixed intervals, the world itself dissolves and evolves anew, repeating the same pattern of what has already taken place and will again take place in the future. And from this game of merry-go-round they could find no exemption for the immortal soul—not even for the soul of a philosopher—but it, too, must be

> ceaselessly on its way to a false beatitude, only to
> return to its genuine misery.[34]

The theory of the Neoplatonists seems meaningless to Augustine,[35] because, in actual fact, it denies the very notion of happiness, which, however, is upheld by most of the ancient philosophers. If happiness is to be sure, it must be undying, part of the true Being, which is eternal,[36] and not ravished by ruthless fortune.[37] The two properties of bliss, eternity and safety, are denied in the doctrine of eternal circles. The soul would attain happiness intermittently, accompanied by ignorance or suffering, depending on whether or not it was aware of the good attained, in the first or the second case. In any case, there would be false happiness or true misery.[38] According to the cyclic vision, every human being would be condemned to an absurd condition: at times he or she would lead a miserable life awaiting happiness, at other times, on the contrary, the person would lead a happy life in expectation of misery. Thus, the expectation of happiness would be miserable and that of misery would become happy. Misery would thereby come to characterize present and future life.[39]

Eternal returns do not exist for Augustine, because time had a beginning and will have an end. With the act of creation, God gave humans a beginning (*exortus*), a path to follow (*excursus*) and a purpose (*finis*) to reach. He brought to reality a design through which he wants human beings to participate in their own happiness. Time is intersected by this divine design that human beings, endowed with intelligence and free will, are called upon to uphold. All that they do is unique and unrepeatable. It follows that history is guided by two protagonists, Divine Providence and human beings, who can support or hinder the divine design.[40] In the Augustinian vision, Providence is identified neither with immanent cosmic law, nor with a particular function of the so-called universal soul. Time is no longer cyclical, it is linear, because the becoming of events, no longer part of an eternal repetition, blind and necessary, is inscribed between the initial creative act and the final purpose.

Looking more closely, one finds that the linear historical process is however, *ambivalent*. The time of history, although guided by a positive design toward the final destination, on the human side is filled with a wide variety and quantity of problems, errors and evils. Humans may know what the object of history actually consists of, but they often fail to decipher the details and secrets. This is the origin of what some have called *the mystery of history*.[41] Plotinus had a different way of conceiving of human vicissitudes. According to him, life of the human race and individuals was predetermined by necessity. The Neoplatonist philosopher left a picture of this vision that was extremely clear and tragic, in the *Enneads*.[42]

According to Augustine, history is not fatality and pessimism as Greek philosophy would have it. On the contrary, human life acquires a positive and dramatic meaning at the same time, with a new opening toward social life:

> (...) there is nothing so social by nature, so antisocial by sin, as man.[43]

The building of social peace thus becomes the task of all humans:

> The peace, then, of the body lies in the ordered equilibrium of all its parts; the peace of the irrational soul, in the balanced adjustment of its appetites; the peace of the reasoning soul, in the harmonious correspondence of conduct and conviction; the peace of body and soul taken together, in the well-ordered life and health of the living whole. Peace between a mortal man and his Maker consists in ordered obedience, guided by faith, under God's eternal law; peace between man and man consists in regulated fellowship. The peace of a home lies in the ordered harmony of authority and obedience between the members of a family living together. The peace of the political community is an ordered harmony of authority and obedience between citizens. The peace

of the heavenly City lies in a perfectly ordered and harmonious communion of those who find their joy in God and in one another in God. Peace, in its final sense, is the calm that comes from order. Order is an arrangement of like and unlike things whereby each of them is disposed in its proper place.[44]

3. "Duo amores": "duae civitates"

Starting from the conception of time as *extensio* and history as the realm of the action of God and human will, Augustine observes that all human events go back to the question of the *city of God* and the *earthly city*. In the fourteenth book of *De civitate Dei* St. Paul's distinction is once again taken up (Gal. 5, 19–21). It concerns the opposition between flesh and the spirit, between living according to the flesh and according to the spirit. Augustine observes that living according to the flesh means living according to the works of the flesh identified not only in the disorders characteristic of the sensual sphere, such as lust, drunkenness, and debauchery, but also in the disorders of the soul, such as hostilities, rivalries, idolatries, witchcraft, etc. Living according to the spirit, on the contrary, means living according to God. Two *amores* are born from these opposing ways of love: love for oneself and love of God, which, like two weights, constitute what Augustine also calls *pondus cupiditatis* and *pondus caritatis* in which *mergimur et emergimus*:[45]

> What we see, then, is that two societies have issued from two kinds of love. Worldly society has flowered from a selfish love which dared to despise even God, whereas the communion of saints is rooted in a love of God that is ready to trample on self.[46]

The two loves find one another in human history like two human beings, two cities, two societies, since the human race was established by God as a sole person (*genus humanum tanquam unum hominem*).[47] What binds each of the two societies together is not exterior but interior: the *amor* that humans cultivate determines the belonging to one of the two cities, which do not identify with any institutional entity:

> There are, then, two loves, of which one is holy, the other unclean; one turned towards the neighbour, the other centred on oneself; one looking to the common good, keeping in view the society of saints in heaven, the other bringing the common good under its own power, arrogantly seeking to dominate; one subject to God, the other rivalling Him; one tranquil, the other tempestuous; one peaceful, the other seditious; one preferring truth to false praise, the other eager for praise of any sort; one friendly, the other envious; one wishing for its neighbour what it wishes for itself, the other seeking to subject its neighbour to itself; one looking for its neighbour's advantage in ruling its neighbour, the other looking for its own advantage. These two loves started among the angels, one love in the good angels, the other in the bad; and they have marked the limits of the two cities established among men under the sublime and wonderful providence of God, who administers and orders all that He creates; and one city is the city of the just, and the other city is the city of the wicked.
>
> With these two cities intermingled to a certain extent in time, the world moves on until they will be separated at the last judgment. The one will be joined to the holy angels and, being united with its King, will attain eternal life; the other will be joined to the wicked angels and, being united with its king, will be sent into eternal fire. Concerning these two cities I shall perhaps write more at length in another book, if the Lord is willing.[48]

This page from *De Genesi ad litteram* provides the key for understanding the nature of the city of God and that of the antithetical earthly city. The city of God is a society of human beings inclined toward humbleness, dependence on and submission to God. It acknowledges common good and justice, and exercises power not for *libido dominandi* but for the benefit of all. It brings with it love oriented toward God and toward the others. The earthly city, on the contrary, can be identified with a society which is in an antagonistic relationship with God and often with others as well.

Anyone can belong to the city of God:

> (…) as the heavenly City is wayfaring on earth, she invites citizens from all nations and all tongues, and unites them into a single pilgrim band. She takes no issue with that diversity of customs, laws, and traditions whereby human peace is sought and maintained.[49]

It transcends differences in time, race, nationality and human institutions.

The two cities cannot be identified with historical institutions such as the Church or the State.[50] Their origin must be sought in two radical and antithetical options, which lead to two ways of conceiving and living existence. They are oriented in opposing directions within the same history.

Civitas, in the broad sense of the word is the synonym of society; that is a unanimous multitude of people united by a determined social relation,[51] by a bond of an interior nature[52] which has historical implications.[53] Departing from this definition, Augustine distinguishes two cities: the city of God and the earthly city, one of which fights for justice and the other for injustice, the former for truth, the latter for vanity. They are antagonists, yet they are mixed together in the present historical situation. They will be separated, like the seed and the chaff of the *Scriptures*, only at the end of a final judgment:

> On earth these two cities are linked and fused together, to be separated only at the Last Judgment.[54]

They are intertwined like the wicker stems of a basket or confused like an emulsion. Nothing can be extricated from this mixture, which at times, is called *permixtio* in Augustine's works and at other times: *commixtio*. The boundary between the two societies is historically not recognizable.⁵⁵ Augustine offers a very concrete image of that mixture:

> All those who have no taste but for the things of this earth, all who prize earthly happiness above God, and all who seek their own ends, not those of Jesus Christ, belong to that city whose mystical name is Babylon, the city that has the devil as its king. But all whose taste is schooled to the things above, who ponder the realities of heaven, who live with circumspection in this world, taking care not to offend God, who are wary of committing sin, but if they do sin are not ashamed to confess it, all who are humble, gentle, holy, just, devout and good—all these belong to the one city whose king is Christ. The former has priority as to time, but no priority in nobility or honor. This is the elder, and that other city is younger. The one began with Cain, the other with Abel. They are two bodies, active under their respective rulers and citizens of their respective cities. They are opposed to one another and will be so until the end of time, until those who are now commingled are separated. (...)
>
> (...) During the present age these two cities are mingled together, but they will be separated at the end. They are in conflict with each other, one fighting on behalf of iniquity, the other for justice; one for what is worthless, the other for truth. This mixing together in the present age sometimes brings it about that certain persons who belong to the city of Babylon are in charge of affairs that concern Jerusalem, or, again, that some who belong to Jerusalem administer the business of Babylon. (...)
>
> (...) Now reflect on how the same things happen in the Church, even in our own day, fulfilling the prophetic type. What about all those concerning whom we are warned, *Do what they tell you, but do not imitate what they do* (Mt 23:3)? They are all citizens of Babylon, but they control the public affairs of the city of Jerusalem. This is incontestable, because if they had no such authority over Jerusalem's business, how could we be commanded, *Do*

what they tell you? And how could it be said of them, *They have taken their place in the chair of Moses* (Mt 23:2)? But then, if they are citizens of Jerusalem, destined to reign for ever with Christ, how can it be said, *Do not imitate what they do?* That must imply that they are to hear one day, *Depart from me, all you who act unjustly* (Mt 7:23; Lk 13:27).

You can see, then, that citizens of the bad city have some control over the affairs of the good city; but now let us see whether the converse is true. Do the citizens of the good city take charge of any business belonging to the bad city? Keep in mind that every earthly state will undoubtedly perish. Its sovereignty will pass away at the coming of the Lord's reign, that reign about which we pray, *Your kingdom come*, and of which it has been foretold that *his kingdom will have no end* (Lk 1:33). In spite of this, every earthly state makes use of some of our citizens to administer its affairs. How many of the faithful are there among its citizens, among its loyal subjects and its magistrates, its judges, generals, governors and even kings?[56]

Some writers have spoken of ethical dualism in reference to the Augustinian conception of history. This expression can be accepted in reference to Paul's distinction between living by the flesh and by the spirit. Historically speaking, this dualism does not exclude the possibility of living together peacefully and even with co-operation among the citizens of one city and the other. This is true because the citizens of the two cities, however dissimilar they may be and despite the fact that they are often struggling with one another, have the same nature[57] with the same *appetitus*. They can share human, family and patriotic affections. The members of both cities have in common the use of temporal goods, obedience to the same laws, the seeking and safeguarding of peace:

> So, too, the earthly city which does not live by faith seeks only an earthly peace, and limits the goal of its peace, of its harmony of authority and obedience

> among its citizens, to the voluntary and collective attainment of objectives necessary to mortal existence. The heavenly City, meanwhile, or, rather, that part that is on pilgrimage in mortal life and lives by faith, must use this earthly peace until such time as our mortality which needs such peace has passed away. As a consequence, so long as her life in the earthly city is that of a captive and an alien (although she has the promise of ultimate delivery and the gift of the Spirit as a pledge), she has no hesitation about keeping in step with the civil law which governs matters pertaining to our existence here below. For, as mortal life is the same for all, there ought to be common cause between the two cities in what concerns our purely human living.[58]

If the celestial city welcomes citizens from all people speaking all languages, because it is not concerned with differences in customs, laws, institutions, it disagrees with the earthly city on the religious question:

> The heavenly City, on the contrary, knows and, by religious faith, believes that it must adore one God alone and (…) she has been unable to share with the earthly city a common religious legislation.[59]

Both use the same temporal goods, yet they have a different faith, different hopes, and a different form of love.[60]

Augustine, then, does not fall into an ethical and radical dualism, conceiving social and political life separated from faith. Ch. Dawson and others have observed that the bishop of Hippo has never separated faith and the ethics from social life, although he acknowledges the distinction between the two areas.[61] The reason for this lies in the fact that his anthropological model, derived from Varro and which he discusses amply in the nineteenth book of *De civitate Dei*, is different from the Neoplatonist one.

Notes

1. Ambrose, *Hexaemeron* I, 5, 18–19.
2. Ibid., I, 6, 20.
3. *Gn. litt. imp.* 3, 7.
4. Ibid., 3, 8; cf. N. Cipriani, *Le opere di sant'Ambrogio negli scritti di sant'Agostino anteriori all'episcopato*, "La Scuola Cattolica", CXXV, 1997, pp. 778–779.
5. *conf.* XI, 10, 12.
6. Plotinus, *Enneads* III, 2, 1.
7. The matter is taken up again in the twelfth book of *De civitate Dei* and the fifth book of *De Trinitate*, where the concept of relationship is explored in depth.
8. Aristotle, *Physica* IV, 10–14, 217b–224a.
9. *conf.* XI, 14, 17.
10. Ibid.
11. F. Chiereghin, *Il tempo come possibilità interiore del male in Agostino*, in *Il mistero del male e la libertà possibile (IV): ripensare Agostino*, Roma 1997, pp. 179–180; the scholar emphasizes the difference in Augustine between *duration*, understood as a qualitative property of time and *measure* understood as a quantitative property of time.
12. *conf.* XI, 14, 17; cf. E. Corsini, *Lettura del libro XI delle "Confessioni"*, in "Le Confessioni" *di Agostino d'Ippona. Libri X–XII*, Palermo 1987, p. 50.
13. *conf.* XI, 15–18.
14. Ibid., XI, 21, 27.
15. Ibid., XI, 21, 28.
16. Ibid., XI, 17, 22.
17. Ibid.
18. F. Chiereghin, *Il tempo* op. cit., p. 182
19. *conf.* XI, 18, 23
20. Ibid., XI, 20, 26; cf. E. Corsini, *Lettura* op. cit., p. 52
21. Ibid., XI, 26, 33; cf. E. Gilson, *The Christian Philosophy* op. cit., p. 194; J. Guitton, *Le temps et l'éternité chez Plotin et saint Augustin*, Paris 1933, pp. 179–193.
22. *conf.* XI, 28, 37.

23. Ibid., XI, 27, 38.
24. Ibid., XI, 29, 39; *trin.* IX, 1, 1; *serm.* 255, 6, 6; 284, 4.
25. G. O'Daly, *Time as* distentio *and St. Augustine's Exegesis of Philippians* 3, 12–14, "Revue des Études Augustiniennes", XXIII, 1977, pp. 265–271.
26. s. 255, 6, 6.
27. Plotinus, *Enneads* III, 7, 11–12.
28. H. I. Marrou, *Teologie de l'histoire,* Paris 1968, pp. 31–35.
29. M. F. Sciacca, *Filosofia e Teologia della storia in sant'Agostino,* in *Atti della settimana agostiniana pavese,* Pavia 1974, p. 35.
30. *civ.* V, 9, 2.
31. Ibid., V, 9, 4.
32. Ibid.; cf. Th. J. Kondoleon, *Augustine and the Problem of Divine Foreknowledge and free Will,* "Augustinian Studies", XVIII, 1987, pp. 171–175.
33. V. Bourke, *The City of God and the christian View of History,* in *Mélanges à la Mémoire del Charles De Koninck,* Québec City 1968, p. 74.
34. *civ.* XII, 13, 1.
35. Ibid., XI, 4, 2.
36. *div. qu.* 35, 2; *civ.* XI, 11.
37. *beata v.* 2, 11.
38. *civ.* XII, 20, 1.
39. Ibid., XII, 20, 2.
40. Ibid., V, 11; cf. P. Miccoli, *Storia e profezia nel pensiero di S. Agostino,* "Augustinian Studies", XVI, 1984, pp.90–106.
41. H. I. Marrou, *Théologie* op. cit., pp. 53–61; see also H. I. Marrou, *The meaning of History,* Montreal 1949, p. 285.
42. Plotinus, *Enneads* III, 2, 15.
43. *civ.* XII, 27, 1.
44. Ibid., XIX, 13, 1.
45. *conf.* XIII, 7, 8; cf. M. F. Sciacca, *Filosofia e Teologia della storia* cit., p. 37.
46. *civ.* XIV, 28.
47. *div. qu.* 58, 2.

48. *Gn. litt.* XI, 15, 20. The text used here is taken from *Ancient Christian Writers, St. Augustine, The Literal Meaning of Genesis*, Newman Press, New York, N.Y./Ramsey N.J., 1982.
49. *civ.* XIX, 17.
50. V. J. Bourke, *The City of God* op. cit., p 71.
51. *civ.* I, 15; XV, 8, 2.
52. A. Trapè, *Introduzione a* Sant'Agostino, *la Città di Dio*, I, Roma 1978, p. XXIX.
53. J. Ratzinger, *Volk und Haus Gottes in Augustins Lehre von der Kirche*, München 1954, pp. 276–295.
54. *civ.* I, 35.
55. H. I. Marrou, *Théologie* op. cit., pp. 71–72.
56. *en. Ps.* 61, 6–8. The text used here is taken from *The Works of St. Augustine, Expositions of the Psalms*, Augustinian Heritage Institute, Inc., New City Press, N.Y., 2001.
57. *civ.* XI, 33. Here it must be observed that Augustine is speaking of two groups of angels. However, the term *natura* can also be applied to two human groups.
58. *civ.* XIX, 17.
59. Ibid.
60. Ibid., XVIII, 54, 2.
61. Ch. Dawson, *St. Augustine and his Age*, in *A Monument to Saint Augustine*, London 1930, p. 75.

IX

POLITICAL PHILOSOPHY

1. Origin and Function of the civil Laws

In the sixth chapter we illustrated Augustine's investigation into the existence and nature of eternal law. This is the fruit both of a knowledge God has of the way realities are ordered and directed toward their goal, and of a divine decision that constantly binds all beings created in the order conceived by Him.[1] It is also identified with the very essence of God which is also true justice,[2] of whom natural law is a reflection. All rational beings must be inspired by this if they wish to promote in the society the virtue of justice, defined as: "Perfect reason according to which humans give to everyone that to which he or she is entitled."[3] Humans are rendered capable, through reason and freedom, of transcribing the natural code into an ethical and juridical system according to positive codifications which we can find within the various civil societies.

In the first book of *De libero arbitrio* Augustine analyzes the nature and goals of positive laws putting forth a doctrine which, as we shall see, will form the basis of his conception of the State. In a purely moral context, without dealing with the political problem, he limits himself to analyzing the relationships between temporal and eternal law and discussing the problem of evil, the nature of *libido*, and other matters. It is not difficult, however, to glean his idea of the State from the analysis he provides of temporal law, its function and limits. This idea will then come out in the letters and, above all, *De civitate Dei*.

Noting the diversity found in human legislations, he observes:

> He who draws up temporal laws, if he is a good and wise man, takes eternal life into account, and that no soul may judge he determines for the time being what is to be commanded and forbidden according to the immutable rules of eternal life.[4]

He once again takes up the same concept In *De libero arbitrio*:

> I think that you also see that it is from the eternal law that men have derived whatever is just and lawful in the temporal law.[5]

It is further underlined that if the author of positive legislation were a wise man, that is, possessing the knowledge of immutable realities, the positive order that would result would be closer to eternal law. If, on the contrary, the author of the positive order were not a wise man, but one who possessed only the knowledge of temporal realities, the resulting positive order would be more or less imperfect, indeed, even permissive. The permissiveness of positive legislation is, in fact, in equal measure to the moral and civil level of the people. Hence, civil legislation may be subject to change, as is inferred from the case described in a dialogue with Evodius, where change is not only desirable, but also proper:

> *Aug.* If therefore, people are found possessing moderation and prudence, vigilant for the common good wherein each one esteems his own private interest of less importance than the public good, is it not right to enact a law permitting such people to set up for themselves magistrates to provide for their welfare, that is, for the public welfare?
> *Ev.* It is absolutely right.
> *Aug.* If after having gradually grown corrupt, these same people should afterward prefer the individual

> to the common good, should offer their vote for sale and, bribed by those who covet honor, should entrust the government to wicked and disreputable men, would it not also be right, provided some honest man of great ability was found at the time to strip these people of the power to elect public officials and to subject them to the rule of a few good men, or even to that of one man?
> *Ev.* That would also be right.
> *Aug.* Since these two laws then appear to be contradictory, insofar as one grants the people the power to elect public officials while the other takes it away and, since the second law was enacted in such a way that both cannot be in force at once in the same city, are we to say that one of them is unjust and should never have been made?
> *Ev.* Not at all.
> *Aug.* Let us then call that law "temporal" which, though just, can yet be justly changed in the course of time.[6]

The reason for this change in temporal legislation also lies in the fact that positive law must take account of the historical conditions under which people live as it accomplishes social peace mediating interests pertaining to temporal goods.[7]

Let us examine another characteristic passage in the dialogue between Evodius and Augustine:

> *Ev.* (...) It seems to me that the law drafted for governing people legally permits such things, while Divine Providence punishes them. A law enacted for the governing of people is concerned with upholding whatever is enough to maintain peace among unenlightened men so far as this is possible by man-made laws. But transgressions against the divine law have other appropriate penalties from which, as I see it, wisdom alone can set them free.
> *Aug.* I commend and approve this distinction of yours. Though it is only a beginning and not fully developed, it nevertheless gives promise of leading us on to higher things. You are of the opin-

> ion that laws enacted for the government of cities make many concessions and leave unpunished many crimes which are nevertheless punished by Divine Providence, and rightly so. And we should not reproach what a law fails to accomplish simply because it does not do everything.[8]

If, on the one hand, civil law must never deviate from natural law, on the other hand, it must be admitted that adaptation of the former to the latter is almost never complete because of the concrete human condition. Despite this limit, however, positive legislation can be improved and can limit the range of arbitrariness and abuse to which the citizens can fall prey. If it is changeable and perfectible, in some ways permissive at times, too, its final goal is to "ensure peace among human beings",[9] to impose discipline and to regulate the use of temporal goods. These goods are:

> (…) first of all, the body and what are called goods of the body, such as sound body, keenness of sense, strength, beauty, and any others there may happen to be. Some are necessary for the useful arts and must therefore be valued more highly; others are of less value. Next comes freedom, which is not true freedom except for those who are happy and who adhere to the eternal law. But I am presently speaking of that freedom which makes men think they are free when they have no masters, or which is desired by those who want to be set free from any human masters. Then come parents, brothers, wife, children, kindred, relatives, friends and those who are joined to us by ties of intimacy. Then there is the state itself which is commonly regarded as holding the place of a parent. Also, honours and praise, and what is called popular favour. Last of all, there is money, a single term including all things of which we are the rightful owners, and which we seem to have the power to dispose of by sale or donation.[10]

Positive law tends to defend what is useful and advantageous for the citizens. It enables distribution of goods to

Political philosophy 235

each one to whom they are entitled. It ensures social harmony and takes away from those who transgress the goods they possess or a portion of them. It does not punish sin, which consists in loving temporal goods in a disorderly way, but does punish the guilt of those who take goods away from their rightful owners. Like most of the Fathers of the Church, Augustine is aware that if, on the one hand, civil law does not deviate completely from natural law, on the other, it does not adapt to it from all points of view.

2. Nature and Limits of the State

Before dealing with the question of nature and limits of the State, a remark of capital importance must be made. Augustine is a complex thinker, especially because of the immense volume of his writings. That complexity explains why some scholars, even renowned ones, misunderstand points, when they do not keep in mind the entire framework in which a particular set of problems is to be placed. One of the most common misunderstandings in which a part of Augustinian historiography has fallen is Augustine's conception of the State and its foundation. On that subject, it should be pointed out that there are two currents of interpretation: on the one hand there are scholars[11] who take account of only a portion of the Augustinian texts, stating that the State is only an institution established as a result of original sin; on the other hand, a group[12] claims, without, in any case, documenting their point adequately, that the State is a natural institution. To resolve the matter, it must be considered that although Augustine shares a conception of the State as an entity established in history, he does not forget the situation of human nature as such, to remark what constantly belongs to it, both in the condition of original integrity, and in the present historical one of corruption. To summarize, there are original tendencies belonging to human nature as such that continue to exist, although distorted, in the present condition of corruption. These original tendencies, as we shall shortly explain, lay the basis for the State. Thus, if the effect of original sin is the coercive apparatus of the State—which, and this should not be forgotten, finds justification only in so far as it manages to ensure social peace and regulate the use of temporal goods—certainly a State which finds its organizational roots, both administrative and juridical ones, in the natural positive tendencies present both before and after original sin, is not the effect of original sin. Typically, Augustine even speaks of a love, present in human nature as such, toward friends and citizens. It was what he calls the "third love".[13]

The appetites (*appetitus*) toward self-preservation, action and reproduction of the species, characteristic of human nature, are the origins of the impulse toward sociability, with which human beings build social bonds and stable structures on various levels, to ensure themselves and others like them the basic conditions in which to lead a quiet life. This tendency toward association drives men and women to seek one another in order to give rise to a family bond:

> (...) the union of male and female is, then, so far as mortal living goes, the seed-bed (*seminarium*), so to speak, from which a city must grow.[14]

For Augustine, family is a *societas amoris* and, to the degree to which family bonds multiply and are strengthened, men and women move from the experience of the home (*domus*) to that of the city (*civitas*) and the State (*res publica*). The natural *milieu* for men and women, then, is the society:

> Since every man is a part of the human race, and human nature is something social and possesses the capacity for friendship as a great and natural good, for this reason God wished to create all men from one, so that they might be held together in their society, not only by the similarity of race, but also by the bond of blood relationship. And so it is that the first natural tie of human society is man and wife.[15]

That social dimension of existence has, as its prime expression, the family experience without which the world would be nothing but a wasteland.[16] The destiny of civil society depends, in large part, on the family, whose stability contributes to the growth of social life. On this matter, Augustine provides a series of remarks:

> Now, since every home should be a beginning or a fragmentary constituent of a civil community, and every beginning related to some specific end, and every part to the whole of which it is a part, it ought to follow that domestic peace has a relation to political peace. In other words, the ordered harmony of authority and obedience between those who live together has a relation to the ordered harmony of authority and obedience between those who live in a city. This explains why a father must apply certain regulations of civil law to the governance of his home, so as to make it accord with the peace of the whole community.[17]

It is the natural order itself that encourages men and women to create the family,[18] children to submit to their parents, brothers and sisters to live in harmony, blood relatives and in-laws to keep the bonds stable. For this reason it is advisable that the most gifted young people be introduced to the study of the *artes*, in so far as this is possible, to prepare themselves for civil administration.[19] Emphasis is placed on the need to defend the common good[20], private property,[21] work,[22] civil freedom, the obligation to pay taxes, and social well-being.[23] As far as the attitude toward material goods is concerned, Augustine upholds the principle according to which *it is better to have fewer needs than to possess more things.*[24]

While the tendency for men and women to associate is gradually realized, the *compositio voluntatum* is consolidated. The hierarchical structure is built with an authority in charge of exercising power, and a sort of *generale pactum societatis humanae* is born.[25]

In the second and nineteenth books of *De civitate Dei*, Augustine deals with the problem of the nature and function of the State. In the twenty first chapter of the second book he quotes some passages from the dialogue *De republica*, in which, as Scipio states, Cicero maintains that "The State is not just any group of individuals but a group associated by consent to the law (*consensus iuris*) and common interests (*communio utilitatum*)".[26] Cicero, and Sallustius for that matter, note that depravity in Roman society began with the fall of Republican ideals. The more power and wealth grew, the more exploitation and injustice spread. The ancient virtues of the citizens of the Republic were replaced by vices. Pleasure seeking had turned the citizens into slaves of their own appetites. The ancient trust in justice and democracy had disappeared, in such a way that there prevailed tyranny, resulting from a decadent monarchy, or an aristocracy no longer concerned with virtue and honor, or a degenerated democracy.[27] Augustine quotes Cicero's *De republica*:

> '(...) By our own vices, not by chance, we have lost the republic, though we retain the name'.[28]

Indeed, he is convinced that, according to Cicero's definition, the Roman State existed neither at the time of "ancient people and customs" nor at the time of "the moral decadence". Thus, he makes this promise to his readers:

> We shall consider this later, God willing. In its proper place I shall endeavor to show that that ancient creation was never a true republic, because in it true justice was never practiced.[29]

In the twenty first chapter of the nineteenth book of *De civitate Dei* the thesis promised to the readers is discussed. Augustine's reasoning can be summarized in the following terms: although there was consensus in the Roman State about temporal interests (*communio utilitatum*), a genuine consensus about true justice was lacking (*consensus iuris*). For that reason, Cicero's definition of the State does not correspond to the facts, since, historically speaking, there

Political philosophy

had not been consensus about true justice but merely about the administration of temporal things. It is not Augustine's intention to claim that justice is useless, even if limited to the needs and rights of human nature, but to underscore the fact that the Roman State did not fulfill Cicero's definition, historically. So, in the light of the nature of the positive law discussed in *De libero arbitrio* a new definition of the State is put forth:

> It is possible to define 'people' not as Cicero does, but as 'a multitude of reasonable beings voluntarily associated in the pursuit of common interests' (*Populus est coetus multitudinis rationalis rerum quas diligit concordi communione sociatus*).[30]

Since, in their present condition, people have as the object of their love not so much what is just in itself but what is useful, the aim of the State, arising from the natural need to guarantee the peace of its members, coincides with mediating, regulating, the use of temporal goods[31] so that the abuse of some against the rights of others will not prevail in the society:

> So, too, the earthly city which does not live by faith seeks only an earthly peace, and limits the goal of its peace, of its harmony of authority and obedience among its citizens, to the voluntary and collective attainment of objectives necessary to mortal existence.[32]

According to this definition, the Roman people are a people and, therefore, also a State. History attests to what interests people pursued in ancient times, and in the times that followed. What has been said of the Roman State could apply to Athens, the other Greek cities, Egypt, etc. The laws governing the lives of these peoples did not correspond totally to what is good and equitable in itself, but corresponded to what was useful and advantageous for them and thus could enhance civil administration and peaceful harmony among the citizens:

> By the very laws of his nature, he seems, so to speak, forced into fellowship and, as far as in him lies, into peace with every man.[33]

When the State forgets the goals for which it had been born, it turns into an organized disorder and becomes

> (...) an organized brigandage (...) for, what are bands of brigands but petty kingdoms? They also are groups of men, under the rule of a leader, bound together by a common agreement, dividing their booty according to a settled principle.[34]

Thus, the State is a society whose basis lies in some primary tendencies of the human being and in the communion of goods useful to all citizens. It is, then, a natural and positive institution which, in its historical task, must not claim to be able to attain eternal law in every aspect and in all things. Although it is inspired by it, in so far as possible, it must aim at the defense of the equitable use of temporal goods, so that abuse will not harm the rights of others, and common good and civil harmony will be safeguarded.

Augustine is aware that if the positive legislation of the State does not always adapt to natural law in every respect, that depends on the fact that only a small number of human beings, in their present condition of sin, are capable of obeying the eternal law. Most humans love what is useful more than what is just in itself. For that reason the role of the State must be limited to keeping social peace and mediating the interests of all citizens. Augustine arrives, as we shall see, at the distinction in roles between religion and the State which, in the Roman world, had remained closely linked for a long time.[35]

The State must acknowledge the Church's freedom to carry on its religious mission in civil society and the Church must respect the positive function of the State.

This political model moves away from the potentially revolutionary eschatology of the vision of Origen, who aimed at delegitimizing the State order, but also from the political theocracy of Eusebius of Cesarea.[36] Augustine assigns a role to the State that could be called neutral, in which the citizens of the terrestrial city and the city of God can live together.[37] The State must govern and take care of its citizens; it lives in peace and harmony when an ordered relationship is established between authorities and subjects. Order, understood as the disposition of equal and unequal things, which assigns to each its proper place, is a necessary condition for peace in society.[38]

Although all three forms of government are recognized, monarchy, aristocracy and democracy,[39] Augustine hints at the superiority of democracy over the other two forms. However, the accomplishment of the democratic ideal depends on the equilibrium and seriousness of the people.[40] He expresses the wish, in any case, that whoever governs, will have pity, and be aware of the common good,[41] although the quality of the State is also determined by the character and love of the citizens who form it.[42] The State guarantees law and the interests of the citizens, also using force within the limits prescribed in the laws.[43] In particular, the exercise of the power to use force[44] is the responsibility of the judge, who possesses the *potestas iudiciaria*:

> (…) it is not without purpose that we have the institution of the power of kings, the death penalty of the judge, the barbed hooks of the executioner, the weapons of the soldier, the right of punishment of the overlord, even the severity of the good father. All those things have their methods, their causes, their reasons, their practical benefits. While these are feared, the wicked are kept within bounds and the good live more peacefully among the wicked.[45]

The judiciary power "does not go beyond forbidding or taking away from the person who is punished all or part of his temporal goods".[46] Since the ultimate source of authority is Divine Providence,[47] the person who wields the power must be circumspect, and inclined to be indulgent. Furthermore, the punishment must be used simply to protect the common good and not feed conflicts and rivalries.[48]

In the light of these principles, the limits of the State in matters of war are also indicated. The right to declare war is acknowledged, on the condition that the war be a just one. War is just when one's own survival must be protected, the pacts among friends and of alliances observed,[49] and wrongs avenged.[50] The duty of declaring war on another State is that of the supreme authority of the State. The cruelty of revenge, the passion of domination and the like must, however, be avoided.[51] The power to use violence to ensure peaceful coexistence is acknowledged to the State even if coercive punishment is required. Even though Augustine was always against the death penalty, due to humanitarian reasons, he acknowledged that the State has the formal power to condemn a person to it,[52] calling, in any case and several times, for *moderatio legum* and the right to *intercessio*.[53] Finally, torture as a method of inquisition in the courts is judged as unacceptable.

3. Relationship between Church and State

At this point, it is advisable to dwell on several facts, even if it may seem like reportage, so that Augustine's political thought in the well-known controversies with the Donatists is given proper emphasis.

As far back as 394 he had reflected on the relationship between Church and State, acknowledging the distinction between the religious and political areas and setting forth their respective roles. He observes in his *Expositio quarundam propositionum ex epistula Apostoli ad Romanos*:

> As far as the present life is concerned, we need to be submissive to temporal authorities, that is to say to those who are in charge of day to day affairs on earth, thereby deriving all due recognition and honors. The opposite holds true, however, for what pertains to our faith in God and our calling to His Reign. In this sphere we must not consider ourselves bound by the authority of man, especially when such authority aims to subvert all that God has granted us pertaining to eternal life. It would

be therefore a severe error for a Christian to take refuge in his Christianity to avoid paying taxes and other monetary demands, or to consider himself exempt from the claims imposed by those authorities in the exercise of public functions. Even more serious would be the error of one who, in his efforts to comply with authorities (which occupy a prominent position in the administration of temporal matters) recognizes them as dictating one's own faith. It is absolutely essential to respect the boundaries between what is temporal and matters of faith. (...).[54]

At the beginning of the fifth century, Augustine is forced by several events to change his practical attitude concerning the problem of the relationship between Church and State, in apparent contradiction with the aforementioned principle.[55] Here are not concerned with dealing with the problem in all its historical and theological implications. On the contrary, some events that may have been at the origin of his change in attitude, ones that required emergency measures, must be presented. On one occasion, as we shall see, he ended by approving and accepting a decision by the political authority which he had originally been decidedly against. It is not difficult to reconstruct these events since we find numerous statements and declarations in his correspondence.[56] Up to the Council of Carthage in 404 Augustine had maintained that reason, discussion and dialectic had to prevail in theological controversies. The exercise of secular force to bring heretics back to the ecclesiastical community was excluded. In his letter to the Donatist bishop Vincent, he writes:

> I have, then, yielded to the facts suggested to me by my colleagues, although my first feeling about it was that no one was to be forced into the unity of Christ, but that we should act by speaking, fight by debating, and prevail by our reasoning, for fear of making pretended Catholics out of those whom we knew as open heretics.[57]

Then, in his letter to Boniface, the Arian Gothic general, he maintains that the bishops must limit themselves to asking the civil authorities to ensure the Catholics' physical safety from the violence of the Donatists. He asks that the law of the emperor Thedosius (392) be enforced, in which any heretic recognized responsible for violence be fined. He points out:

> Our idea was that if the Donatists were frightened in this manner, and so did not dare to commit such acts, there would be freedom for the Catholic truth to be taught and embraced, so that no one would be forced to it, but any who wished might follow it without fear, and thus we should not have any false or feigned Catholics.[58]

At the beginning of the fifth century the controversy between Catholics and Donatists became dramatic because of the violence of the latter. Addressing the Donatist bishop Petilianus, Augustine reminded him that at Hippo, some years back, Catholics were even forbidden to buy bread.[59]

Despite the climate of intolerance, the Catholic bishops decided, in the Council at Carthage in 401, that their response should be meek and mild. The Catholic peace offer was not reciprocated by the other party which, on the contrary, actively opposed it. After refusing to take part in another council, which took place later in Carthage in 403 on the suggestion of Augustine, Possidius, and other fellow bishops, the Donatists began to practice forms of physical aggression especially against the most prominent exponents of Catholicism in Numidia.[60]

The Circumcellions, a faction which ended up forming the terrorist wing[61] of Donatism, attempted to attack the bishop of Hippo several times. Finding out that Augustine was to pay a visit to one of the villages in the diocese, they gathered in a hidden place along the road to ambush him and his followers. Fortunately, the cart driver took the wrong road and this avoided a massacre. Some time later, the unfortunate Possidius was to undergo a different fate and Augustine himself recorded the ambush in a letter. Possidius was assailed by the Circumcellions, while on the way to visit some Christian communities in his diocese, but he managed to escape and take refuge in the house of a Catholic family. The terrorists "in a manifest act of violence in the farm of Liveti, tried to burn him alive in the house where he had taken refuge. He would not have been saved if the peasants in that same farm, attempting to avoid the dangers they themselves faced, had not put out the flames relit three times!".[62]

Possidius was captured and beaten by the Donatist priest Crispinus. The local bishop, also Donatist and with the name of Crispinus, refused to punish his namesake, having rejected the conciliatory invitation officially sent to him by Possidius. The misdeed was reported and he was forced to pay the civil authority a fine of ten gold pounds for being a heretic. He immediately appealed the decision, however. At the same time, Augustine and Possidius proposed a public debate, at the end of which Possidius succeeded in proving the accusation of heresy against the Donatist. The bishop Crispinus then turned to the emperor who confirmed the sentence. This was later condoned thanks to the intervention of the two Catholic bishops.[63]

Acts of violence broke out all over Numidia. The Catholic bishops, meeting once again in Carthage at the Council of 404, agreed to ask for intervention from the emperor. In the assembly discussion, two points of view emerged: the older bishops suggested harsh action by the emperor while Augustine and just a few colleagues were opposed. They felt that the best thing to do was to provide only for defending the Catholics from the acts of violence, without demanding a decree to suppress the Donatist heresy. According to Augustine it was sufficient to apply the law of Theodosius of 392, that obliged the bishops and other Donatist ministers to pay a fine, "but only in those regions where the Catholic Church suffered acts of violence by the clergy, the Circumcellions, or the Donatist faithful, so that the bishops and other ministers of their sect were obliged to pay the fine by order of the judges in charge, upon suit from the Catholics who had been victims of those excesses".[64]

In the Council discussion the bishop of Hippo was able to have his moderate and reasonable proposal accepted. A delegation was then sent to the imperial court, but at this point, the emperor had been made aware of some of the serious acts, and had already decided to adopt a stricter position. Augustine wrote to Boniface the tribune:

> Ours were anticipated by some very serious complaints from bishops of other districts, who had suffered many outrages and been turned out of their sees by the Donatists; particularly revolting and unbelievable was the maltreatment of Maximian, Catholic Bishop of Bagai. It left our embassy with nothing to transact (....).[65]

Before the official delegation of the Council of Carthage reached the imperial court, some bishops had already reported the news of the aggression against Maximian to the emperor. The latter took note of the repeated and unheard of acts of violence, and on 12 February 405, decided to issue the decree of union which called for the exile the Donatist bishops and ministers as well as a fine.[66] On 23 August 405, the Council of Carthage accepted the decree and adopted every provision requested to enact the sentence. The edict was accompanied by a letter to the Prefect Adrianus, in which emperor Onorius expressed his desire to eliminate the Donatist heresy. Augustine reports as follows:

> (...) for a law had already been promulgated to the effect that the Donatist heresy was guilty of such monstrous conduct that to spare it seemed a greater cruelty than any perpetrated by it; that it should not only be restrained from violence but should not be allowed to exist at all under the protection of the laws. However, the death penalty was not to be invoked, because Christian moderation was to be observed even toward those unworthy of it,

but fines were to be imposed and exile was decreed against their bishops and ministers.[67]

Despite the emperor's intervention, the Circumcellions continued to persecute the Catholics in a new form. In about 407 Augustine wrote to the Donatist bishop Ianuarius:

> (...) your people are now doing even worse things to us. They not only beat us with clubs and stab us with swords, but, with an unspeakable refinement of cruelty, they try to blind us by throwing into our eyes lime mixed with vinegar. They pillage our homes, and they have made for themselves dangerous and terrible weapons, armed with which they run here and there, threatening and breathing out murder, theft, fire, blindness.[68]

The Catholic bishops realized that, in a situation of emergency of that sort, "imperial vigilance (*regia diligentia*) rather than private violence (*privata violentia*) was preferable".[69]

Around 407, in a letter to the schismatic bishop Vincent, Augustine, conscious as always of the fact that he should not exceed the bounds of his jurisdiction,[70] wrote a defense of the position taken, justifying *post factum* the positive nature of the imperial decision. He accounted for his change in attitude bringing two reasons. First of all he pointed out how dramatic the situation was: the moment required special measures to hold back the violence of the Donatists. The emperor's intervention was not aimed at favoring one church over another, but simply reestablishing order;[71] secondly, it must be recalled that after 405 Augustine realized the sincerity of many Donatist conversions, hence, the arguments of colleagues among the bishops on behalf of underscoring the positive results of the intervention should be accepted.

> I have, then, yielded to the facts suggested to me by my colleagues (...).[72]

Augustine's thought cannot be fully understood if his action pertaining to the decree of union is not carefully examined. It must be kept in mind that Augustine is not a philosopher and theologian indifferent to practical life, but in addition to being a thinker, he is also a bishop, pastor and spiritual master. He accepted the decree of union but, at the same time, asked that it be applied with moderation by the civil authorities, insisting with Marcellinus, the imperial officer, that the judges act with humanity[73] and that torture as well as the death penalty be forbidden.[74] He begs the officer not to take away the freedom from the Donatists that have merited death, but just their citizenship, employing them in some task (*utile opus*) such as the building of public services, roads, baths or furnaces.[75]

The final position of Augustine cannot be considered a sort of "apologia of the State's right to eliminate the non-Catholics",[76] nor is it a "pastoral strategy",[77] but simply a new and practical attitude brought about by a situation of emergency. Augustine has no intention of having the Donatists punished as heretics, but because they have become a threat to public order.[78]

The conclusion reached by P. Brown and R. A. Markus is rather surprising, when first-hand knowledge of the history of the beginning of the fifth century and of Augustinian literature is available. On the contrary, it is meaningful to quote in its entirety the judgment of an author whose sources are unquestionable. Bonner writes:

> It is difficult to see how any state could have tolerated Donatism in the form in which it expressed itself, or that the Church is to be condemned for welcoming the action of the state in putting down a movement in which savage violence was so prominent a characteristic. Indeed, if Augustine had been content merely to accept and to apply the legislation against the Donatists, he would have escaped a good deal of the odium which has been heaped upon his name by scholars who never knew the nature of a life lived under the threat of the terrorist

or experienced any conditions other than those procured by the existence of a well-drilled police force. Unfortunately for himself Augustine, with characteristic honesty, admitted that he had changed his mind — a change which no one, in the circumstances could condemn — but then proceeded to rationalize his outlook, thereby providing ammunition both for those who wished to justify persecution on religious grounds, and for those who wished to denounce it in the person of the man to whom the persecutors appealed. In this, he has had an unfortunate destiny, and the Donatists have proved better propagandists than they knew.

It is to be hoped that it is possible today to take a more balanced view of Augustine's teaching about the repression of Donatism than was possible a few generations ago.[79]

Notes

1. P. Brezzi, *I fondamenti filosofici del diritto e dello Stato in S. Agostino*, in *S. Agostino e le grandi correnti della filosofia contemporanea. Atti del Congresso Italiano di Filosofia Agostiniana*, Roma 1955, p. 196.
2. *vera rel.* XLVIII, 93.
3. *civ.* XIX, 4, 4; *div. qu.* 30; 31.
4. *vera rel.* XXXI, 58.
5. *lib. arb.* I, VI, 15.
6. Ibid., I, VI, 14.
7. *conf.* III, 7, 13–8, 15.
8. *lib. arb.* I, 5, 13.
9. Ibid., I, 5, 13.
10. Ibid., I, 15, 32; *civ.* XIX, 13, 2.; *b. coniug.* 9, 9.
11. We refer in particular to: P. Brown, *Augustine* op. cit., pp. 234–235; R. A. Markus, *Saeculum. History and Society in the Theology of St. Augustine*, Cambridge 1970, p. 98; K. Flash, *Augustin* op. cit., pp. 394–395.

12. In this group we can mention: P. Brezzi, *I fondamenti* op. cit., p. 206; D. X. Burt, *Friendship and Society. An Introduction to Augustine's Practical Philosophy*, Grand Rapids, Michigan 1999, p. 135.
13. *s.* 349, 1, 2.
14. *civ.* XV, 16, 3.
15. *b. coniug.* 1, 1; *civ.* XII, 21 and 27; XIX, 5; cf. W. J. Bourke, *The political Philosophy of St. Augustine*, in *Proceedings of the Annual Meeting of the American Catholic Philosophical Association*, St. Louis (Missouri) 1931, pp. 51–52.
16. *ep. Jo.* 7, 1.
17. *civ.* XIX, 16.
18. *b. coniug.* 1, 1.
19. *ord.* II, 8, 25; II, 20, 54; cf. V. J. Bourke, *The political Philosophy* op. cit., p. 52.
20. *ep.* 137, 17; *ep.* 211, 12.
21. Ibid., 153, 6, 26.
22. *mor.* I, 33, 70.
23. *ep.* 138, 2, 15.
24. Ibid., 211, 9.
25. *conf.* III, 8, 15; cf. H. A. Deane, *The Political and Social Ideas of St. Augustine*, New York 1963, pp. 117–153.
26. *civ.* II, 21, 2.
27. Ibid., II, 18, 1–2; cf. G. J. Lavere, *The Problem of Common Good in Saint Augustine's* Civitas Terrena, "Augustinian Studies", XIV, 1983, p. 2.
28. *civ.* II, 21, 3.
29. Ibid., II, 21, 4.
30. Ibid., XIX, 24.
31. Ibid.; *ep.* 153, 6, 26; cf. N. Cipriani, *Il ruolo della Chiesa nella società civile: la tradizione patristica*, in *I cattolici e la società pluralistica. Il caso delle leggi imperfette*, Bologna 1996, p. 145.
32. *civ.* XIX, 17.
33. Ibid., XIX, 12, 2.
34. Ibid., IV, 4.

35. A. Di Berardino, *I cristiani e la città antica nell'evoluzione religiosa del IV secolo*, in *Chiesa e Impero da Augusto a Giustiniano*, Roma 2001, pp. 213–223.
36. J. Ratzinger, *Die Einheit der Nationen: eine Vision der Kirchenväter*, München 1971; it.tr. *L'unità delle nazioni. Una visione dei padri della Chiesa*, Brescia 1973, pp. 104–109; E. Gilson, *La città di Dio e i suoi problemi*, Milano 1959, pp. 80–82; R. Pezzimenti, *Società aperta e i suoi amici*, Messina 1995, p. 98 .
37. G. Bonner, "Quid imperatori cum Ecclesia?" *St. Augustine on History and Society*, "Augustinian Studies", II, 1971, pp. 238–241.
38. *civ.* XIX, 13, 1.
39. Ibid., II, 21, 2.
40. *lib. arb.* I, 6, 14.
41. *civ.* V, 19.
42. N. H. Baynes, *The political Ideas of St. Augustine's "De Civitate Dei"*, London 1955, p. 16.
43. *trin.* XIII, 13, 17.
44. *en. Ps.* 108, 4.
45. *ep.* 153, 6, 16.
46. *lib. arb.* I, 15, 32.
47. *civ.* V, 1.
48. Ibid., V, 24.
49. Ibid., XXII, 6, 2.
50. *in Hept.* VI, 10.
51. *c. Faust.* XXII, 74–75.
52. *s.* 302, 13; cf. G. Combès, *La doctrine politique de Saint Augustin*, Paris 1927, p. 188.
53. *ep.* 152, 2; 153, 2–3; cf. N. Cipriani, *La violenza nel pensiero di S. Agostino*, in *La violenza*, Bologna 1998, pp. 251–253.
54. *exp. prop. Rm.* 64 [72].
55. E. Lamirande, *Church, State and Toleration: an Intriguing Change of Mind in St. Augustine*, Villanova (Pennsylvania) 1975, p. 18; pp.70–76.
56. Ch. Boyer, *Sant'Agostino e i problemi dell'ecumenismo*, Roma 1969, pp. 106–112.

57. *ep.* 93, 5, 17.
58. Ibid., 185, 7, 25.
59. *c. litt. Pet.* II, 83, 184.
60. *ep.* 105, 4; Possidius, *Vita Augustini*, 12; cf. Ch. Boyer, *Sant'Agostino e i problemi* op. cit., p. 108; W. H. C. Frend, *The Donatist Church*, Oxford 1952, p. 260.
61. R. A. Markus, Saeculum op. cit., p. 141.
62. *ep.* 105, 2, 4.
63. Ibid., 88, 7; 105, 2, 4; cf. G. Bonner, *St. Augustine* op. cit., pp. 263–264.
64. *ep.* 185, 7, 25.
65. Ibid., 185, 7, 26.
66. Ibid., 93, 3, 10.
67. Ibid., 185, 7, 26.
68. Ibid., 88, 8.
69. *c. ep. Parm.* I, 10, 16.
70. *ep.* 133, 3. In *Epistula 100* Augustine writes: "I wish that the Church of Africa were not afflicted by such severe tribulations, so that it would not need the help of any terrestrial authority".
71. *ep.* 93, 1, 2; cf. N. Cipriani, *La violenza* op. cit., pp. 264–268.
72. *ep.* 93, 5, 17.
73. Ibid., 133, 2; 134, 1–2.
74. Ibid., 139, 2.
75. Ibid., 133, 1.
76. P. Brown, *Augustine* op. cit., p. 231.
77. R. A. Markus, Saeculum op. cit., p. 140.
78. N. Cipriani, *La violenza* op. cit., p. 266.
79. G. Bonner, *St. Augustine* op. cit., pp. 307–308.

Biography

354   Augustine, son of Patricius and Monica, was born on November 13, in the village of Thagaste in the Roman territory of Numidia (present day Sank-Ahras in Algeria).

361   Begun his education under the guide of a *litterator*.

367   Sent to Madaura to continue his education.

370   Returned to Thagaste putting his studies on hold due to financial difficulties in his family.

371   With the aid of Romanianus as a benefactor he moved to Carthage to be tutored in rhetoric and lived with a young woman. In the same year his father died.

372   A son named Adeodatus was born from the common law union.

373   Studied Cicero's *Hortensius* which set the tone for his philosophical ideas, and adhered, as *auditor*, to Manichaeism.

374   Returned from Carthage to teach grammar. His mother, Monica, refused him entry to the maternal home. Became the house guest of Romanianus.

375   Returned once more to Carthage where he opened a school for rhetoric.

383   Met Faustus of Milevi, a Manichaean Bishop. Began to have doubts about Manichaeism. Departed for Rome. While continuing to frequent Manichaean circles, his orientation began to shift towards the Skepticism of the Academics.

384   Appointed official orator in Milan. Met Bishop Ambrose.

385	In January delivered the eulogy for the consulate of Bautone. In the spring Monica arrived in Milan. On November 22 he gave the eulogy for Valentinian II.
386	Listened to the sermons of Ambrose. Read some *Platonic books*. Met a priest by the name of Simplicianus, an old friend of the deceased rhetorician Marius Victorinus, and was visited by Ponticianus. Read Paul's letters and returned to Catholic faith. In mid October refused the position of teacher. In the beginning of November made a retreat to Cassiciacum in Brianza region with friends and family. Wrote *Contra academicos, De beata vita, De ordine* and *Soliloquia*.
387	Returned to Milan. On the night of Holy Saturday (April 24–25) was baptized by Ambrose, along with his son Adeodatus and his friend Alypius. In the summer decided to return to Africa. During his stay in Rome wrote *De quantitate animae, De moribus ecclesiae catholicae et de moribus manichaeorum* and the first book of *De libero arbitrio*. Death of Monica in Ostia Tiberina.
388	Returned to Africa to live with friends in his father's house in Thagaste in keeping with his ideals of communal life.
389	Composed *De magistro*.
389–391	Wrote *De vera religione*; his son Adeodatus died; one year later he was ordained a priest in Hippo by Bishop Valerius and completed *De libero arbitrio*.
395–396	Succeeded Valerius as Bishop of Hippo and studied St Paul anew.
399–419	Wrote his *De Trinitate*.
400–412	Augustine's polemic against the Donatists. In the year 411 the conference between Catholic and

	Donatists Bishops took place in Chartage; Augustine played a pivotal role.
412	Controversy against the Pelagians began.
413–427	Wrote his *De Civitate Dei* over various intervals of time.
426	Appointed as his successor a priest by the name of Eraclius.
427	Completed his *Retractationes*.
430	Vandals laid siege to Hippo. Death and burial of Augustine.

Appendix

CRITICAL INTERPRETATIONS OF AUGUSTINIAN PHILOSOPHY

1. The mediaeval Heritage of Augustine

Augustine is unquestionably the master of the West: "he is absolutely without rivals" (Portalié). His influence on mediaeval philosophy is enormous because many of his insights continue to be alive and vital, even after Aristotle's irruption into the Latin and Germanic world.

A history of mediaeval Augustinism has yet to be written. An in-depth investigation on at least three levels would be needed to accomplish this:

1. the study of Augustinism in the authors who expressly refer to Augustine (the Franciscan current, for example);
2. the study of Augustine's quotations and the use made of his doctrines by authors differently oriented in their thinking;
3. the presence of Augustine in texts that have assimilated his doctrine in depth, without making explicit reference to him.

In short, mediaeval Augustinism is a complex problem which cannot be dealt with in all its implications or resolved here. Here, we limit ourselves to a *specimen*. By way of example, a distinction must first be made, as a hermeneutic criterion, not only between Avicennist Augustinism and Averroesian Augustinism, but also Dionysian and Platonizing Augustinism. Let us take things in order in this brief overview.

As far as Augustine's mediaeval heritage is concerned, four ages should be identified: (a) the first embraces the first four centuries after the death of Augustine, from 430 to the mid-ninth century; (b) the second from the mid-ninth century to the end of the twelfth; (c) the third covers the thirteenth century; (d) the fourth–the fourteenth and fifteenth centuries.

(a) The first four centuries after the death of Augustine

The first era is characterized by Encyclopaedism. The inspiration comes from Augustine's program, as seen in *Retractationes* (I, 6) and *De doctrina christiana* (II, 25 ff). All the Authors of the great syntheses of early mediaeval knowledge are inspired by Augustine's program, although drawing in content on Plinius and other ancient Authors: Cassiodorus (d. ca. 570) with the *Institutiones divinarum et saecularium litterarum*, Isidore of Seville (d. 630) with the *Origines* or *Etymologiae* and with the *De natura rerum*, Bede (d. 735) with *De rerum natura*, Rabano Maurus (d. 856) with *De clericorum institutione* and *De rerum naturis*. The need for encyclopaedia, that reflected the spirit of Augustine, would be felt in the centuries that followed, when the cultural and scientific conditions had changed. William of Conches (d. 1145), Hugh of St Victor (d. 1141) and Roger Bacon (d. 1292 or 1294) are examples. Although Augustine was the undisputed authority, and as such, the study of his works more than sufficient to meet the needs of the times, the need was felt to delve more deeply into some aspects of his thought, for example, the theme of spirituality and the immortality of the soul. That took place in two distinct periods, far off in time, specifically with the *De anima* of Cassiodorus, which came down to us as book XIII of the *Variae*, and with *De animae ratione* of Alcuin (d. 804).

(b) From the mid-ninth century to the end of the twelfth

We can identify five distinct orientations in the second period: Dionysian Augustinism or to phrase it better, Augustinizing Dionysianism; the original rethinking of Augustinian philosophy in the spirit of Augustine; Augustinizing Platonism; speculative and mystical Augustinism; rhetorical and mystical-literary Augustinism.

The first exponent of Dionysian Augustinism, a current running throughout the Middle Ages to the Renaissance, was John Scotus Eriugena, who died after 870. In his mammoth work *De divisione naturae* he seeks to reconcile the Neoplatonism of the Pseudo-Dionysius that comes from Proclus with the Christian use of Neoplatonism by Augustine. This was the source of continuing variations and ambiguities. For example, Eriugena seems to follow in the wake of Augustine as far as the relationship between faith and reason is concerned—suffice it to compare *De praedestinatione* I, 1 with *De vera religione* V, 8, and *De divisione naturae* with *De ordine* 9, 26. As far as the divine essence is concerned he takes a radical distance. The following shows this: in *De divisione naturae* II the primordial causes such as goodness in itself, essence in itself, life in itself, wisdom in itself (...), eternity in itself are not part of the divine essence but occupy an intermediate position between God and things created. In other words, there is a return to Plotinus by way of a line that harks back to Pseudo-Dionysius and to Proclus, in those very points where Neoplatonism had been criticized and surpassed by the bishop from Hippo.

The first great genius of the Scholastics is undoubtedly Anselm of Aosta (d. 1109). The *Opera omnia* of this thinker is a highly original reconsideration of the entire set of issues surrounding Augustine, performed in the spirit of Augustine, but aided by a subtle and shrewd logic, expressed in curt, basic prose, far from that of the African rhetorician. To obtain an idea of the Augustinism of Anselm one could compare, as a *specimen*, *Monologion* I, 1–6 with *Confessiones* X, 6–26 and *Proslogion* II, 1–5 with *De doctrina christiana* I, 7.

With the School of Chartres (990–up to the end of the twelfth century) a rebirth of Platonism took place, although it was contaminated by Aristotelian elements. The founder of the Academy was rediscovered through Boethius, Augustine, Seneca, and, directly, through *Timeus*. The dangers of pantheism are almost always avoided because the reading of *Timeus* is performed from the Augustinian point of view. Variations remain, however. For example, in Bernard of Chartres (who lived between the eleventh and twelfth centuries) ideas are immanent in the thought of God, but they are eternal, not coeternal with Him. The heritage of Scotus Eriugena can be perceived in this vision.

Totally following orthodoxy and the essentially Augustinian orientation is the philosophical and mystical speculation of the followers of the Victor. Aside from the fact that the *Didascalicon* of Hugh of St Victor (d. 1141) is a reworking of Augustine's encyclopedia project—it is interesting that, along with the liberal arts, Hugh also takes the technical ones into consideration (*Didascalicon* II, 18), a sign of a change in social, economic and cultural conditions—Augustine's heritage can be found above all in the metaphysics of the soul and the mysticism of the Victor school. This is clear from the three degrees of knowledge *cogitatio, meditatio, contemplatio* which Hugh speaks of (PL CLXXVI, col. 764 b) or the division into three of *imaginatio, ratio, intelligentia* that we find in the *De gratia contemplationis* of Richard. Here we even find another division into three in the spirit of Augustine in the final phase: the *dilatatio mentis*, which takes place when God is seen figuratively; the *sublevatio mentis*, which takes place when he is seen as in a mirror; the *alienatio mentis*, when he is contemplated "in his pure truth". Augustine was so totally assimilated by the Victorines that one of their texts could be taken for one by Augustine. Compare, for example, *Didascalicon* II, 20 with *De civitate Dei* XIV, 28.

(c) The thirteenth century

The thirteenth century was the golden age of Scholasticism. At the same time it was the culmination of speculation into the most profound motifs of Augustinism, but also the beginning of a new era in the philosophy of the Roman and Germanic West with the advent of Aristotle, Arab and Hebrew philosophy. A new event occurred, however, curi-

Critical interpretations of Augustinian philosophy 261

ous at first sight: at a time when Augustinism is dying as a philosophical current, it showed its vitality. Many of its aspects survive, and in the crucial points or at least in those that are anything but secondary, in currents of thought that would, at first sight, seem thousands of miles away from that of Augustine. This would be the case of Thomism and, starting from the fourteenth century, Scotism and Occamism.

Various currents of thought must be distinguished in the thirteenth century. William of Auvergne (d. 1249) demonstrates a first-hand knowledge of Aristotle and the Arabs which he makes use of in the *Magisterium divinale*, but the author who inspires the entire work and provides the framework is Augustine. There are no theses from Augustine that are not followed by William, but knowledge of the interests and issues in the new cultural climate confer new relevance on it, as can be seen in the Augustinian interpretation of the separate acting intellect (*De anima*, VII, 6). In Henry of Ghent, too, (d. 1293) we find the use of Avicenna but his Augustinism is purer. The following statement is an example: "If any divine illumination is excluded, human beings cannot know the truth using their pure natural aptitudes. These cannot act in such a way as to arrive at the rules of the eternal light that God presents to and takes away from anyone he wishes, without any natural necessity". (*Summa theologica*, I, 2, 19).

Thirteenth-century Franciscan thought follows two paths: philosophical and theological on the one hand, the most prominent one considering the number of scholars involved; scientific and theological on the other. Alexander of Hales (d. 1245), whose *Summa* is the most organic synthesis of the Augustinian system before Aristotle's advent, John of La Rochelle (d. 1245), in whose *Summa de anima* the Avicennist Augustinism appears in the Minorite Order for the first time, belong to the first category; Bonaventure of Bagnoregio (d. 1274), who speculated on issues without ever departing from Augustine in all his works from the *Commentarii in quattuor libros Sententiarum Petri Lombardi* to the *Collationes in Hëxaemeron*, to the point of adopting his method as can be seen in *De reductione artium ad theologiam* and, above all, in *Itinerarium mentis in Deum*, which is a true summary of his thought and which belongs to this tradition as well. Although Bonaventure's philosophy uses the Pseudo-Dionysius and Avicenna, it is constructed in the spirit of Augustine: observation of what has been created, inwardness, transcendence of changeable human nature "extra per vestigium, intra per imaginem et supra per lumen" (*Itinerarium*, V, 1). This itinerary of the soul comes closer and closer to God through the *vestigia* and in the *vestigia* to be found in the world (*Itinerarium*, ch. II); through the *imago* and in the *imago* to be found in the soul (chs. III–IV); through the *lumen* and in the *lumen* where God is contemplated as Being and as Good, followed by the mystical ecstasy of the soul (chs. V–VII). It cannot be forgotten that the itinerary of Bonaventure, like that of Augustine, is both intellectual and existential.

Although a few Franciscans take their distance from Augustine on this or that particular point of the doctrine, a basic fidelity remains as far as the basic structure of the philosophy of Augustine is concerned: the conception of God as a Being and place for ideas, knowledge understood as an activity of the soul which makes use of the body, the theory of illumination, spirituality and immortality of the soul, the positive nature of matter, and the *rationes seminales*. An enormous number of thinkers perform their speculations in the spirit of Augustine. Here a mention is to be made of Thomas of York (d. 1260) who left behind a work in six books under the title *Sapientiale*; Walter of Bruges (d. 1307) the author of a *Comment on the Maxims* and *Quaestiones disputatae*; Matthew of Acquasparta (d. 1302) he too an author of A *Comment on the Maxims* of *Quaestiones*; Roger Marston (d. 1303) who wrote *Quaestiones disputatae*.

Among the most illustrious personalities in the second scientific and theological path of the Minorite Order are Roberto Grossatesta (d. 1253) and Roger Bacon (d. 1292 or 1294). If these thinkers are primarily interested in scientific and theological matters, this is especially clear in the case of the latter, the root and goal of their investigations clearly show the hand of Augustine. This can be seen in the *Letter to Adam of Exeter*, in the tract *De veritate*, the treatise *De libero arbitrio*, writings in which Grossatesta shows a first-hand knowledge of the *Opera omnia* of Augustine whose point of view he fully shares. The position of Roger Bacon in his *Letter to Clement IV* is more singular. He explicitly states that he is drawing on the *De doctrina christiana* of Augustine in his gigantic research program—the first idea of working in an *équipe* organized scientifically—which goes from morals to experimental science, optics, mathematics, and the knowledge of languages,

What is most surprising is, upon first glance, paradoxical: the 'Aristotelian' Thomas Aquinas (d. 1274) is closer in many points to Augustine than the 'Augustinian' Bonaventure and all of the Franciscan Augustinism. The theory of the plurality of forms ascribed to Augustine came, in actual fact, from Ibn Gebirol. One need only compare *Tractatus in Joannem*, XIX, 1, 15; *Epistolae* CXXXVII, III, 11; CCXXXVIII, II, 12; *De Trinitate*, V, 8, 8; XV, 7, 11 with *Summa Theologiae*, Pars I, Quaestio 75, to be aware of the Augustinism of Thomas. This is not a sporadic case. All Thomist theodicy is constructed in Augustinian terms, from the conception of God as "ipsum esse subsistens" to the immanence of ideas in the divine mind. Aside from the numerous times when Aquinas quotes Augustine in the "Sed contra"—a sign that he embraces the cause, as can then be inferred from "Respondeo dicendum"—one often has the impression that Thomas uses Aristotelian language to express the concepts of Augustine, since the language of the latter was now obsolete in the new cultural situation. What is most disconcerting is that, here and there, while Augustine is not cited, there are entire passages of Augustine quoted by Thomas, so deep the assimilation had been. Compare *Summa contra Gentiles*, I, 4, with *De ordine* II, 5, 15, for example.

Among the Domenicans, too, there are followers of Augustine such as Richard Fishacre (a teacher in Oxford between 1240 and 1248) and Robert Kilwardby (d. 1279), the Archbishop of Canterbury, famous for having emulated his colleague from Paris, Stephen Tempier, in condemning several theses of Aristotelian origin in which Thomas Aquinas was also condemned.

(d) The fourteenth and fifteenth centuries

Augustine's presence in the philosophy and culture of the fourteenth and fifteenth centuries was multifarious. No longer was there a pure Augustinism. There are those who reconcile Augustine with the most convincing results of Thomism, such as the Augustinian Egidio Romano; others, referring to Augustine see in God the *intellectus agens* who enlightens and assists *formaliter* our intellect, like the other Augustinian Ugolino Malabranca of Orvieto; who, finally, identifies the acting intellect of Averroes with God, such as Richard Fitz Ralph, giving rise to another type of Augustinism, that which Gilson calls 'in the style of Averroes'.[1] Augustinism then underwent a complete change to Rhine mysticism (Eckhart, Tauler, Suso). It often crossed the boundary of heresy. Cases of a return to the Pseudodionysius, Proclus and Plotinus are not rare.

The use of Augustine in John Duns Scotus (d. 1308) and his successors is more interesting. All the *Ordinatio* of this genius of philosophy who died at an early age is a radical rethinking of Augustine in the light of a new concept: that of the univocity of being. The prologue of this monumental work is already Augustinian in tone: there is an imbalance between the desire of humans for the Infinite, and the impossibility for the *homo viator* to obtain it solely using natural instruments. Thus philosophy is necessary but insufficient at the same time. The opposition between the intentional correlation of the Scotist expression *ex natura potentiae* and that of the equally Scotist expression *pro statu isto* once again brings to the forefront the Augustinian dichotomy between the status of human beings before and after original sin, in the new cultural climate.

How alive and vital Augustinism still was in what Huizinga referred to as "the Waning of the Middle Ages" can be inferred from the fact that Augustinian insights survived in currents of thought that were, in many ways, poles apart from the mentality of Augustine, Occamism for example. Various times, William of Ockham (d. 1349) quotes Augustine in support of his theses in the *Epistola proemiale*, in the *Summa logicae* (the reference is to *De doctrina christiana* II, 31, 48) or when he distinguishes the *terminus conceptus*, from *prolatus* and *scriptus*. Here, in *Summa logicae* I, 1, he makes explicit reference to *De Trinitate* XV, 10, 19. Nor can that come as a surprise: no thinker had ever dealt with the issues of signs as had Augustine (*De Magistro* 1, 1–2; 4, 8; 2, 3; 2, 4, for example, etc.), and, as is well known, those issues were fundamental in scholastic semiotics in general and Occamist in particular. How Augustinism functioned in thinkers such as Peter Aureolus (d. 1322) was more complex. In Aureolus' *Comment on the Maxims* a *contaminatio* between Augustinism and phenomenism took place. The position of the Augustinian Gregory of Rimini (d. 1358), varied between those of Ockham and Augustine.

The pre-humanistic rediscovery of Augustine must also be recalled. While Francesco Petrarca (d. 1374), Coluccio Salutati (d. 1406), Giovanni Dominici (d. 1419), and Leonardo Bruni (d. 1444), albeit lacking in speculative genius, attempted to remain in the Augustinian realm, such was not to be the case for Cusano (d. 1464), Ficino (d. 1499), or Giovanni Pico della Mirandola (d. 1494). They made use of Augustine but to formulate their own visions of the world. These latter authors, however, are fifteenth century ones, but they belong to another cultural climate: humanistic and Renaissance.

2. Augustine in the Renaissance and the first Centuries of the Modern Era

The history of printed books is related to the first editions of Augustine's works. The volumes of the *Opera omnia* appeared in Basel in 1506 in the printing types of Johann Amerbach. The edition is almost complete although it contains various books that are not authentic. Many of the future protagonists of the Reformation can be found involved in printing, as correctors of proofs and compilers of indexes. In 1529 Erasmus of Rotterdam completed the second edition of the *Opera omnia* of Augustine. Unlike Amerbach, Erasmus possesses good and ancient codes as well as a richer experience with critical work which he acquired from publishing classical writers.[2]

The sixteenth century is marked by the work of Luther (d. 1546) and Calvin (d. 1564) who aimed at rediscovering St Paul's teachings surrounding original sin, concupiscence and justification, departing from several Augustinian theses rigidly and severely interpreted. In reference to his monastic period, Luther, an Augustinian monk, recognized that "Augustinum vorabam non legebam", but with *De servo arbitrio* he increasingly radicalized some theses which, in Augustine, were occasional expressions. He definitively kept his distance from the bishop from Hippo.[3] Calvin seems closer to the Father of the Church, but also ended up distancing himself from Augustine, carrying ideas on grace and predestination stated in opposition to Pelagius to the extreme, and conserving the Lutheran principle concerning justification by faith alone.[4] In the seventeenth century new theological controversies on the doctrine of Grace flared up in France due to Baius (d. 1589) and Jansen (d. 1638). Baius appeals to Augustine to confuse grace and nature, with a primarily juridical interpretation of the notions of grace and merit. Jansen actually betrays Augustine's teaching, despite ample textual correspondences. He underscores the radical corruption of present human nature and free will, sacrificing liberty to grace.

As these theological controversies raged, Augustinism played a determining role in the philosophy of Tommaso Campanella (d. 1639), as shown by the strong presence of Augustine in the *Metaphysica*, but this presence operated especially in the reawakening of philosophy in France.

Two Augustinian doctrines in particular, self-awareness and illumination, fed the philosophical speculation. The historians of philosophy see in the *si fallor, sum* of Augustine an anticipation of the *cogito ergo sum* of Descartes (d. 1650). After the publication of the *Discours de la méthode* and the *Meditationes de prima Philosophia*, Marcenne in 1637 and Arnauld in 1648 bring to attention of the French philosopher similarities in thought and expressions with some passages in Augustine's writings, in particular with *De libero arbitrio* II, 3, 7, *De civitate Dei* XI, 26, and *De Trinitate* X, 10, 14. At first, Descartes found it gratifying to have the authority of Augustine in his favor. Some time later, in a letter to Marcenne, he wrote, more precisely: "il ne me semble pas s'en servir à même usage que je fais" and for good reason. In fact Augustine had formulated a different concept of self-awareness. It should be recalled that although Descartes never acknowledged having been directly influenced by Augustine's writings, the echo of Augustinian thought in his philosophy aroused such great interest among his contemporaries that Cartesianism would come to be considered by some as a development of Augustinism.[5] It is no accident that many thinkers discovered some themes from Augustinian philosophy through the Cartesian prism. Malebranche (d. 1715) is an example. Although he was inspired by the theory of illumination, he arrived at an ontologist interpretation thereby distorting the Augustinian metaphysical system. Pascal (d. 1662) is another important philosopher, who was certainly influenced by Augustine. Pascal's anthropological thought, especially in the *Pensées* and treatises, owes a debt to *Confessiones* in many ways. Without quoting Augustine, the French philosopher nonetheless reveals considerable familiarity with Augustinian texts.

Between 1679 and 1690 the Benedictine monks of the congregation of St Maurus raised the most enduring monument to Augustine's memory. They published a complete edition of all his works. This work marks a definitive step forward in the history of Augustinian texts and was to be reproduced and published in 1841 by J. P. Migne. These fifteen volumes in the well-known series *Patrologia latina* constitute the basis of the two large, modern critical editions still in the process of completion: the *Corpus scriptorum ecclesiasticorum latinorum* (CSEL), published by the Academy of Vienna (1887–), and the *Corpus Christianorum, Series Latina* (CCL), published by Brepols of Turnhout (1954–).

3. Liberal Interpretation and Viewpoint of the historiography of Catholic Origin

Subsequent to publication of the *Opera omnia* by Migne, in the second half of the nineteenth century a first study appeared. It is by G. F. Nourisson,[6] who investigated in depth Augustinian philosophy. Approximately twenty years later, the German scholar G. Storz[7] published another in-depth introduction to Augustine the philosopher. The two scholars laid particular emphasis on the critical use made of Platonic philosophy by Augustine. Their studies led to a new field of research: the nature of the relationship between Platonism and Christianity. A controversy arose in 1888 over the historical value of the *Confessiones*, and the relationship between these and the writings of Cassiciacum, when two essays were published by G. Boissier[8] and A. Von Harnack[9] respectively. As exponents of the critical and philological method they emphasized two radical questions: one concerned the legitimacy of calling a Christian a philosopher, and the other, the nature of Augustine's intellectual evolution. A. Von Harnack, departed from the assumption that Christianity should only have an ethical and religious dimension without a philosophical character. He pointed out that the true Augustine is what comes out of the intense experience of faith alien to any manifestation of a philosophical nature. Boissier retraced the entire existential journey of Augustine, observing that the account of the conversion in *Confessiones*, in which the penitent Christian speaks, is not in agreement with the philosophical Dialogues of Cassiciacum. Boissier and Von Harnak agree in placing Augustine the thinker of Cassiciacum in opposition to the mature bishop of Hippo. Discussing the problem of the veracity of *Confessiones* the two scholars intended to put forth a new point of view in the interpretations of Augustinian thought.[10] A whole series of scholars, following Boissier and Harnack, placing the actual conversion of Augustine in the period following his ordination as a priest, went so far as to theorize the existence of 'two Augustines': the Neoplatonic thinker on the one hand, and the theologian of the Catholic Church on the other.

In 1900, L. Gourdon, with a comparative study of the *Confessiones* and the *Dialogues* maintained that the two moments in fact reveal two conversions and two different men. He summarizes the results of his research as follows:

1) after Augustine abandoned his profession as rhetorician, he retired to Cassiciacum to regain his health;

2) here he continued to enhance his knowledge of literature, poetry and philosophy, conserving his same profane needs and exigencies;

3) he adopted Neoplatonic philosophy and only because of this he chose the path of chastity.

Only from 390 on, could Augustine be called genuinely Christian because this was the year in which he wrote a work whose contents were totally Christian.[11] H. Becker[12] put aside the account of *Confessiones*, rejecting the traditional point of view. W. Thimme attempts to demonstrate that not *Confessiones* but just the first writings have historical value in reference to accepting Catholic dogma, which, in 386, Augustine was far from doing.[13] But P. Alfaric[14] was the scholar who dealt with all these theses in the most decided and rigorous way. In 1918, he published a study on Augustine's intellectual development. The author intended this to be the first part of a trilogy. Here it is maintained that the African had embraced Neoplatonism in 386 and that he would convert to Christianity only a few years later, after recognizing that it was in conformity with the philosophy of Plotinus. In Alfaric's words: "Morally as intellectually,

(Augustine) converted to Neoplatonism rather than to the Gospel".[15] Alfaric was convinced of the existence of an opposition between the *Dialogues* of Cassiciacum and the story of Augustine's conversion as is recorded in *Confessiones*, which Alfaric maintained should be examined critically if not indeed with suspicion.

The series of interpretations beginning with G. Boissier and A. Von Harnack, and culminating in the study of P. Alfaric, met with fierce resistance especially in the Catholic world, to such a degree that P. Alfaric was obliged to give up the pursuit of his work. The first reply to this series of interpretations came with E. Portalié, who, under the item *Augustin* in the *Dictionnaire de Théologie Catholique* (1902) distanced himself from the positions of A. Von Harnack and G. Boissier. The second reply was that of E. Gilson[16], who judged P. Alfaric's work to be totally arbitrary. He maintained that Augustine was already in possession of a sure Christianity in the first dialogues, even though this had traces of Neoplatonism. After E. Gilson there followed the reaction of Ch. Boyer. He claimed the historicity of *Confessiones* on the one hand, and the numerous traces of Christian faith scattered through the first writings. These document the submission of Augustine to the rule of Christian faith as well as the continuity between the young and the mature Augustine.[17]

The controversy over the evolution in Augustinian thought and the nature of the conversion aroused the interest of Augustine scholars in all of the philosophical production and the first writings in particular. From the nineteen-twenties on, a series of studies was published which examined in greater depth the point of view of Ch. Boyer. We mention in particular the introductions to Augustine of E. Gilson[18] and M. F. Sciacca,[19] to which we shall return shortly, and the study of A. Guzzo,[20] according to which the philosophical reflections of the first dialogues constitute the original core out of which all the later theological activity would grow. The heritage of Augustine in philosophers who certainly do not belong to mainstream of Christian philosophy should not be forgotten, either. For example, there is E. Husserl—see the conclusion to the *Cartesianische Meditationen*—and G. Gentile. It should be observed, however, that this is an immanentized Augustine used in a spirit which is not Augustinian.

The fifteen-hundredth anniversary of the death of Augustine was the occasion for numerous collective works, among which we point out *Aurelius Augustinus* (edited by M. Grabman and J. Mausbach, Köln 1930), *Miscellanea Agostiniana* (edited by the Augustinian Order, Roma 1930) and *A Monument to Saint Augustine* (edited by Ch. Dawson, C. C. Martindale, E. Przywara, M. Blondel and others, London 1930). In the nineteen thirties H. I. Marrou, published a long study on Augustine and the end of ancient culture, thereby widening the area of Augustinian historiographical discussion in comparison to the previous years. This distinguished scholar pointed out that Augustine's personality, which is the most meaningful expression of *late antiquity*, was fully enlightened as he made reference both to the philosophical tradition of the Hellenistic and Roman era and the no-less-important classical rhetoric, which had made of Augustine a man of letters, a grammarian, and man of learning.[21] In those same years, J. Guitton[22] published a study on the relationship between time and eternity in Plotinus and Augustine. According to the scholar, even though a similarity of language may be found, there exists a profound difference in conception between Augustine and Plotinus.

In 1954 the sixteen-hundredth anniversary of Augustine's birth was commemorated with two international conferences. The first[23], held in Paris, summarized the Augustinian studies carried out in the main areas of research. The second,[24] in Rome, dealt with a few particular themes in speculation about Augustine and his influence on contemporary philosophy.

The period from the end of the nineteen forties to the beginning of the new millennium are marked by a threefold turning point in Augustine studies: a philosophical, a philological, a logical-formal, and an analytic-linguistic turning point. In the first one, philosophical issues and the trend in Augustine's thinking are not only of great interest historiographically speaking, but also constitute a new point of departure in theoretical investigation. Augustine is reconsidered after Kant, Fichte, Hegel and Gentile. In the second turning point, a direct reading of the *opera omnia* of Augustine, without leaping recklessly into difficult passages—alas, a more widespread custom than one might imagine—the original figure of Augustine the philosopher is reconstituted without the many commonplaces that had accumulated over the centuries being repeated, ones which had ended up creating a stock of stereotypes uncritically repeated by a few scholars. The use of logic and rigour in argumentation was rediscovered in the third turning point along with the relevance of the Augustinian thought from the point of view of the modern philosophy of language.

4. Philosophical Turning Point

As has already been indicated, M. F. Sciacca (1908–1975), was among the main interpreters of Augustine in the twentieth century along with Ch. Boyer, H. J. Marrou, R. Holte, J. Guitton, G. Madec, G. O'Daly, N. Cipriani. He is the only one who assumed the main points and themes of Augustine's thought, theoretically as well. His first studies on Rosmini (1936) and those on Plato at the same time culminated with those on Saint Augustine. M. F. Sciacca published only one of the three planned volumes (*Sant'Agostino*, Brescia 1949). This was enhanced with studies in part for the Augustinian hundredth anniversary celebration of 1954 in his Spanish translation (Barcelona, 1955). He did not, however, have time to collect all his specific studies for Augustine—as he had done for the Platonic studies in 1967 (*Platone, nos.* 26 and 27 of the forty volumes of his *Opere complete*, assembled between 1957 and 1975). The Course held at the Chaire Mercier in 1954, among other things, was not included and, above all, the studies on philosophy and theology of history, with the introduction to

De trinitate that came out in 1973 in the edition edited by A. Trapè, were also not included.

The reason why M. F. Sciacca did not publish the other two volumes as planned is purely a matter for speculation: from *Pascal* (1944) to the first works such as *Filosofia e metafisica* (1950), *L'interiorità oggettiva* (1952) and *Atto ed essere* (1956), M. F. Sciacca went from being an Augustine scholar to the main, theoretically fruitful interpreter. In *Filosofia e metafisica* the existence of God is assumed to be the root of the very problem of knowledge, without which this remains unfounded, and metaphysically unintelligible. The "objective interiority" is Augustinian, taken up as a determining factor in overcoming immanentist rationalisms and subjectivisms, idealisms and existentialisms. Augustine, "experienced" through Pascal and Blondel as well, frees M. F. Sciacca from spiritualisms, phenomenologies, existentialisms, and personalisms metaphysically unfounded. Moreover and above all, he is encouraged to construct a "metaphysics of integrality", which will take organic Augustinian form, in particular, in the works *L'uomo, questo squilibrato* (1958) and *Morte e immortalità* (1959). The theses of the transcendence of the objective being, with respect to the finite existing and of infinite truth with respect to the thinking existing, are the foundation of his anthropological metaphysics. This is accomplished in two other fundamental works marked by Augustine's presence, which finally led Sciacca to Thomas Aquinas (1974): *La libertà e il tempo* (1965) and *Ontologia triadica e trinitaria* (1972). The problem of evil and the two *civitates* is central to all the works of Sciacca, from *L'ora di Cristo* (1954) to *L'oscuramento dell'intelligenza* (1970).

5. Philological Turning Point

In the fifties and sixties P. Courcelle put an end to the dilemma surrounding the conversion of Augustine first to Neoplatonism and then to Christianity. Through painstaking philological analyses of Augustine's writings, he drew scholars' attention to the Milanese environment where the African rhetorician had come into contact with Christianity. According to the French author, there was a cultural circle in Milan in 386 which had formulated a synthesis between Neoplatonism and Christianity.[25] The thinkers behind this operation were several members of the Milanese clergy, the bishop Ambrose and the priest Simplicianus, as well as some lay people, in particular, Manlius Teodorus and Zenobius. Here Augustine is thought to have accepted the formula briefly referred to as *Christian Neoplatonism*.[26] Those same years, A. Solignac,[27] assessed the status of research on the role of Neoplatonism in Augustinian thought, bringing out, among other things, the existence of a Milanese circle which went beyond the Christian area and involved people of diverse convictions attracted by the reading of Plotinus' books.

In 1962 the Swedish scholar R. Holte[28] published his doctoral thesis on Augustine and the problem of the aim of human beings in ancient philosophy. He identified the point of contact between Pagan and Christian wisdom in the problem concerning the *télos* of human life. For the first time, he put the doctrine of the *appetitus* in the framework of Augustine's ontological vision, emphasizing the fact that every natural *appetitus* has an aim of its own.

Instead of putting an end to the dispute over the conversion of Augustine, the conclusions of P. Courcelle and R. Holte inflamed it once again. At the end of the sixties, O. Du Roy published a voluminous study on the birth and development of the Trinitarian doctrine of Augustine, from the dialogues of Cassiciacum up to the end of 391. Following a phenomenological, genetic and structural method, the author maintained that the conversion had, in actual fact, been a moral event and that the Trinitarian doctrine of the Dialogues was only partly inspired by the New Testament.[29] O. Du Roy stated that Augustine moreover confused the Holy Spirit with the *anima mundi* of which Plotinus had spoken[30] and maintained that the solution of the problem of evil proposed by Augustine himself in his first writings was clearly of Neoplatonic origin. These theses were shared by several authors, among whom were K. Flash[31] and R. J. O'Connell,[32] while others, like L. Hölscher[33] and G. O'Daly,[34] firmly disassociated themselves from such interpretations. The latter insisted, rather, on several connections in the thought of Augustine with Cicero and the Stoics, thereby minimizing the Neoplatonic influence on Augustine.

In the seventies G. Madec, in a study,[35] was the first to raise doubts about several theses of O. Du Roy. With a subsequent article[36], published in 1975 he gave Augustinian historiography a new orientation and maintained that it was not Plotinus but Simplicianus who had offered Augustine the point of departure for his speculation, suggesting to him that the principle of coherence (*principe de cohérence*) of Christian doctrine is provided by the Prologue of the Gospel of John. Augustine was thus able to bring together in the person of Christ the *sapientia* of *Hortensius*, the *intellectus* of the *Libri Platonicorum* and the *Verbum* of the Prologue of the Gospel of John. From that moment on he was in possession of the principle that would give order to his doctrine. Two texts allude to this intuition, the *Contra Academicos* III, 19, 42, and the *De ordine* II, 5, 16. A few years later, the French scholar gave a report[37] in which he further explained his interpretation of Augustine's relationship with Neoplatonism. He pointed out that the African was never, strictly speaking a Neoplatonist, and that the *Dialogues* of Cassiciacum are a radical minimization of Platonism. Only within this framework should his debt toward Plotinus and Porphyrius be evaluated. The influence of Neoplatonism on Augustine remains important, in any case, but confined to the free use of some themes. The French scholar once again made this observation in his general introduction to the *Retractationes*: in Augustine's literary activity periods and developments must be distinguished which, however, do not imply reversals in doctrine. In short, not only had Augustine read the *Enneads* in 386 as a Christian, but also pronounced a Christian judgment on *Libri Platonicorum*, discerning the good philosophy to be found therein and distinguishing it from the bad religious practices.[38]

The sixteen-hundredth anniversary of Augustine's conversion was celebrated in 1986. This event was organized and directed by A. Trapè, and held at the *Istituto Patristico Augustinianum* of which he was the head. This was an international congress comparable to the one held in Paris in 1954. In 1987 another large international symposium followed. It was set up by the research team from the *Augustinus-Lexicon* in Würzburg. The two events offered an in-depth updating of the Augustinian studies of the preceding decades, thereby giving a new impulse to further research.

In the nineteen-nineties, the research of N. Cipriani was at the forefront of scholarship. It was aimed at identifying new sources of Augustinian thought. In a study of 1994[39], the scholar demonstrated that the Trinitarian doctrine of the first Dialogues of Augustine came not so much from Plotinus as from several Christian sources, in particular, from the anti-Arian treatises of Marius Victorinus and the *De fide* of Ambrose. A later study in 1996, by Cipriani[40], took up hypotheses put forth by A. Dyroff and R. Holte. Cipriani identified points in the first writings of Augustine that, via the meditation of Varro, go back to the philosophers of the ancient Academy and from these to Stoicism and Aristotle himself. In particular, he demonstrated that the anthropological and moral model exposed by Varro in his *De philosophia*, attributed to Antiochus of Ascalon and investigated in the nineteenth book of *De Civitate Dei*, was kept in mind by Augustine from the very first works on. In a study[41] published in 2000 N. Cipriani drew attention to numerous conceptual and lexical parallels in the encyclopedic section of *De ordine* and the more ample one of *De doctrina christiana*, which always lead back to Varro as the source.

There is little point in citing other contributions, however numerous they may be, since they have little significance from the point of view of the history of criticism,

Critical interpretations of Augustinian philosophy 277

and because they repeat commonplaces without adding new and original insights.

6. Logical-formal and analytical-linguistic Turning Point

The final quarter of the twentieth century saw an authentic revolution in Augustinian studies: the logical-formal and analytical-linguistic investigation of the texts of the African.

The credit for having performed the first examination of Augustine's works using the tools of modern mathematical logic goes to T. G. Bucher. In an article of fundamental importance which came out in 1982 the Swiss scholar not only identified the various passages in which Augustine uses Stoic logic, translating it into schemes of inference, but established, with the help of modern symbolic techniques, a useful comparison with Cicero and M. Capella.[42] A second fundamental contribution concerning the connections between the *cogito* and formal logic was presented by the scholar in Rome at the International Symposium, on the sixteen-hundredth anniversary of the conversion of Augustine.[43] Bucher's studies are important not only because they show that symbolization constitutes a hermeneutic aid, complementary to, and clarifier of the philological one, but also because it makes it possible to test the correctness of the way in which Augustine proceeds in his argumentation. Independently of the Swiss scholar, M. Malatesta devoted two monographic courses to the *Contra Academicos* at the University *"Federico II"* of Naples, one in the first half of the eighties and the other approximately ten years later. Malatesta has very much at heart the relevance of Augustine. This is why his investigation is not limited to formal logical but extends to the analysis of the Augustinian reasoning in the light of the modern theories of linguistic acts and propositional aptitudes.[44] The analyses of Malatesta show that certain passages of the first philosophical dialogue written by Augustine just after the conversion, were anything but an accumulation of rhetorical exchanges. They reveal themselves to be intersubjective philosophical investigations whose depth can be perceived and appreciated only if one digs deeply into the various linguistic layers, one on top of the other, in which various areas of heterodoxical logic are intertwined, from indexical to bulomatic, from optative to erotetic, from epistemic to doxastic, to modal.

It is especially with G. Balido, a student of S. D'Elia and M. Malatesta, a Marius Victorinus scholar, that multi-layered logical linguistic analysis began to extend to the entire Augustinian *corpus* and did not remain circumscribed in the early works. Numerous contributions presented by Balido starting from the beginning of the nineties bear witness to this fact, as in the *Lectio Augustini* at the University of Pavia and the international Seminar of Augustinian studies organized by the Faculty of Letters and Philosophy of the University of Perugia. They are collected in an extremely interesting volume.[45] Balido's investigations are far from over.

7. Conclusion

The twentieth century had opened with a fierce controversy over the cultural and human identity of Augustine, and came to a close with the publication of an encyclopedia[46] which constitutes a new instrument for scholarship and yet another monument to the memory of Augustine. It is edited, with the collaboration of an international team of scholars, by A. D. Fitzgerald, professor of Patrology at the *Istitutum Patristicum Augustinianum* of Rome and editor of the journal *Augustinian Studies*.

Notes

1. E. Gilson, *Le philosophie au moyen âge*, Paris 1952; it. tr. *La filosofia nel Medioevo*, Firenze 1998, p. 823.
2. For further discussion cf. G. Pani, *L'Opera omnia di S. Agostino in Lutero e nei riformatori*, "Augustinianum", XXX, 2000, pp. 519–566.
3. L. Cristiani, *Luther et Saint Augustin*, in *Augustinus magister*, II, Paris 1954, pp. 1029–1031.

Critical interpretations of Augustinian philosophy 279

4. Ch. Boyer, *J.Calvin et Saint Augustin*, "Augustinian Studies", III, 1972, p. 34.
5. G. Lewis, *Augustinisme et cartésianisme*, in *Augustinus magister*, II, Paris 1954, pp. 1087–1104.
6. J.F. Nourisson, *La philosophie de Saint Augustin*, Paris 1865.
7. J.Storz, *Die Philosophie des hl. Augustinus*, Freiburg 1882.
8. G. Boissier, *La conversion de saint Augustin*, "Revue des Deux Mondes", LXXXV, 1888, pp. 43–69.
9. A. Von Harnack, *Augustins Konfessionen. Ein Vortrag*, Giessen 1888 (reprinted in *Reden und Aufsätze*, I, Giessen, 1904, pp. 51–79).
10. V. Mannucci, *La conversione di sant'Agostino e la critica recente*, in *Miscellanea agostiniana*, vol. II, Roma 1931, pp. 23–47.
11. L. Gourdon, *Essai sur la conversion de saint Augustin*, Paris 1900, pp. 44–46.
12. H. Becker, *Augustin. Studien zu seiner geistigen Entwicklung*, Leipzig 1908.
13. W. Thimme, *Augustins geistige Entwicklung in den ersten Jahren nach seiner Bekehrung (386–391)*, Berlin 1908, pp. 11–24.
14. P. Alfaric, *L'évolution intellectuelle de saint Augustin*, vol. I, *Du Manichéisme au Néoplatonisme*, Paris 1918.
15. Ibid., p. 399.
16. E. Gilson, *Compte-rendu de P. Alfaric*, "Revue philosophique", LXXXVIII, 1919, pp. 497–505.
17. Ch. Boyer, *Christianisme et néoplatonisme dans la formation de saint Augustin*, Paris 1920, pp.190–195.
18. E. Gilson, *The Christian Philosophy* op. cit.
19. M. F. Sciacca, *S. Agostino* op. cit.
20. A. Guzzo, *S. Agostino* op. cit.
21. H.-I. Marrou, *Saint Augustin* op. cit., pp. 541–543.
22. J. Guitton, *Le temps* op. cit.
23. *Aurelius Augustinus*, in 3 voll. edited by A. Mandouze, Paris 1954.
24. *S. Agostino e le grandi correnti della filosofia contemporanea*, edited by the Augustinian Order, Roma 1955.

25. P. Courcelle, *Les Confessions de Saint Augustin dans la tradition littéraire. Antécédents et postérité*, Paris 1963, p. 31.
26. P. Courcelle, *Recherches* op. cit., pp. 252–253.
27. A. Solignac, in *Bibliothèque Augustinienne*, vol. 4, pp. 529–536.
28. R. Holte, *Béatitude* op. cit.
29. O. Du Roy, *L'intelligence* op. cit., p. 466.
30. Ibid., p. 148.
31. K. Flash, *Augustin* op. cit.
32. R. J. O'Connell, *St. Augustine's early Theory of Man, A.D. 386–391*, Cambridge (Massachusetts) 1968.
33. L. Hölscher, *The Reality of the Mind* op. cit.
34. G. O'Daly, *Augustine's Philosophy* op. cit.
35. G. Madec, *À propos d'une traduction du De Ordine II, 5, 16"*, "Revue des Études Augustiniennes", XVI, 1970, pp. 182–183.
36. G. Madec, "Christus scientia et sapientia nostra". *Le principe* op. cit., pp. 77–85.
37. G. Madec, *Augustin et le néoplatonisme*, "Revue de l'Institut Catholique de Paris", XIX, 1986, pp. 41–52.
38. G. Madec, *Introduzione generale* a S. Agostino, *Le ritrattazioni*, Roma 1994, p. XC.
39. N. Cipriani, *Le fonti cristiane* op. cit., pp. 253–312.
40. N. Cipriani, *L'influsso di Varrone* op. cit., pp. 369–400.
41. N. Cipriani, *Sulla fonte varroniana* op. cit., pp. 203–224.
42. T. G. Bucher, *Zur formalen Logik* op. cit., pp. 3–45.
43. T. G. Bucher, *Augustinus und der Skeptizismus* op. cit., pp. 381–392.
44. In addition to these courses, two lessons were held for the inauguration of the *Giornate Agostiniane Urbinati* in 1994 and not yet published. In the meantime, M. Malatesta *St. Augustine's Dialectic* op. cit., pp. 91–120 and M. Malatesta *La problematica linguistica* op. cit., pp. 46–63 can be consulted.
45. G. Balido, *Strutture logico-formali* op. cit., Roma 1998.
46. A. D. Fitzgerald (General Editor), *Augustine through the Ages. An Encyclopedia*, Grand Rapids (Michigan) 1999.

Conclusion

The purpose of this volume is to illustrate the Augustinian philosophical outline starting from the most interesting outcomes as evidenced by the three turning points, the philosophical, the philological and the formal-logical, that have distinguished the Augustinian studies in the past decades. To draw together the threads of this subject and underlying previously suggested observations, I think it is opportune to dwell on the three themes presented in this volume and that, in my opinion, constitute an innovation in the Augustinian historiographical circle: the peculiarity of Augustine's epistemology, certain elements of anthropology and some aspects of politics.

As far as the first point is concerned, I recall the declaration found at the end of the third book of *Contra Academicos* where Augustine affirms his decision to pursue the philosophical ideal and, at the same time, his resolve not to stray from the authority of Christ. He underlines, moreover, that he will not be satisfied with believing only but he wishes to understand through the intellect, as far as it is possible to do so, that which he believes. He adds that in his search he is certain to find in the Platonic philosophers some ideas and doctrines not at odds with Christian faith. What emerges from this premise, is that Augustinian philosophy is not anchored solely in reason, but in faith in the authority of Christ, *Scriptures* and reason.[1]

This method of inquiry has been an object of disappointment on the part of certain modern thinkers, Karl Jaspers to name one. K. Jaspers has harshly criticized this decision of Augustine. In *The Great Philosophers*, the existentialist German philosopher expresses great admiration for Augustine and ranks him among the greatest philosophers while at the same time distinguishing two groups of philosophers, the creative philosophers and the systematic philosophers. In his opinion, Augustine falls under the first group, alongside Plato and Kant. Augustine is a creative philosopher, says Jaspers, because he has taught others to think, revealing to human being his true essence such as self-awareness for example. Unfortunately, Jaspers goes on to say, after showing a new way to philosophical reflection, Augustine submits himself to the authority of Christ and Plato, thereby giving up the essential principle fundamental to all philosophical research: the refusal of any authority.[2]

To understand this methodological presupposition, one must remember that Augustine, at the beginning of his education in Africa, had tied himself to the Manichaean Gnosis, thereby distancing himself from Christian faith as taught by the Catholic Church which places faith as the point of departure in any rational understanding. The Manichaean Gnostics had convinced him to reject the *auctoritas* of the Church and to seek truth solely through rational clarity. Convinced by this point of view, Augustine remained embroiled in the Manichaean Gnosis for nine years. It was in Milan where he had obtained the Chair in Rhetoric that he became aware of the Manichaean trickery after hearing St. Ambrose. Augustine's return to the Catholic Church coincided with the recovery of the reasonableness of faith in general and of the Christian faith in particular.

The autobiographical tale of the *Confessiones*, the *Dialogues of Cassiciacum*, other later writings such as the *De utilitate credendi, De fide rerum quae non videntur*, all bear witness to the attempt of Augustine to search for the reasons which render reasonable both faith in its general sense, and faith more appropriately Christian. To understand Augustinian philosophy, it is important to bear in mind this "*Hermeneutical circle*": Augustine wishes "to believe in order to understand and to understand prior to believing".

Augustine is not a fundamentalist. He came to believe only after having verified that it is not unreasonable to believe in Christ. This is the first point of view that I have highlighted in my inquiry.

The second point of view I outlined concerns anthropology. In the past century many scholars of Augustinian thought have seen the first Augustine (the philosopher) under the light of neoplatonism more so than Christianity. For example, P. Alfaric maintained that in 386 Augustine became a convert not to the Gospel but to neoplatonism. This theory was justified in part by certain readings relating to themes such as, the Trinitarian the Anthropological as well as other themes. I have emphasized that neoplatonism, at the start of Augustinian speculative thought, is not as all encompassing as is sometimes thought to be the case. Undoubtedly, Augustine, had hoped to find in the Platonics, ideas and doctrines that would not be at odds with the Christian faith. This concerned above all, those intelligible truths such as soul and God. In *Sententiae ad intelligibilia ducentes*, Porphyrius had taught to think the presence of God, and the soul in the body that lives in the world, and had elaborated a type of metaphysics regarding *Incorporea*, which Augustine embraces. Nevertheless, Augustine was not at all neoplatonic in so far as the conception of the nature of man is concerned, and this right from the beginning of his inquiry.

Departing from the presupposition that Augustine, in Milan, had converted to Christianity, and upon reading carefully the first philosophical *Dialogues*, one discovers that the Augustinian Trinitarian doctrine pointed out in the *Dialogues of Cassiciacum*, decidedly was not that of Plotinus. We should remember at this point, that according to some scholars, O. Du Roy for example, in the *Dialogues* of *Cassiciacum* Augustine confused the Holy Spirit with the "reason of the universal soul," referred to in the Enneades. On the contrary, in the Trinitarian themes mentioned in the *De Beata Vita*, in *De Ordine*, Augustine is inspired by *De Fide* of St. Ambrose and the anti-Arian treatises of Marius Victorinus.[3]

This was an important discovery. We find lexical expressions, in addition to concepts clearly inspired by these two Christian authors, which lead us to conclude that it is not possible to speak of Trinitarian doctrine inspired by Plotinus in the first *Dialogues* written in Cassiciacum.

More interesting still is the point of view relative to anthropology. From the beginning, for example, in *De Ordine*, Augustine accuses certain great minds of pride (he is referring to the Neoplatonists) who consider it too vile and humiliating that God should take on a human body. In *De quantitate animae*, written in Rome in the years 387–388, Augustine underlines at the end of the book, that no one must show disdain or in any way complain that the soul has been given by God to a body. Plotinus in fact, uses the Greek term corresponding to the Latin term *stomachari* which Augustine adopts in a polemic way.

According to the Egyptian philosopher, it is regrettable that the soul be closed within the body. In other texts, Augustine also criticizes the Neoplatonists who are discontent with the idea that the soul is to be found in the body. The polemic references are additionally supported by positive affirmations concerning the doctrine that the body, like the soul, is an integral part of the human being. This theory is already present in the *De beata vita* dialogue written in Cassiciacum. The terms used in this text, even more explicitly in the work *De moribus ecclesiae catholicae*, hark back to Varro's *De philosophia* that we know sufficiently well from the quotations which Augustine uses as references in the book XIX of *De civitate Dei*. Attempts were made, in the early nineties, to utilize the text of *De philosophia* to reinterpret the philosophical *Dialogues* of Augustine.[4] One has been able to discover that the Augustinian anthropological conception in this first period is inspired not by Plotinus or Porphyrius but by Varro. In *De Ordine*, for example, there is a statement that is the exact opposite of what one reads in the third *Ennead*. Plotinus maintained that the wise man is not composed of body and soul but only of a rational soul. In *De Ordine*, Augustine asserts the contrary: the wise man is composed not only of body and soul, but also of the whole soul (the rational and the sensitive one). Many texts can be quoted where Augustine maintains that the body is an *integral part* of man, unlike the view maintained by the Neoplatonists. Augustine does not stop here. He goes beyond this doctrine by accepting the Aristotelian distinction of the *goods*, the goods of the soul, but also the goods of the body and the *external goods*. For Augustine, the goods of the body are real goods, even if in the hierarchy of values they occupy an inferior level: life itself, health of the body, integrity of the limbs—all are true goods that man must pursue.

I point out another theory that is found neither in Plotinus nor in the surviving books of Porphyrius, that is, the theory of *oikeiosis*. Augustine underlines this theory quite often, in *De immortalitate animae*, in *De Vera religione*, in the *Confessiones* and in *De doctrina christiana*. According to this doctrine, the soul is not all extraneous to the body. On the contrary, it has an *appetitus*, that is to say, a natural tendency to give life to the body, to govern and to give it order. This means that the human being has a tendency towards self-preservation; to live, seeking in every way that which is useful for its life, for its health, while rejecting all that is harmful. In addition, it possesses other tendencies: to know truth, not to be exposed to trickery, and finally to live in society.

The need to live in society, a trait unknown to Neoplatonists, constitutes for Augustine from the very beginning of his research, an essential element of his anthropology.

I have delved into the question of politics in the last two chapters. In the past, the political thought of Augustine was often connected with a theocratic vision sometimes theorized, maybe even utilized in the Middle Ages. Political Augustinism has often been placed as the foundation of the strict connection between Church and temporal authority.

I have disclaimed a similar interpretation in the light of an Augustinian text previously overlooked by scholars of Augustinian thought. I choose again to bring to the attention of the reader this text whose relevance is paramount:

> (...) as far as the present life is concerned, we need to be submissive to temporal authorities, that is to say to those who are in charge of day to day affairs on earth, thereby deriving all due recognition and honors. The opposite holds true, however, for what pertains to our faith in God and our calling to His Reign. In this sphere we must not consider ourselves bound by the authority of man, especially when such authority aims to subvert all that God has granted us pertaining to eternal life. It would be therefore a severe error for a Christian to take refuge in his Christianity to avoid paying taxes and other monetary demands, or to consider himself exempt from the claims imposed by those authorities in the exercise of public functions. Even more serious would be the error of one who, in his efforts to comply with authorities (which occupy a prominent position in the administration of temporal matters) recognizes them as dictating one's own faith. It is absolutely essential to respect the boundaries between what is temporal and matters of faith (...).[5]

In the light of this text we can conclude that the relationship between Church and State is essentially a problem of co-existence. I reaffirmed with great conviction that for Augustine, the State is a structure that comes into being due to the primordial tendency of human nature and not because of original sin, as some modern scholars have maintained. The ultimate aim of the State is that of guaranteeing peace among its members by regulating the use of temporal goods in order to curb abuse by some against the rights of others.

I have investigated Augustinian political theory having as my starting point the outcomes of the philological research regarding the anthropological Augustinian model brought out by N. Cipriani, and the analyses which I conducted over the years on the nature of the positive laws or imperfect, illustrated by Augustine in the first book of *De Libero Arbitrio* largely ignored by scholars.

Notes

1. *C. Acad.*III 20,43.
2. K. Jaspers, *Drei Grunder des Philosophierens, Plato, Augustin, Kant,* München 1957, *passim.*
3. See N. Cipriani, *Le fonti cristiane* op. cit., pp. 253–312.
4. See N. Cipriani, *L'influsso di Varrone* op. cit., pp. 369–400.
5. *exp. prop. Rm.* 64 [72].

Bibliography

1. Repertories

For the bibliography up to 1928 see E. Nebreda, *Bibliographia augustiniana*, Rome 1928. Bibliographies up to the beginning of the nineteen sixties are listed in D. A. Perini, *Bibliographia augustiniana*, Firenze 1936 and C. Andresen, *Bibliographia Augustiniana*, Darmstadt 1962. To further investigate Augustinian literature of the nineteen-fifties, see T. Van Bavel and F. Van Der Zande, *Répertoire bibliographique de saint Augustin* (1950–1960), Instrumenta Patristica III series, Steenbrugis 1963. For updating to the nineteen eighties, we point out T. L. Miethe, *Augustinian Bibliography 1970–1980* (with an introduction by J. V. Bourke), Westport Connecticut—London 1982; also *Fichier Augustinien*, 4 vol., edited by the *Institut des Études Augustiniennes*, Paris 1972.

We also note the bibliographical bulletins in the following journals: "Augustinus", Madrid 1956 ff; "Revue des Études Augustiniennes", Paris 1956 ff, a continuation of l'"Année Théologique Augustinienne"; "Augustiniana", Louvain 1960 ff.

We refer those who do not have access to the aforementioned bibliography to: "Année Philologique", Paris 1951 ff, item *Augustinus*; "Bibliographia Patristica", Berlin 1959 ff; *Répertoire bibliographique de la philosophie de la Société philosophique de Louvain*, and *The Philosopher's Index*.

2. Miscellanies

Aurelius Augustinus: Festschrift der Görresgesellschaft zum 1500. Todestage des hl. Augustinus, hrsg. von M. Grabman und J. Mausbach, Köln 1930.

Miscellanea Augustiniana, XV centenario della morte di Agostino, Rotterdam 1930.

S. Agostino. Pubblicazione commemorativa del XV centenario della morte. Supplemento speciale della "Rivista di filosofia neoscolastica", Milano 1931.

Miscellanea Agostiniana. Testi e studi pubblicati dall' Ordine eremitano di Sant'Agostino nel XV centenario della morte del santo Dottore, Roma 1930–1931, 2 vol.

A Monument to Saint Augustine. Essays on some Aspects of his Thought written in Commemoration of his 15th Centenary by M. C. D'Arcy, M. Blondel, Ch. Dawson, C. C. Martindale, London 1930.

Acta hebdomadis augustinianae-tomisticae, Torino 1931.

Sant'Agostino e le grandi correnti della Filosofia contemporanea. Atti del Congresso italiano di Filosofia agostiniana, Roma 1955.

Augustinus Magister, Congrès international Augustinien, 3 vol., Paris 1954–1955.

Atti del Congresso internazionale su S. Agostino nel XVI centenario della conversione, edited by the Istituto Patristico Augustinianum, 3 vol., Roma 1987.

Internationales Symposion über den Stand der Augustinus-Forschung, hrsg. von C. Mayer und K. H. Chelius, Würzburg 1989.

3. Works of Augustine

Among the very numerous works of Augustine, those relevant to the philosophical perspective are indicated here, while those whose importance is connected strictly with Augustine's pastoral activity are not included. The title of the work is accompanied by 1) the abbreviation used in the text and, in round brackets, the year of writing; 2) in square brackets the indication of the locations in *Patrologia latina* (PL), *Corpus Scriptorum Ecclesiasticorum Latinorum* (CSEL) and *Corpus Christianorum. Series Latina* (CCL) respectively.

Confessiones = *conf.* (397–401); [PL 32, 659; CSEL 33, 1; CCL 27].
Contra Academicos = *Acad.* (386); [PL 32, 905; CSEL 63, 3; CCL 29].
Contra epistolam Parmeniani = *c. ep. Parm.* (400); [PL 43, 33; CSEL 51, 17].

Bibliography

Contra Faustum manichaeum = *c. Faust.* (397–399); [PL 42, 519; CSEL 25].

Contra Felicem manichaeum = *c. Fel.* (404); [PL 42, 519; CSEL 25, 2].

Contra Iulianum = *c. Iul.* (421–422); [PL 44, 641].

Contra Iulianum Opus Imperfectum = *c. Iul. imp.* (429–430); [PL 45, 1049; CSEL 85, 1].

De beata vita = *beata v.* (386); [PL 32, 959; CSEL 63, 89; CCL 29].

De bono coniugali = *b. coniug.* (400–401); [PL 40, 373; CSEL 41, 185].

De catechizandis rudibus = *cat. rud.* (399); [PL 40, 309; CCL 46].

De civitate Dei = *civ.* (412–427); [PL 41, 13; CSEL 40; CCL 47–48].

De dialectica = *dial.*; a B. D. Jackson editus 1975.

De diversis quaestionibus octoginta tribus = *div. qu.* (388–397); [PL 40, 11; CCL 44].

De doctrina christiana = *doctr. chr.* (397–427); [PL 34, 15; CSEL 80, 3; CCL 32].

De duabus animabus = *duab. an.* (391–392); [PL 42, 93; CSEL 25, 51].

De fide et symbolo = *f. et symb.* (393); [PL 40, 181; CSEL 41, 3].

De fide rerum invisibilium = *f. invis.* (400); [PL 40, 171; CCL 46].

De Genesi ad litteram = *Gn. litt.* (400–416); [PL 34, 245; CSEL 28/1, 1].

De Genesi ad litteram imperfectus liber = *Gn. litt. imp.* (393–394); [PL 34, 219; CSEL 28/1, 419].

De Genesi adversus Manichaeos = *Gn. adv. man.* (388–390); [PL 34, 173; CSEL 91].

De immortalitate animae = *imm. an.* (387); [PL 32, 1021; CSEL 89].

De libero arbitrio = *lib. arb.* (388–391); [PL 32, 1221; CSEL 74; CCL 29].

De magistro = *mag.* (388–390); [PL 32, 1193; CSEL 77/4, 1; CCL 29].

De moribus Ecclesiae catholicae et de moribus manichaeorum = *mor.* (387–388); [PL 32, 1309, CSEL 90].

De musica = *mus.* (388–390); [PL 32, 1081].

De natura boni = *nat. b.* (398); [PL 42, 551; CSEL 25, 853].

De natura et gratia = *nat. et gr.* (413–415); [PL 44, 247; CSEL 60, 231].

De ordine = *ord.* (386); [PL 32, 977; CSEL 63, 121; CCL 29, 87].

De philosophia (lost) = *phil.*

De praedestinatione Sanctorum = *praed. Sanct.* (428–429); [PL 44, 959].

De pulchro et apto (lost) = *pulch.*
De quantitate animae = *an. quant.* (387–388); [PL 32, 1035, CSEL 89].
De spiritu et littera = *spir. et litt.* (412); [PL 44, 201; CSEL 60, 153].
De Trinitate = *trin.* (399–426); [PL 42, 819; CCL 50].
De utilitate credendi = *util. cred.* (391–392); [PL 42, 65; CSEL 25, 3].
De vera religione = *vera rel.* (390); [PL 34, 121; CSEL 77/5, 1; CCL 32].
Disciplinarum libri = *discipl.* (387)
Enarrationes in psalmos = *en. Ps.*; [PL 36, 67; CCL 38].
Enarrationes in psalmos = *en. Ps.*; [PL 37, 1033; CCL 38].
Epistulae = *ep.*; [PL 33, 61; CSEL 34. 44. 57. 88].
Epistulae ad romanos inchoata expositio = *ep. Rm. inch.* (393–395); [PL 35, 2087; CSEL 84, 145].
Expositio quarundam propositionum ex epistula Apostoli ad Romanos = *exp. prop. Rm.* (394); [PL 35, 2063; CSEL 84, 3].
Retractationes = *retr.* (427); [PL 32, 583; CSEL 36, 1; CCL 57].
Sermones = *s.*; [PL 38, 23; CCL 41, Dolbeau 1996].
Sermones = *s.*; [PL 38, 1493; CCL 41, Dolbeau 1996].
Soliloquia = *sol.* (386–387); [PL 32, 869; CSEL 89].
In epistulam Johannis ad Pathos tractatus = *ep. Jo.* (413–418); [PL 35, 1977; CSEL 75].
In Johannis evangelium tractatus = *Jo. ev. tr.* (406–419); [PL 35, 1379; CCL 36].

4. Editions

The first edition of Augustine's *Opera omnia* appeared in Basel in 1506. This eleven-volume edition was printed by Johann Amerbach. The works were chronologically assembled into a single *corpus*. In 1517 the edition was enhanced in Nuremberg with indexes prepared by Johann Teuschlein. The *corpus* was, however, published without the appropriate critical distinction being made between the various codes, so that non-authentic writings were attributed to Augustine. A later edition of the work, edited by Erasmus of Rotterdam, came out in 1529, also in Basel, where the publisher Johann Froben had taken over Amerbach's printing house. This second edition was provided with a two-hundred page index and one indicating quotations from the *Scriptures*. Erasmus' edition was then published again in Paris in 1532, Venice in 1552 and Lyons in 1570. In 1577, in Louvin, another, more complete edition of the *Opera omnia*, appeared in ten volumes. It was edited by Plantin Moretus from Antwerp. In a Papal bull of 1587 Sixtus V ordered that the works of the Fathers of the Church be published, starting with those of Augustine. The work, commissioned to the Benedictines, was, however, completed between 1679 and 1690, and would be reproduced and again published in 1841 by J. P. Migne, in 16 volumes, in the well-known series *Patrologia latina*.

At the end of the nineteenth century, the Austrian Academy of Sciences in Vienna began publication of a critical edition of Augustine's writings in the *Corpus Scriptorum Ecclesiasticorum Latinorum* (CSEL); in the mid-twentieth century the publisher Brepols of Turnhout (Belgium) initiated a new critical edition of the patristic texts, called *Corpus Christianorum. Series Latina* (CCL). Thus far, only a part of Augustine's works have been published in it.

5. Lexicons and Encyclopedias

For the indexes, the concordances and the lexicon, see D. Lenfant, *Concordantiae Augustinianae*, 2 vol. , Paris 1656 and the *Catalogus verborum quae in operibus Sancti Augustini inveniuntur*, 5 vol. , Eindhoven 1976–1985.

To facilitate direct access to Augustine's works, a team of scholars directed by C. Mayer devised an *Augustinus-lexicon*, establishing the outline of the work and assigning the writing of the various items to the greatest experts in Augustinian thought. Concepts, people, places and institutions significant in Augustine's life and thought are dealt with in alphabetical order. Thanks to the *German Province* of the Augustinian Order and the *Augustinus Institut* of Würzburg it has been possible to initiate the work. The first volume came out in 2003.

At present, a convenient encyclopedia is also available in English: *Augustine through the Ages. An Encyclopedia*, Grand Rapids (Michigan) 1999, directed by A. Fitzgerald. L' work.

Several cultural institutions have set up internet sites, whose addresses are listed below:

www.augustinus.it, edited by a team of Augustinian scholars from Tolentino Italy). It has made the *opera omnia* available in Latin and Italian, in the translation of the *Nuova Biblioteca Agostiniana* (NBA) of the publisher *Città Nuova*, and is enhanced with comparison tables, tables of content, indexes, selected sentences, translations into various language, etc.;

www.aug.org/augustinianum, offers information on the cultural, scientific and publishing activities of the *Istituto Patristico Augustinianum*;

www.library.villanova.edu/sermons/augustiniana.html, with news pertaining to the journal "Augustinian Studies" and annual meetings, *Augustinian Lectures*;

www.augustinus.de, (in German) with a bibliography of over 25 thousand titles divided into seven categories; the editors (C. Mayer and the University of Giessen) have also produced a CD-Rom containing all the works of Augustine.

6. Translations into modern languages

In English

Not all of the *Opera omnia* has been translated, but some partial collections exist with others under way. Among all of them we can cite:

Nicene and Post-Nicene Fathers of the Christian Church, Buffalo 1886; containing the oldest and most numerous collection of Augustinian works in English;

Writings of Saint Augustine, in *The Fathers of the Church*, Washington 1947 ff, vol. 29, under way;

Augustine: Earlier Writings, in *The Library of Christian Classics*, Philadelphia and London 1953–66;

Ancient Christian Writers, New York 1946 ff. This series has already published various works of St. Augustine;

The Works of Saint Augustine, A Translation for the 21st Century, New York 1990 ff, a series edited by the *Augustinian Heritage Institute*.

In Italian

The first edition of the *Opera omnia* is the one that was never completed because of the World War. It is from the Biblioteca Agostiniana, and prepared under the "Bollettino Storico Agostiniano", Florence 1930.

In the nineteen-sixties the founder of the *Istituto Patristico Augustinianum* of Rome, A. Trapè, began the publication of the entire body of Augustine's works, in a critical edition with the Latin text on facing pages for the co-edition "Città Nuova/Nuova Biblioteca Agostiniana". 48 volumes were available as of 2003.

Alongside the above-mentioned edition of the *Opera omnia* we single out:

La città di Dio, tr. L. Alici, Milano 1984; *Dell'Ordine*, tr. A. M. Moschetti, Firenze 1941;

La vera religione, tr. M. Vannini, Milano 1987;

Il maestro, tr. E. Riverso, Roma 1990;

Le Confessioni, tr. R. De Monticelli, Milano 1990; *Il* "De Libero Arbitrio" *di S. Agostino*, tr. F. De Capitani, Milano 1987.

In German

There is no translation of the *Opera omnia*, however, several works have been translated. In particular:

Drei Bücher gegen die Akademiker, tr. R. Emmel, Paderborn 1927; *Vom seligen Leben*, tr. J. Hessen, Leipzig 1923; *Gottes Weltregiment. Zwei Bücher von der Ordnung*, tr. P. Keseling. Münster 1940;

Selbstgespräche, tr. L. Schopp and A. Dyroff, Münster 1938;

Der Lehrer, tr. C. J. Perl, Paderborn 1958;

Bekenntnisse, tr. J. Bernhart, München 1955;

Der Gottesstaat, 3 vol. , tr. C. J. Perl, Salzburg 1951–1953.

In French

Oeuvres de Saint Augustin, 51 vol. with Latin text on facing pages in *Bibliothèque Augustinienne*, Paris 1949 ff, unfinished.

In Spanish

Obras completas de San Augustín, 41 vol. with Latin text on facing pages, in *Biblioteca de autores cristianos*, Madrid 1944 ff, unfinished.

7. Monographs and Critical Studies

a) *Monographs and general critical Studies*

Alfaric, P., *L'évolution intellectuelle de Saint Agustin. 1: Du Manichéisme au Néoplatonisme*, Paris 1918 (single volume).

Alici, L., *Il linguaggio come segno e come testimonianza. Una rilettura di Agostino*, Roma 1976.

Baguette, Ch., *Une période stoïcienne dans l'évolution de Saint Augustin*, "Revue des Études Augustiniennes", XVI, 1970, pp. 47–77.

Balido, G., *Strutture logico-formali e analisi linguistiche di testi agostiniani*, Roma 1998.

Beierwaltes, W., *Agostino e il neoplatonismo cristiano*, Milano 1995.

Biolo, S., *La coscienza nel "De Trinitate" di S. Agostino*, Roma 1969.

Bodei, R., *"Ordo amoris". Conflitti terreni e felicità celeste*, Bologna 1991.

Bonner, G., *St. Augustine of Hippo. Life and Controversies*, Norwich (UK) 1986.

Bourke, V.J., *Augustine's Quest of Wisdom*, Milwaukee (Wisconsin) 1945.

Boyer, Ch., *Christianisme et néoplatonisme dans la formation de saint Augustin*, Paris 1920.

Boyer, Ch., *L'idée de vérité dans la philosophie de saint Augustin*, Paris 1921.

Boyer, Ch., *Sant'Agostino filosofo*, Bologna 1965.

Brown, P., *Augustine of Hippo*, Berkeley and Los Angeles 1967.

Bucher, T. G., *Zur formalen Logik bei Augustinus*, "Freiburger Zeitschrift für Philosophie und Theologie", XXIX, 1982, pp. 3–45.

Bucher, T. G., *Augustinus und der Skeptizismus zur Widerlegung in "Contra Academicos"*, in Atti del Congresso internazionale su S. Agostino nel XVI centenario della conversione, vol. II, Roma 1987, pp. 381–392.

Cayré, F., *Initiation à la philosophie de saint Augustin*, Paris 1947.

Chadwick, H., *Augustine*, Oxford 1986.

Cipriani, N., *L'ispirazione tertullianea nel "De libero arbitrio" di S. Agostino*, in *Il mistero del male e la libertà possibile: lettura dei dialoghi di S. Agostino*, Roma, 1994, pp. 165–178.

Cipriani, N., *Il rifiuto del pessimismo porfiriano nei primi scritti di sant'Agostino*, "Augustinianum", XXXVII, 1997, pp. 113–146.

Cipriani, N., *Le opere di sant'Ambrogio negli scritti di sant'Agostino anteriori all'episcopato*, "La scuola cattolica", CXXV, 1997, pp. 763–800.

Cipriani, N., *Il problema del male in S. Agostino*, in *Agostino non è (il) male*, edited by G. Fidelibus, Chieti 1998, pp. 27–41.

Courcelle, P., *Les lettres grecques en Occident de Macrobie à Cassiodore*, Paris 1948.

Courcelle, P., *Recherches sur les Confessions de Saint Augustin*, Paris 1968.

Crosson, F.J., *The Structure of "The Magistro"*, "Revue des Études Augustiniennes", XXXV, 1989, pp. 120–127.

Doignon, J., *Etat des questions relatives aux premiers dialogues des Saint Augustin*, in *Internationales Symposion über den Stand der Augustinus-Forschung*", Würzburg 1989, pp. 47–86.

Du Roy, O., *l'intelligence de la foi en la Trinité selon s. Augustin. Genèse de sa théologie trinitaire jusqu'en 391*, Paris 1966.

Dyroff, A., *Über Form und Begriffsgehalt der augustinischen Schrift "De ordine"*, in *Aurelius Augustinus*, hrsg. von M. Grabmann, J. Mausbach, Köln, 1930, pp. 15–62.

Evans, G. R., *Augustine on Evil*, Cambridge 1982.

Fidelibus, G., *Grazia e storicità nel disegno del "De civitate Dei": un percorso di ragione*, "Augustinianum", XL, 2000, pp. 225–254.

Fidelibus, G., *Ragione, religione, città. Una rilettura filosofica del libro VIII del "De civitate Dei" di Sant'Agostino*, Teramo 2002.

Flash, K., *Augustin. Einführung in sein Denken*, Stuttgart 1980.

Gilson, E., *The Christian Philosophy of Saint Augustine*, New York 1960.

Guardini, R., *Die Bekehrung des Aurelius Augustinus. Der innere Vorgang in seinen Bekenntnissen*, München 1950.

Guitton, J., *Le temps e l'éternité chez Plotin et saint Augustin*, Paris 1933.

Guzzo, A., *S. Agostino dal "Contra Academicos" al "De vera religione"*, Torino 1957.

Henry, P., *La vision d'Ostie. Sa place dans la vie et l'oeuvre de saint Augustin*, Paris 1938.

Henry, P., *Plotin et l'Occident. Firmicus Maternus, Marius Victorinus, Saint Augustin et Macrobe*, Louvain 1934.

Hölscher, L., *The Reality of the Mind. Saint Augustine's Philosophical Arguments for the Human Soul as a Spiritual Substance*, London/New York 1986.

Holte, R., *Béatitude et Sagesse. Saint Augustin et le problème de la fin de l'homme dans la philosophie ancienne*, Paris 1962.

Jaspers, K., *Drei Gründer des Philosophierens. Plato, Augustin, Kant*, München 1957.

Jackson, B.D., *The Theory of Signs in St. Augustine's "De Doctrina Christiana"*, "Revue des Études Agustiniennes", XV, 1969, pp. 9–49.

Jolivet, R., *Dieu, soleil des esprits. La doctrine augustinienne de l'illumination*, Paris 1934.

Kneale, W. C. – Kneale, M., *The Development of Logic*, Oxford, Clarendon 1962.

König, E., *Augustinus Philosophus, Christlicher Glaube und philosophisches Denken in den Frühschriften Augustins*, München 1970.

Madec, G., *"Christus, scientia et sapientia nostra". Le principe de cohérence de la doctrine augustinienne*, "Recherches Augustiniennes", X, 1975, pp. 77 – 85.

Madec, G., *The notion of philosophical Augustinianism: an attempt of clarification*, "Mediaevalia", IV, 1978, pp. 125–145.

Madec, G., *La délivrance de l'esprit, Confessions VII*, in *Le Confessioni di Agostino di Ippona. Libri VI–IX*, Palermo 1985, pp. 45–69.

Madec, G., *Le néoplatonisme dans la conversion d'Augustin*, in *Internationales Symposion über den Stand der Augustinus Forschung*, Würzburg 1989, pp. 9–25.

Madec, G., *La Patrie et la Voie*, Paris 1989.

Madec, G., *Saint Augustin et la philosophie. Notes critiques*, Paris 1996.

Malatesta, M., *Logistica I. Introduzione alla logica degli enunciati*, Napoli 1976.

Malatesta, M., *Dialettica e logica formale*, Napoli 1982.

Malatesta, M., *The Primary Logic*, Leominster (UK) 1997.

Mandouze, A., S*aint Augustin. L'aventure de la raison et de la grâce*, Paris 1968.

Mannucci, U., *La conversione di S. Agostino e la critica recente*, in *Miscellanea Agostiniana*, vol. II, 1931, pp. 23–47.

Markus, R. A., Saeculum. *History and Society in the Theology of St. Augustin*, Cambridge 1970.

Markus, R. A., *Augustine: a collection of critical essays*, New York 1972.

Marrou, H.-I., *Saint Augustin et la fin de la culture antique*, Paris 1958.

Martin, J., *Saint Augustin*, Paris 1923.

Nash, R. H., *The light of the mind: St. Augustine's theory of knowledge*, Lexington (Kentucky) 1969.

O'Daly, G., *Augustine's Philosophy of Mind*, Berkeley and Los Angeles 1987.

O'Meara, J. J., *The Historicity of the Early Dialogues of St. Augustine*, "Vigiliae Christianae", V, 1951, pp. 150–178.

O'Meara, J. J., *The young Augustine*, London 1965.

O'Meara, J. J., *Porphyry's Philosophy from Oracles in Eusebius' "Praeparatio Evangelica" and Augustine's Dialogues of Cassiciacum*, "Recherches Augustiniennes", VI, 1969, pp. 103–139.

Pacioni, V., *La presenza di Sant'Agostino nell'opera letteraria e filosofica di Albert Camus*, in *Congresso Internazionale su S. Agostino nel XVI Centenario della conversione*, vol. III, Roma 1987, pp. 369–379.

Pacioni, V., *La struttura logica del principio di autocoscienza*, in *Interiorità e intenzionalità in Sant'Agostino*, Roma 1990, pp. 59–69.

Pacioni, V., *L'unità teoretica del "De ordine" di sant'Agostino*, Roma 1996.

Parma, Ch., Pronoia *und* Providentia. *Der Vorschungsbegriff Plotins und Augustins*, Leiden 1971.

Pépin, J., Ex Platonicorum persona, *Études sur les lectures philosophiques de Saint Augustin*, Amsterdam 1977.

Pépin, J., *Saint Augustin et la dialectique*, Villanova (Pennsylvania) 1976.

Perler, O., *Les voyages de Saint Augustin*, Paris 1969.

Piemontese F., *La* Veritas *agostiniana e l'agostinismo perenne*, Milano 1963.

Pinborg, J., *Das Sprachdenken der Stoa und Augustins Dialektik*, "Classica et mediaevalia", XXIII, 1962, pp. 148–177.

Pizzani, U., *L'enciclopedia agostiniana e i suoi problemi*, in *Congresso Internazionale di S. Agostino nel XVI centenario della conversione*, vol. I, Roma 1987, pp. 331–361.

Portalié, E., *Augustinisme*, in *Dictionnaire de théologie catholique*, vol. I, Paris 1902, pp. 2501–2561.

Portalié, E., *A Guide to the Thought of Saint Augustine*, Chicago 1960.

Reale, G., *Introduzione ad* Aurelio Agostino. *Natura del Bene*, Milano 1995.

Reardon, K., *The Relation of Philosophy to Faith in the Teaching of S. Augustine*, "Studia Patristica", II, 1957, pp. 288–294.

Rief, J., *Der Ordobegriff des jungen Augustinus*, Tübingen 1962.

Rist, J. M., *Augustine. Ancient thought baptized*, Cambridge 1994.

Samek Lodovici, E., *Dio e il mondo. Relazione, causa, spazio in S. Agostino*, Roma 1979.

Sciacca, M. F., *Il principio della metafisica di S. Agostino*, "Humanitas", IX, 1954, pp. 947–960.

Sciacca M. F., *S. Agostino*, Brescia 1949.

Simone V., *Semiologia agostiniana*, "La Cultura", VII, 1969, pp. 88–117.

Solignac, A., *Doxographies et manuels dans la formation philosophique de S. Augustin*, "Recherches Augustiniennes", I, 1958, pp. 113–148.

Sparrow Simpson, W.J., *St. Augustine's Conversion*, London 1930.

Steppat, M. P., *Die Schola von Cassiciacum, Augustinus "De ordine"*, Darmstadt 1980.

Stock, B., *Augustine the Reader. Meditation, Self-Knowledge and the Ethics of Interpretation*, Cambridge (Massachusetts)–London 1998.

Svoboda, K., *L'esthétique de saint Augustin et ses sources*, Brno 1933.

TeSelle, E., *Augustine the Theologian*, New York 1970.

Teske, R. J., *The World-Soul and Time in St. Augustine*, in "Augustinian Studies", XIV, 1983, pp. 75–92.

Theiler, W., *Porphyrios und Augustin*, Halle 1933.

Trapè, A., *La nozione del mutabile e dell'immutabile secondo sant'Agostino*, Roma 1959.

Trapè, A., *S. Agostino. L'uomo, il pastore, il mistico*, Fossano (Cuneo) 1976.

b) Monographs and critical Studies of individual Subjects

Studies on the Dialogues of Cassiciacum

Cipriani, N., *Le fonti cristiane della dottrina trinitaria nei primi dialoghi di S. Agostino*, "Augustinianum", XXXIV, 1994, pp. 253–312.

Cipriani, N., *Sulla fonte varroniana delle discipline liberali nel "De ordine" di S. Agostino*, "Augustinianum", XL, 2000, pp. 203–224.

Cutino, M., *I dialoghi di Agostino dinanzi al "De regressu animae" di Porfirio*, "Recherches Augustiniennes", XXVII, 1994, pp. 41–74.

Doignon, J., *Notes de critique textuelle sur le "De Beata vita" de saint Augustin*, "Revue des Études Augustiniennes", XXIII, 1977, pp. 63–82.

Doignon, J., *Problèmes textuels et modèles litteraires dans le livre I du "De ordine" de S. Augustin*, "Revue des Études Augustiniennes", XXIV, 1978, pp. 71–86.

Doignon, J., *Points litigieux dans la tradition du texte du "De ordine" (Livre II) de S. Augustin*, "Revue des Études Augustiniennes", XXV, 1979, pp. 230–244.

Doignon, J., *Le "De ordine": son déroulement, ses thèmes*, in *L'opera letteraria di Agostino tra Cassiciacum e Milano*, Palermo 1987, pp. 113–150.

Dyroff, A., *Über Form und Begriffsgehalt der augustinischen Schrift "De ordine"*, in *Aurelius Augustinus*, hrsg. M. Grabmann, J. Mausbach, Köln 1930, pp. 15–62.

Gunermann, H. H., *Literarische und philosophische Tradition im ersten Tagesgespräch von Augustinus "De ordine"*, "Recherches Augustiniennes", IX, 1973, pp. 183–226.

Hübner, W., *Der Ordo der Realien in Augustins Frühdialog* "De ordine", "Revue des Études Augustiniennes", XXXIII, 1987, pp. 23–48.

Madec, G., *À propos d'une traduction de* "De ordine" *II, 5, XVI*, "Revue des Études Augustiniennes", XVI, 1970, pp. 179–186.

Madec, G., *L'historicité des "Dialogues" de Cassiciacum*, "Revue des Études Augustiniennes", XXXII, 1986, pp. 207–231.

Malatesta, M., *St. Augustine's Dialectic from the Modern Logic Standpoint. Logical Analysis of* "Contra Academicos" III, 10, 22 –13, 29, "Metalogicon", VIII, 1995, pp. 91–120.

Malatesta, M., *La problematica linguistica del* "Contra Academicos" *alla luce della filosofia del linguaggio contemporanea*, "Metalogicon", X, 1997, pp. 46–63.

Pacioni, V., *Un caso di utilizzazione di logica stoica:* "De ordine", *II, 3, 8–9*, in *Ripensare Agostino, interiorità e intenzionalità*, Roma 1993, pp. 175–181.

Pacioni, V., *La provvidenza divina e il male nella storia: a proposito di un testo controverso,* "De ordine", *I, 1, 2*, in *Il mistero del male e la libertà possibile: lettura dei dialoghi di Agostino*, Roma 1994, pp. 137–148.

Reale, G., *Agostino e il* "Contra Academicos", in *L'opera letteraria di Agostino tra Cassiciacum e Milano*, Palermo 1987, pp. 13–30.

Solignac, A., *Réminescences plotiniennes et porphyriennes dans le début du "De ordine" de saint Augustin*, "Archives de philosophie", XX, 1957, pp. 446–465.

Winkler, K., *La théorie augustinienne de la mémoire à son point de départ*, in *Augustinus Magister*, vol. I, Paris 1954, pp. 511–519.

Studies on Method

Camelot, T. H., "Quod intelligimus, debemus rationi". *Note sur la méthode théologique de saint Augustin*, "Historisches Jahrbuch", LXXVII, 1958, pp. 397–402.

Crosson, F., *Philosophy, Religion and Faith*, in *Proceedings of the American Catholic Philosophical Association*, Saint Louis (Missouri) 1978, pp. 165–176.

Cushman, R. E., *Faith and Reason in the Thought of St. Augustine*, "Church History", XIX, 1950, pp. 271–294.

Jess, W. G., *Reason as Propaedeutic to Faith in Saint Augustin*, "International Journal for Philosophy of Religion", V, 1974, pp. 225–233.

Lütcke, K. H., Auctoritas *bei Augustin*, Stuttgart 1968.

Madec, G., *Notes sur l'intelligence augustinienne de la foi*, "Revue des Études Augustiniennes", XVII, 1971 pp.119–142.

O'Meara, J. J., *S. Augustine's View of Authority and Reason in A. D. 306*, "Irish Theological Quarterly", XVIII, 1951, pp. 338–346.

Pacioni, V., Auctoritas e ratio: *la via alla vera libertà*, in *Il mistero del male e la libertà possibile: linee di antropologia agostiniana*, Roma 1995, pp. 81–109.

Thonnard, F. J., *La philosophie et sa méthode rationnelle en augustinisme*, "Revue des Études Augustiniennes", VI, 1960, pp.11–30.

Van Fleteren, F. E., *Authority and Reason, Faith and Understanding in the Thought of St. Augustine*", "Augustinian Studies", IV, 1973, pp. 33–71.

Studies on Anthropology

Cipriani, N., *L'influsso di Varrone sul pensiero antropologico e morale nei primi scritti di S. Agostino*, in *L'etica cristiana nei secoli III e IV: eredità e confronti*, Roma 1996, pp. 369–400.

Cipriani, N., *Lo schema dei* tria vitia (voluptas, superbia, curiositas) *nel "De vera religione": antropologia soggiacente e fonti*, "Augustinianum", XXXVIII, 1998, pp. 157–195.

Cipriani, N., *Il modello antropologico nel libro I delle* Confessioni, in Le Confessioni *di Agostino (402–2002): bilancio e prospettive*, Roma 2003, pp. 421–433.

Couturier, Ch., *La structure métaphysique de l'homme d'après saint Augustin*, in *Augustinus Magister*, I, Paris 1955, pp. 543–550.

De Durand, G. M., *L'homme raisonable mortel: pour l'histoire d'une définition*, «Phoenix», XXVII, 1973, pp. 328–344.

Dempf, A., *Die Menschenlehre Augustins*, "Münchener theologische Zeitschrift", VI, 1955, pp. 21–31.

Di Martino, C., *La* intentio *nella psicologia di Agostino dal "De libero arbitrio" al "De Trinitate"*, "Revue des Études Augustiniennes", XLVI, 2002, pp. 173–198.

Fortin, E. L., *Augustine's "De quantitate animae" or the spiritual Dimensions of Human Existence*, in "De moribus ecclesiae catholicae et de moribus manichaeorum", "De quantitate animae" *di Agostino d'Ippona*, Palermo 1991, pp. 133–169.

Fortin, E. L., *Saint Augustin et la doctrine néoplatonicienne de l'âme (Ep. 137, 11)*, in *Augustinus Magister*, vol. III, Paris 1955, pp. 371–380.

Henry, P., *St. Augustine on Personality*, Villanova (Pennsylvania) 1960.

Jolivet, R., *San Agustín y la preexistencia platonica de las almas*, "Augustinus", I, 1956, pp. 49–51.

Palmieri, D., *La persona umana nel pensiero di s. Agostino*, "Studia Patavina", I, 1954, pp. 370–399.

Salmon, E., *The Nature of Man in St. Augustine's Thought*, in *Proceedings of the American Catholic Philosophical Association*, Saint Louis (Missouri) 1951, pp. 25–41.

Sciacca, M. F., *Il composto umano nella filosofia di Sant'Agostino*, "Studia Patavina", I, 1954, pp. 211–226.

Sciacca, M. F., *L'origine dell'anima secondo Sant'Agostino*, "Giornale di metafisica", IX, 1954, pp. 542–550.

Stefanini, L., *Il problema della persona*, in *Sant'Agostino e le grandi correnti della filosofia contemporanea*, Tolentino 1956, pp. 52–68.

Thonnard, F. J., *Les fonctions sensibles de l'âme humaine selon saint Augustin*, "Année theologique augustinienne", XII, 1952, pp. 335–345.

Studies on Ethics

Alvarez, T., *S. Agustín y la teoría de la* "lex aeterna", "Annuario de Filosofia del Derecho", VI, 1958–1959, pp. 245–290.

Barth, H., *Die Freiheit der Entscheidung im Denken Augustins*, Basel 1935.

Brachtendorf, J., *Cicero and Augustine on the Passions*, "Revue des Études Augustiniennes", XLIII, 1997, pp. 289–308.

Capone, G., *La concezione agostiniana della libertà*, Padova 1931.

Cechini, L., *Il problema morale in Sant'Agostino*, Reggio Emilia 1934.

Clark, M. T., *Augustine. Philosopher of Freedom*, New York–Paris 1958.

Deman, Th., *Le traitement scientifique de la morale chrétienne selon S. Augustin*, Montréal–Paris 1957.

De Plinval, G., *Aspects du déterminisme et de la liberté dans la doctrine de saint Augustin*, "Revue des Études Augustiniennes", I, 1955, pp. 345–378.

Kondoleon, Th. J., *Augustine and the Problem of divine Foreknowledge and free Will*, "Augustinian Studies", XVIII, 1987, pp. 171–175.

Lorenz, R., Fruitio Dei *bei Augustin*, "Zeitschrift für Kirchengeschichte", LXIII, 1950–1951, pp. 75–132.
Mausbach J., *Die Ethik des hl. Augustinus*, Freiburg 1909.
O'Connor, W. R., *The uti/frui. Distinction in Augustine's Ethics*, "Augustinian Studies", XIV, 1983, pp. 45–62.
Roland-Gosselin, B., *La morale de saint Augustin*, Paris 1925.

Studies on the Theory of Knowledge

Acworth, R., *God and human Knowledge in St. Augustine. The Theory of Illumination*, "The Downside Review", LXXV, 1957, pp. 207–214.
Boyer, Ch., *L'idée de vérité dans la philosophie de S. Augustin*, Paris 1921.
Bourke, V. J., *Wisdom in the Gnoseology of St. Augustine*, "Augustinus", III, 1958, pp. 331–336.
Campus, M. A., *Il problema gnoselogico in Sant'Agostino*, Firenze 1943.
Cioconardi, J., *De cognitione sensibili apud S. Augustinum*, Roma 1939.
Incardona, N., *Fondamenti teologici e limiti teoretici dell'atto del pensare in S. Agostino*, in *Augustinus Magister*, vol. I, 1954, pp 463–475.
Manferdini, T., *Comunicazione ed estetica in S. Agostino*, Bologna 1995.
Markus, R. A., *St. Augustine on Signs*, "Phronesis", II, 1957, pp. 60–83.
Pegis, A. C., *The Mind of Saint Augustine*, "Medieval Studies", VI, 1944, pp. 8–29.
Pépin, J., *Univers dionysien et univers augustinien*, "Recherches de Philosophie", II, 1956, pp. 179–224.
Pialat, E., *La théorie de la sensation chez saint Augustin*, "Archives de Philosophie", IX, 1932, pp. 95–127.
Pizzani, U., *Il sesto libro*, in "De musica" *di Agostino d'Ippona*, Palermo 1990.
Pryzwara, E., *Das Gnoseologisch-Religiöse bei St. Augustin*, "Augustinus", III, 1958, pp. 331–336.
Riverso, E., *Introduzione a Sant'Agostino*, "Il maestro", Roma 1990.
Schützinger, C. E., *German Controversy of S. Augustine's Illumination Theory*, New York 1960.

Thonnard, F. J., *La* cognitio per sensus *chez s. Augustin*, "Augustinus", III, 1958, pp. 193–203.

Van Der Linden, L. J., Ratio *et* intellectus *dans les premiers écrits de s. Augustin*, "Augustiniana", VII, 1957, pp. 6–32.

Vanni Rovighi, S., *La fenomenologia della sensazione in Sant'Agostino*, "Rivista di Filosofia neoscolastica", LIV, 1962, pp. 18–32.

Zepf, M., *Augustinus und das philosophische Selbstbewusstsein der Antike*, "Zeitschrift für Religions und Geistesgeschichte", XI, 1959, pp. 105–132.

Studies on the Nature and Existence of God

Anderson, G. F., *St. Augustine and Being. A Methaphisical Essay*, The Hague 1965.

Aubin, P., *Plotin et le christianisme. Triade plotinienne et Trinité chrétienne*, Paris 1992.

Bochenski, I. M. , *De cognitione existentiae Dei apud Augustinum*, Poznan 1936.

Bochet, I., *Saint Augustin et le désir de Dieu*, Paris 1982.

Boyer, Ch., *L'esistenza di Dio secondo S. Agostino*, "Rivista filosofica neoscolastica", XLVI, 1954, pp. 321–331.

Boyer, Ch., *Les voies de la connaissance de Dieu selon s. Augustin*, "Augustinus", III, 1958, pp. 227–245.

Cayré, F., *Dieu prouvé par la vie de l'esprit. Avantages de cette position*, "L'Année Théologique", XI, 1951, pp. 13–24.

Cayré, F., *La preuve de l'existence de Dieu*, "Revue de Philosophie", XXXVI, 1936, pp. 306–328.

Cipriani, N., *Dio nel pensiero di S. Agostino*, in *Dio nei Padri della Chiesa*, Roma 1996, pp. 257–274.

De Capitani, F., "Quomodo sit manifestum Deum esse". *Lettura del libro II del "De libero arbitrio"*, in "De libero arbitrio" *di Agostino d'Ippona*, Palermo 1990, pp. 35–57.

Duquesnois, H., *Une preuve de l'existence de Dieu dans saint Augustin. Dialogue "De libero arbitrio"*, "Annales de philosophie chrétienne", XXV, 1855, pp. 286–302.

Hübner, G., *Das absolute Sein bei Augustin*, "Studia Philosophica", VI, 1955, pp. 117–160.

Kälin, B., *Augustin und die Erkenntnis der Existenz Gottes*, "Divus Thomas", XIV, 1936, pp. 331–352.

Madec, G., *Connaisance de Dieu et action de grâces. Essais sur les citations de l'Ép. aux Romains, I, 18–25, dans l'oeuvre de Saint Augustin*, "Recherches Augustiniennes", II , 1962, pp. 273–309.

Ritter, J., Mundus intelligibilis. *Eine Untersuchung zur Aufnahme und Umwandlung der neuplatonischen Ontologie bei Augustinus*, Frankfurt 1937.

Sciacca, M. F., *L'existence de Dieu*, Paris 1951.

Tolley, W. P., *The Idea of God in the Philosophy of S. Augustine*, New York 1930.

Verbeke, G., *Connaissance de soi et connaissance de Dieu*, "Augustiniana", IV, 1954, pp. 279–299.

Studies on the Notions of Time and History

Amari, G., *Il concetto di storia in S. Agostino*, Roma 1951.

Brezzi, P., *Il carattere ed il significato della storia nel pensiero di S. Agostino*, "Revue des Études Anciennes, I, 1955, pp. 149–160.

Chaix-Ruy, J., *Le problème du temps dans les* Confessions *et dans* La Cité de Dieu, "Giornale di metafisica", IX, 1954, pp. 464–477.

Chaix-Ruy, J., *S. Augustin. Temps et Histoire*, Paris 1956.

Chiereghin, F., *Il tempo come possibilità interiore del male in Agostino*, in *Il mistero del male e la libertà possibile (IV): ripensare Agostino*, Roma 1997, pp. 177–190.

Corsini, E., *Lettura del libro XI delle "Confessioni"*, in "Le confessioni" *di Agostino d'Ippona, libri X–XIII*, Palermo 1987, pp. 35–65.

D'Elia, S., *Storia e teologia della storia nel "De Civitate Dei"*, in *La storiografia ecclesiastica nella tarda antichità. Atti del convegno di Erice*, Messina 1980, pp. 391–481.

Hoffmann, E., *Platonism in Augustine's Philosophy of History*, in *Philosophy and History, Essay presented to Ernest Cassirer*, Oxford 1936, pp. 173–190.

Marrou, H.-I., *The Meaning of History*, Montreal 1949.

Marrou, H.-I., *L'ambivalence du temps de l'histoire chez S. Augustin*, Paris 1950.

Marrou, H.-I., *Théologie de l'histoire*, Paris 1968.

Miccoli, P., *Storia e profezia nel pensiero di S. Agostino*, "Augustinian Studies", XVI, 1984, pp. 90–106.

O'Daly, G., *Time as a* distentio *and St. Augustine's Exegesis of Philippians' 3, 12–14,* "Revue des Études Augustiniennes", XXIII, 1977, pp. 265–271.

Petruzzellis, N., *La visione agostiniana della storia,* "Rassegna di scienze filosofiche", XII, 1959, pp. 1–17.

Raviez, M. E., *St. Augustine: Time and Eternity,* "Thomist", XXII, 1959, pp. 542–554.

Ruotolo, G., *La filosofia della storia e la Città di Dio,* Roma 1930.

Sciacca, M. F., *Interpretazione del concetto di storia in S. Agostino,* Tolentino 1960.

Von Balthasar, H. U., *Das Ganze im Fragment. Aspecte der Geschichtstheologie,* Einsiedeln 1963.

Studies on Political Philosophy

Arquillière, H. X., *L'augustinisme politique. Essai sur la formation des théories politiques du moyen âge,* Paris 1934.

Baynes, N. H., *The political Ideas of St. Augustine's* "De Civitate Dei", London 1955.

Bonner, G., *Quid imperatori cum Ecclesia? St. Augustine on History and Society,* "Augustinian Studies", II, 1971, pp. 231–251.

Borghesi, M., *L'età dello spirito e la metamorfosi della città di Dio,* "Il Nuovo Areopago", XIII, 1994, pp. 5–27.

Bourke, V. J., *The political Philosophy of St. Augustine,* in *Proceedings of the VIIth Annual Meeting of the American Catholic Association,* St. Louis (Missouri) 1931.

Boyer, Ch., *Sant'Agostino e i problemi dell'ecumenismo,* Roma 1969.

Brezzi, P., *I fondamenti filosofici del diritto e dello Stato in S. Agostino,* in *S. Agostino e le grandi correnti della filosofia contemporanea. Atti del Congresso Italiano di Filosofia Agostiniana,* Roma 1955, pp. 191–214.

Burt, D. X., *Friendship and Society. An Introduction to Augustine's Practical Philosophy,* Grand Rapids (Michigan), 1999.

Cipriani, N., *Il ruolo della Chiesa nella società civile: la tradizione patristica,* in *I cattolici e la società pluralista. Il caso delle leggi imperfette,* Bologna 1996, pp. 132–148.

Cipriani, N., *La violenza nel pensiero di S. Agostino,* in *La violenza,* Bologna 1998, pp. 241–268.

Combès, G., *La doctrine politique de Saint Augustin,* Paris 1927.

D'Agostino, F., *L'antigiuridismo di S. Agostino*, "Rivista internazionale di filosofia del diritto", LXIV, 1987, pp. 30–51.

Deane, H. A., *The Political and Social Ideas of St. Augustine*, New York 1963.

Dessì, G., *Reinhold Niebuhr e la "Città di Dio". La critica al perfettismo*, in *Interiorità e intenzionalità nel "De Civitate Dei" di Sant'Agostino*, Roma 1991, pp. 195–205.

Figgis, N., *The political Aspects of St. Augustine's City of God*, London 1921.

Fortin, E. L., *Political Idealism and Christianity in the Thought of St. Augustine*, Villanova (Pennsylvania) 1972.

Garilli, G., *Aspetti della filosofia giuridica, politica e sociale di s. Agostino*, Milano 1957.

Giorgianni, V., *Il concetto del diritto e dello Stato in s. Agostino*, Padova 1951.

Lamirande, E., *Church, State and Toleration. An intriguing Change of Mind in St. Augustine*, Villanova (Pennsylvania), 1975.

Monceaux, P., *Saint Augustin et le donatisme*, in *Histoire littéraire de l'Afrique chrétienne*, Paris 1923.

Pezzimenti, R., *Società aperta e i suoi amici*, Messina 1995.

Ratzinger, J., *Die Einheit der Nationen: eine Vision der Kirchenväter*, München 1971.

Roberti, G., *Il diritto romano in s. Agostino*, "Rivista filosofica neoscolastica", XXIII, 1931, pp. 305–366.

Tosatti, Q., *Agostino e lo Stato romano*, "Studi Romani", III, 1955, pp. 532–547.

Wytzes, J., *Enige gedachten van Augustinus over de Staat*, "Philosophia Reformata", III, 1938, pp. 25–43.

Index of Names

Abbagnano, N., 149, 172
Alcuin, 258,
Alexander of Hales, 261
Alfaric, P., 269, 270, 279, 283
Alici, L., 145, 147, 173
Ambrose of Milan, 13, 17, 19, 29, 118, 159, 207, 208, 213, 227, 253, 254, 271, 276, 282, 283
Anselm of Aosta, 259
Antiochus of Ascalon, 51, 85, 103, 107, 132, 133, 159, 276
Antiseri, G., 45, 47
Apuleius, 1, 83, 153, 172, 202
Arcesilaus, 51
Aristotle, 7, 39, 75, 84, 103, 109, 119, 133, 144, 176, 188, 203, 209, 227, 261
Aulus Gellius, 7
Averroes, 264
Avicenna, 261, 262

Bacon, R., 258, 262, 263
Baguette, Ch., 23
Baius, M., 266
Balido, G., 111, 144, 147, 278, 280
Baynes, N. H., 251
Becker, H., 269, 279
Bede, 258
Beierwaltes, W., 202, 203
Beretta, L., 24
Bernard of Chartres, 260
Bockénski, J. M., 73
Blondel, M., 271, 273

Boethius, 259
Boissier, G., 268, 270, 279
Bonaventure of Bagnoregio, 261, 262, 263
Bonner, G., 22, 251, 252
Bourke, V. J., 143, 228, 229, 250
Boyer, Ch., 140, 142, 201, 202, 204, 251, 252, 270, 272, 279
Brachtendorf, J., 172
Brezzi, P., 173, 249, 250
Brown, P., 23, 248, 249, 252
Bruni, L., 265,
Bucher, T.G., 74, 277, 280
Burt, D. X., 250

Calvin, J., 266
Campanella, T., 266
Carlini, A., 46, 109, 110
Carnap, R., 45
Carneades, 51, 53, 55
Cassiodorus, 258
Cayré, F., 110, 205
Chadwick, H., 102
Chiereghin, F., 227
Cicero, 3, 4, 6, 7, 13, 30, 50, 51, 58, 59, 75, 83, 85, 108. 109, 150, 153, 155, 159, 161, 169, 171, 172, 173, 190, 216, 217, 238, 239, 253, 277
Cipriani, N., 22, 24, 45, 47, 75, 76, 77, 81, 84, 103, 108, 109, 111, 112, 113, 132, 144, 147, 201, 227, 250, 251, 252, 276, 280, 286, 287
Colombo, S., 25

Coluccio Salutati, 265
Combès, G., 251
Corsini, E., 227,
Courcelle, P., 22, 23, 45, 273, 274, 280
Cristiani, L., 278
Crosson, F. J., 144
Cusano, N., 265
Cutino, M., 46

Darrell Jackson, B., 144
Dawson, Ch., 226, 229, 271
Deane, H. A., 250
De Capitani, F., 204, 205
De Durand, G. M., 108
D'Elia, S., 278
Deman, Th., 174
Descartes, R., 267
Di Berardino, A., 251
Dihle, A., 79, 108
Di Martino, C., 108
Doignon, J., 76, 83, 108
Dominici, G., 265
Duns Scotus, G., 264
Du Roy, O., 24, 45, 274, 275, 280, 283
Dyroff, A., 76, 276

Eckhart, J., 264
Egidio Romano, 264
Epicurus, 83
Erasmus of Rotterdam, 266
Eusebius of Caesarea, 240
Evans, G. R., 76

Ficino, M., 265
Fidelibus, G., 202
Fishacre, R., 263
Fitzgerald, A.D., 278, 280
Fitz-Ralf, R., 264
Flash, K., 249, 275, 280

Fortin, E. L., 111, 112
Frend, W. H. C., 252

Gentile, G., 271, 272
Gilson, E., 47, 48, 109, 142, 143, 147, 148, 204, 205, 227, 251, 264, 270, 278, 279
Gourdon, L., 269, 279
Grassi, O., 46, 146
Gregory of Rimini, 265
Grossatesta, R., 262, 263
Guitton, J., 227, 271, 272, 279
Guzzo, A., 91, 95, 110, 111, 270, 279

Hadot, I., 109
Hadot, P., 179
Henry, P., 23
Henry of Ghent, 261
Hölscher, L., 145, 146, 147, 275, 280
Holte, R., 45, 47, 48, 74, 75, 112, 173, 272, 274, 276, 280
Hugh of S. Victor, 258, 260
Huizinga, 265
Husserl, E., 271

Isidore of Seville, 258

Jansen, 266
Jaspers, K., 21, 25, 46, 281, 287
John of la Rochelle, 261
Jolivet, R., 140, 148

Kant, I., 133, 134, 272, 282
Kilwardby, R., 264
Kneale, M., 73
Kneale, W. C., 73
Kondoleon, Th. J., 228

Lamirande, E., 251

Index of Names

Lavere, G. J., 250
Lewis, G., 279
Luther, M., 266
Lütke, K. H., 46

Madec, G., 17, 22, 23, 24, 46, 47, 48, 202, 272, 275, 280
Malatesta, M., 45, 46, 73, 74, 111, 135, 144, 147, 277, 278, 280
Malebranche, N., 267
Mandouze, A., 279
Manetti, G., 144
Manferdini, T., 143
Mannucci, V., 279
Markus, R. A., 248, 249, 252
Marrou, H-I., 47, 228, 229, 271, 272, 279
Marston, R., 262
Martianus Capella, 277
Martindale, C. C., 271
Mates, B., 144
Matthew of Acquasparta, 262
Mazzarelli, C., 109
Miccoli, P., 228

Nicomachus of Gerasa, 7
Nourisson, J. F., 268, 279
Nygren, A., 169, 173

O'Connell, R. J., 275, 280
O'Connor, W. R., 166, 173
O'Daly, G., 79, 108, 111, 112, 142, 143, 144, 145, 148, 214, 228, 272, 275, 280
O'Meara, J. J., 23, 46, 73
Origen, 240

Pacioni, V., 47, 73, 77, 108, 109, 146, 203
Pani, G., 278

Pascal, B., 267, 273
Pelagius, 152, 266
Pépin, J., 144, 147
Petrarca, F., 265
Pezzimenti, R., 251
Pico della Mirandola, G., 265
Piemontese, F., 140, 148
Peter Aureolus, 265
Philo of Larissa, 132
Pythagoras, 109
Pizzani, U., 144, 145
Plato, 32, 39, 44, 46, 51, 60, 75, 95, 103, 177, 179, 181, 201, 202, 203, 282
Plinius, 28
Plotinus, 24, 30, 64, 65, 66, 68, 69, 71, 75, 76, 80, 81, 86, 89, 97, 108, 116, 118, 143, 175, 176, 178, 179, 181, 190, 201, 211, 214, 215, 220, 227, 228, 259, 269, 271, 274, 275, 276, 284
Pohlenz, M., 113, 174, 201
Porphyrius, 24, 37, 38, 84, 118, 176, 179, 180, 202, 275, 283, 284, 285
Portalié, E., 45, 257, 270
Poseidonius, 132
Possidius, 21, 245, 252
Proclus, 259
Protagoras, 178
Przywara, E., 271
Pseudo-Dionysius, 259, 262
Puech, H. C., 22

Quintilian, 83, 108

Rabano M., 258
Radice, R., 110, 113
Ratzinger, J., 229, 251

Reale, G., 23, 45, 46, 47, 112, 113, 172, 179, 202, 203
Riverso, E., 144, 145
Rohmer, J., 143
Roland-Gosselin, B., 174
Rosmini, A., 272
Ruch, M., 22
Russo, A., 108
Russell, R. P., 75

Sciacca, M. F., 22, 46, 108, 140, 142, 143, 144, 145, 147, 148, 228, 270, 272, 273, 279
Scotus Eriugena, G., 259, 260
Seneca, 171, 260
Sextus Empiricus, 83, 108, 112, 144, 147
Socrates, 86
Solignac, A., 22, 127, 146, 274, 280
Suso, B., 264
Stock, B., 22
Storz, J., 268, 269
Svoboda, K., 22, 143

Thales, 86
Tauler, 264
Tempier, S., 264
Tertullian, 19, 72
Testard, M., 22
Theiler, W., 24
Thimme, W., 269, 279
Thomas Aquinas, 139, 263, 264, 273
Thomas of York, 262
Trapè, A., 22, 23, 146, 203, 229, 273, 276

Ugolino Malabranca of Orvieto, 264

Van der Linden, L. J., 146
Varro, 7, 60, 62, 63, 81, 82, 84, 85, 97, 101, 103, 107, 109, 132, 133, 154, 155, 159, 171, 226, 276, 284
Victorinus, M., 14, 19, 276, 278, 283
Von Harnack, A., 268, 270, 279

Walter of Bruges, 262
William of Auvergne, 261
William of Conches, 258
William of Ockham, 265

Zeno of Citium, 51

www.ingramcontent.com/pod-product-compliance
Lightning Source LLC
Chambersburg PA
CBHW030333240426
43661CB00052B/1619